D1715032

Ecosystem Succession

MIT Press/Wright-Allen Series in System Dynamics

Ecosystem Succession
A General Hypothesis and a
Test Model of a Grassland

Luis T. Gutierrez
Willard R. Fey

The MIT Press
Cambridge, Massachusetts, and
London, England

093993

This book was set in VIP Times Roman
by Northeast Typographic Services, Inc.,
printed and bound by
Halliday Lithograph Corp.,
in the United States of America

Library of Congress Cataloging in Publication Data

Gutierrez, Luis T
    Ecosystem succession.

(MIT Press/Wright-Allen series in system dynamics)
    Bibliography: p.
    Includes index.
    1.   Ecological succession—Statistical methods—Data processing.
    2.   Ecological succession—Mathematical models.   3.   Ecological
succession—Colorado—Pawnee National Grassland—Statistical methods—Data
processing.   4.   Grassland ecology—Colorado—Pawnee National Grassland
—Statistical methods—Data processing.   5.   Ecological succession
—Colorado—Pawnee National Grassland—Mathematical models.
    6.   Grassland ecology—Colorado—Pawnee National Grassland—Mathe-
matical models. I. Fey, Willard R., joint author.
II.   Title. QH541.15.S72G84   574.5   79-20932
ISBN 0-262-07075-8

Contents

5

6

7

List of Illustrations

List of Tables

Preface

Succession is the process undergone by natural ecosystems such as lakes, grasslands, and forests as they proceed from early stages of development to maturity, when the community of plants and animals achieves a condition of equilibrium with its physical environment. Ecosystems succeed in response to either natural or man-made disturbances. Therefore it is important to understand how successional behavior arises and how to control it in order to avoid irreversible deterioration of systems that are indispensable for survival in spaceship Earth. At a time when intensive methods of utilizing ecosystem food production are becoming prohibitive due to short supply and soaring costs of fossil fuels, it is critical that man understand how to use succession as a constructive ecological force.

Empirical study of successional behavior has led over the years to several hypotheses to explain this phenomenon. Although long successional time periods make it difficult to compile complete time histories, several investigators have collected data that serve to identify the basic patterns of behavior. In this book we integrate the available empirical evidence on succession into a dynamic model that accounts for successional modes of behavior as they arise from the internal structure of the ecosystem. The numerical quantification of the model approximates the values of biomass and other variables typical of a grassland ecosystem. Our computer simulations with the model confirm that, within the limitations imposed by the physical environment and other open-loop factors, secondary succession is generated by the closed-loop structure of the ecosystem. They also show that successional modes of behavior are relatively insensitive to parametric and exogenous perturbations as long as they are not exceptionally large and that, while climatic factors are certainly influential on range productivity in the short run, the internal feedback structure that is responsible for succession is also responsible for the performance of the range ecosystem in the long run.

The authors are not biologists or ecologists. We are engineers who share the conviction that system dynamics provides a methodology that is particularly applicable to analysis and modeling of large-scale ecosystems for the purpose of designing better ecosystem utilization policies. We have endeavored to review the pertinent ecological literature and several ecologists were consulted while the model was under development. Needless to say, our model is by no means definitive. In this book the model is fully documented so that each assumption and parameter used can be reviewed and criticised by the community of ecologists and land-use managers. It is hoped that the experience of reviewing and using the present model may lead to a better one. After all, science also advances by a succession of sorts; any good model should eventually lead to a better model.

This book is intended primarily for ecologists and land-use managers interested in the quantitative analysis of dynamic ecological processes, succession in particular. The book can be used either as a reference or more appropriately as a case study that can be dissected in courses of quantitative ecology. More generally, it is intended for system dynamics students and practitioners interested in applying this tool to land-use management.

As mentioned before, several ecologists were consulted during model development. In particular, Eugene P. Odum of the University of Georgia provided extremely useful guidance in the early stages of the work. Arthur C. Benke of Georgia Tech and Bernard C. Patten of the University of Georgia also provided valuable advice. Anthony C. Picardi of Development Analysis Associates, Inc., Cambridge, Mass., read the complete manuscript and offered suggestions of substance. George M. Van Dyne of Colorado State University also read and commented on the manuscript and brought to our attention several important references. We are also grateful to William Bossert of Harvard University for bringing to our attention the Drury-Nisbet hypothesis on succession. John Kominski of the Library of Congress was instrumental in making library resources available to the senior author. The time and clerical support provided by IBM and Georgia Tech is gratefully acknowledged. In particular, the excellent editorial assistance of Mr. Robert C. Service at IBM was of great value. Needless to say, responsibility for errors is fully ours.

Ecosystem Succession

Introduction

Nature abhors a vacuum
—Spinoza (ca. 1677)

1.1 Objectives

When a forest is cut, the land cultivated for a period of time and then abandoned, the resulting "old-field" or bare area is gradually colonized anew by vegetation. After a number of years, the vegetation may come to exhibit the density and composition of the original forest, but not without first passing through a succession of stages with different dominant species. This process whereby nature covers denuded lands with vegetation and, consequently, with animal life as well, is termed ecological succession.

Ecological succession is responsible for the dynamic behavior of ecosystems as they proceed from their early stage of development to maturity—when the biotic community achieves a condition of equilibrium with its physical environment. It is the process of ecosystem development. Succession is a universal, exceedingly complex process that involves the ecosystem as a whole and may be examined from many points of view (Clements, 1916). Odum (1959) has described the process as follows:

Ecological succession is the orderly process of community change; it is the sequence of communities which replace one another in a given area. Typically, in an ecosystem, community development begins with pioneer stages which are replaced by a series of more mature communities until a relatively stable community is evolved which is in equilibrium with the local conditions. The whole series of communities which develop in a given situation is called the sere; the relatively transitory communities are called seral stages or seral communities, and the final or mature community is called the climax. . . . If succession begins on an area which has not been previously occupied by a community (such as newly exposed rock or sand surface), the process is known as primary succession. If community development is proceeding in an area from which a community was removed (such as a plowed field or cutover forest), the process is called secondary succession. Secondary succession is usually more rapid because some organisms, at least, are present already. Furthermore, previously occupied territory is more receptive to community development than are sterile areas. This is the type which we see all around us. In general, when we speak of ecological succession, we refer to changes which occur in the present geological age, while the pattern of climate remains essentially the same.

There appears to be general agreement, however, that secondary succession is a critical process to understand and control if we are to manage ecosystems successfully (see Ellison, 1960; Odum, 1969; Horn, 1975). The basic issues involved are those of productivity and stability. Climax (mature) ecosystems typically exhibit low productivity and high stability, while seral (immature) ecosystems are typically very productive, but also very unstable. Therefore a mature ecosystem such as a climax forest maintains itself and protects itself from environmental perturbations, but does not produce much excess biomass that can be harvested frequently by man. Conversely, if the forest is cut, the land can become very productive if properly cultivated, but then the ecosystem becomes dependent on man's protection and supplementary inputs of energy.

From an ecosystem management perspective, there is a wide spectrum of important cases between conserving an ecosystem in climax condition and sustaining it when the natural vegetation is completely removed and substituted by crops. The importance of gaining a better understanding of successional dynamics arises from the fact that ecosystems succeed in various ways under various modes of human utilization. An excellent case example is provided by the successional response of grasslands when the natural equilibrium between plants and animals is perturbed by the introduction of livestock. It has long been recognized that plant succession results from sustained grazing (Sampson, 1919). The long-range effects of secondary succession triggered by grazing may be beneficial or detrimental to the grassland. In his comprehensive survey on the influence of grazing on range succession, Ellison (1960) refers to unregulated livestock overgrazing as the principal cause for deterioration of portions of the western range, and then he states:

Much of this area is too difficult of access or too low in productivity to warrant intensive pastoral practices, so that improvement of its protective plant cover and forage value must be achieved extensively—that is, by natural successional processes. Ecological understanding of these processes, which must form the basis for effective management, is therefore imperative. The achievement of such understanding is a scientific challenge of the first order.

Furthermore, Ellison points out that such understanding cannot be restricted to the destructive effects of overgrazing. What is most needed from the viewpoint of range ecosystem management is an analysis of secondary succession as provoked by light or moderate grazing, so that we can learn to what extent grazing can be manipulated as a constructive ecological force. Unfortunately the successional response to moderate grazing is difficult to observe under actual operating conditions, and field data with regard to small differences (i.e., differences between moderate grazing and no grazing) are both scant and ambiguous. In that it would be practically unfeasible to arrange for controlled (i.e., constant environment) experimental conditions in the field over enough time and space for secondary succession to be observed after an exogenous perturbation, such experimentation must be carried out in the model world.

Some additional considerations that delimit the scope of the present volume are in order. Our research is concerned with explaining successional dynamics as they arise from the internal, closed-loop feedback structure of the ecosystem. Open-loop environmental factors such as temperature and precipitation do have an influence on succession. For example, grasslands are characteristic of regions where precipitation is neither abundant enough to support a forest nor scarce enough to result in a desert. Thus the average level of precipitation in a given region sets a limit on how far succession can proceed in that particular biome. These open-loop aspects of succession are generally well known and well understood. The present contribution focuses on how successional dynamics arise from the internal structure of the ecosystem under a given set of fairly stable environmental conditions. This focus immediately brings to mind another important consideration: if a meaningful quantification of the test model is to be achieved, it must be ecosystem-specific. Once a dynamic model for ecological succession has been structured and tested for a given ecosystem, its generalization for other ecosystems can be inductively attempted.

The Pawnee national grassland in northeastern Colorado was chosen as the subject ecosystem for the test model. A general description of this ecosystem is given by Jameson and Bement (1969). The Pawnee national grassland is under the management of the Forest Service, U.S. Department of Agriculture (USDA). The Central Plains Experimental Range, managed by the Agricultural Research Service, USDA, is located in the southwest corner of the national grassland. As part of the U.S. International

Biological Program (IBP) Grassland Biome Study, the Pawnee site was developed to serve as focus for intensive data collection activity. The Pawnee site consists of portions of the Central Plains Experimental Range and the Pawnee National Grassland. Therefore the Pawnee ecosystem is part of the western grassland biome and, ecologically speaking, is classified as a shortgrass prairie. From the viewpoint of land-use management, it is subject to a single use (i.e., grazing), and it is classified as a year-long range, with livestock feeding almost exclusively from native forage plants. The primary concern of the IBP Grassland Biome study was data collection on intraseasonal as opposed to successional dynamics. Nevertheless, there now exists, as a result, a wealth of functional and structural information about this ecosystem that made it a natural choice as the subject ecosystem for quantification of the test model. Complete long-term successional time histories do not exist for Pawnee or any other large-scale ecosystem. However, fragments exist that permit identification of certain generic time patterns of succession in both aquatic and terrestrial ecosystems. In our work, Pawnee data served to quantify some of the model parameters that determine the physical and biological limits to succession in the shortgrass prairie environment. Descriptive data on succession of grasslands and other ecosystems was used to approximate the model parameters which determine the time constants of succession.

1.2 Ecosystem Analysis Background

There are two reservoirs of knowledge from which the present research draws: the literature of ecological succession and the literature of feedback dynamics. Available accounts of ecological succession are based on numerous field observations, as well as on the general literature of ecology, a venerable body of knowledge under development since ancient times. Feedback dynamics, on the contrary, is a relatively recent development based on cybernetics and computer simulation methods. It is hoped that this study may prove of use to both ecology-oriented and systems-oriented readers. With this objective in mind, the present section is primarily dedicated to the system-oriented reader unfamiliar with the ecological background underlying the study. It also serves to document the ecological foundations for the research. Ecology-oriented readers unfamiliar with the technical background of feedback dynamics will find the relevant literature discussed in the next section, together with a discussion of research methodology.

Ecology has been defined as the study of the structure and function of nature (Odum, 1963). The spectrum of ecology has traditionally covered natural levels beyond that of the individual organism, i.e., populations, communities, and the biosphere. There appears to be a consensus that the term "ecology" was the first introduced in the nineteenth century (Haeckel, 1866), although it was not recognized as a discipline until the beginning of this century (Odum, 1971). Generally speaking, ecology remained a vaguely defined science until quite recently. The British ecologist Macfadyen (1957) has stated:

Ecology concerns itself with the interrelationships of living organisms, plant or animal, and their environments; these are studied with a view to discovering the principles which govern the relationships. That such principles exist is a basic assumption—and an act of faith—of the ecologist. His field of inquiry is no less wide than the totality of the living conditions of the plants and animals under observation, their systematic position, their reactions to the environment and to each other, and the physical and chemical nature of their inanimate surroundings . . . It must be admitted that the ecologist is something of a chartered libertine. He roams at will over the legitimate preserves of the plant and animal biologist, the taxonomist, the physiologist, the behaviourist, the meteorologist, the geologist, the physicist, the chemist, and even the sociologist: he poaches from all these and from other established and respected disciplines. It is indeed a major problem for the ecologist, in his own interest, to set bounds to his divagations.

In 1935 Tansley introduced the concept of ecosystem (ecological system) as a focus for the study of ecological phenomena. Evans (1956) presented the ecosystem as the basic unit of study in ecology. The ecosystem is defined as the biotic community standing in interaction with its physical environment. This important concept provides for the comparative study of similarities and dissimilarities between different kinds of ecosystems, for example, a lake, a tundra, or a grassland. Thus it would seem more precise to define ecology as the study of the structure and function of ecosystems.

The ecosystem concept is central to all modern presentations on ecology (see Odum, 1959, 1963, 1971; Gates, 1968; Major, 1968; Kormondy, 1969; McNaughton and Wolf, 1973; Watt, 1973). It also appears to be central to applied ecology, the use of ecological principles for managing natural environments (Van Dyne, 1968). Of primary interest for the purpose of the test model to be developed is the literature concerned with grassland ecosystems and their utilization. Grassland ecology has been studied by Hanson (1938, 1950), Carpenter (1940), Barnard (1964), Klapp (1964), Moore (1966), Allen (1967), Daubenmire (1968a), Coupland et al.

(1969), Costello (1969), Spedding (1971), and Duffey et al. (1974). Extensive field research has been conducted on the effects of grazing and different grazing systems on range conditions (Pickford, 1932; Albertson et al., 1957; Klipple and Costello, 1960; Ellison, 1960; Reed and Peterson, 1961; Paulsen and Ares, 1962; Jameson, 1963; Smith, 1967; Frischknecht and Harris, 1968; Steger, 1970). The ecological basis for range management is also well developed (Dyksterhius, 1949; Parker, 1954; Osborn, 1956; Costello, 1957; Dyksterhius, 1958; Goekel and Cook, 1960; Humphrey, 1962; DeVos, 1969; Lewis, 1969; Jameson, 1970; Fridrikson, 1972), resulting in enlightened practices of range management whereby many grasslands appear to improve rather than deteriorate under grazing (Williams, 1966; Semple, 1970; Steger, 1970; Vallentine, 1971; Coleman et al., 1973).

An abundance of descriptive information on successional dynamics in grasslands and other ecosystems has been accumulating for many years in the ecological literature, starting with early studies such as those by Cowles (1899, 1901, 1911), Shelford (1911a, 1911b), Clements (1916), Shantz (1917), Cooper (1926), and Tansley (1929, 1935). In his classical paper, Lindeman (1942) was the first ecologist to couple the open-loop flow of energy with the closed-loop cycling of matter as an important aspect (i.e., the trophic-dynamic aspect) contributing to the dynamics of ecological succession. More recently, several authors have elaborated on the dynamics of community diversity as another crucial aspect of successional processes leading to climax ecosystems (Margalef, 1963, 1969; Odum, 1969; Preston, 1969; Whittaker, 1970). Drury and Nisbet (1973) have attempted to explain succession as the outcome of competitive interactions at the organism level. The most comprehensive of recent accounts on succession is possibly that provided by Daubenmire (1968b). He points out that what is known about successional processes has been found by one or more of the following methods of study: repeated observation of permanent plots over a period of time, comparisons of existing vegetation with old records, analysis of age-class distribution in a stand, analysis of the nature and occurence of relics, studies of bare areas of different ages, and analysis of fossil sequences. Another method, involving experiments with laboratory microcosms (Cooke, 1967) has provided empirical evidence that succession arises from the internal structure and function of the ecosystem even when it is completely closed to all external inputs except light.

In recent years, increasing recognition of the ecosystem concept and progressive maturity of systems science has led to systems-ecology research, the application of systems science methodologies to the study of ecosystems (Odum, 1960; Watt, 1966, 1968; Van Dyne, 1968; Dale, 1970; Odum, 1971; Patten, 1971, 1972; Watt, 1973; de Wit and Goudriaan, 1974). In the area of grasslands, a significant amount of research has been conducted at Pawnee and other sites by the **IBP Grassland Biome Study**. Beyond data collection, systems-ecology research is directed at casting into mathematical models all the knowledge available on the structure and function of grassland ecosystems. This activity has resulted in several large-scale state space models (Bledsoe et al., 1971; Innis, 1972a; Patten, 1972) to account for the steady-state dynamics of the Pawnee grassland ecosystem. While the inclusion of fuzzy biological laws coupled with their largeness severely limits the utility of these models (Innis, 1972b), they are contributing significant new insights about the steady-state dynamics of ecosystems.

Comprehensive models to account for the transient (i.e., successional) dynamics, on the other hand, are thus far wanting, although some theoretical models have been presented to account for selected aspects. For example, Monsi and Oshima (1955) contributed a theoretical analysis of production during plant succession. Leak (1970, 1971), Bledsoe and Van Dyne (1971), and Bartos (1973) have presented dynamic models of species substitution during succession. These models, however, are formulated in open-loop form with respect to nutrient cycling and other ecosystem processes. Williams (1971) developed a computer simulation to quantify Lindeman's classical studies of energy flow and trophic equilibrium in a lake (Lindeman, 1942) but did not account for trophic dynamics during succession. Indeed, a comprehensive model to account for the dynamics of ecosystem succession has been reported only recently by the authors (Gutierrez and Fey, 1975a, b, c) and is presently reported in full detail for the first time. We believe that simulation experiments with computer models, if properly used in conjunction with field and laboratory experiments, offer a tremendous potential to advance the study of succession.

1.3 Research Methodology

It must be recognized that simulation experiments cannot possibly provide positive proof of the validity of a given hypothesis. There is always the danger of circular inferences or deductions. However, this danger is also present in other succession analysis methods (Horn, 1975), and computer simulation offers a potential vehicle for hypothesis generating and testing when the size of the system or the duration of the process under study (or both, as in the case of ecosystem succession) make controlled field experimentation difficult. Simulation is rapidly coming of age as a research method in ecology. Watt (1973) already discusses computer simulation, together with the classical inductive and deductive methods and the comparative method of Darwin, as a method of ecological research. He states:

In the last few years, another method of testing hypotheses has become available: computer simulation. For example, we could program a computer with a mathematical model which mimics the behavior of a forest. Then we could test the hypothesis that of five alternative strategies for managing a forest, over a 100-year period, strategy 5 maximized the long-term productivity of pulpwood from the forest. The hypothesis would be tested by using the computer to simulate, or mimic, the behavior of the forest over the 100-year period, using each of the five alternate strategies. Clearly, this is a type of test that would not be feasible in nature because it would take too long and be too expensive, but using traditional mathematical deduction would not be possible either, because of the great complexity of the system of equations required to describe the behavior of the forest.

The essence and utility of dynamic simulation models have been summarized by ecologists de Wit and Goudriaan (1974) as follows:

A system has a pattern of behavior which implies that the system changes with time, that it is dynamic. A simplified representation of a dynamic system is a dynamic model. An operational definition of simulation is the building of a dynamic model and the study of its behavior. Simulation is useful if it increases one's insight of reality by extrapolation and analogy, if it leads to the design of new experiments and if the model accounts for most relevant phenomena and contains no assumptions that are proven to be false. The latter requirement seems obvious, but is nevertheless formulated because such assumptions are often made to enable analytical solutions of mathematical models. With more recent simulation techniques this limitation can often be overcome, so that attention may be shifted from solution techniques to the study of behaviour of model and system.

There are, of course, many different types of simulation techniques available to the investigator. The method we have chosen is that originally known as "industrial dynamics" (Forrester, 1961). Industrial dynamics is a philosophy about systems in general which is essentially qualitative in character, takes the notion of accumulation as the basic building block in the universe, and recognizes that the dynamic behavior of systems is dominated by their feedback loop structure which, in turn, is influenced by the system's performance patterns through time. It is also gradually becoming a body of theory that relates system structure to dynamic behavior (Forrester, 1968b). Due to the vast generality of the subject, the term "industrial dynamics'' has become a misnomer. The term ''system dynamics'' has been adopted more recently (Forrester, 1971). In that it is more descriptive of the fundamental assumption guiding the whole approach, ''feedback dynamics'' appears to be a better term, and it will be used consistently in this book.

There is a research methodology associated with the systems philosophy of feedback dynamics. Forrester (1961) originally stated this methodology as follows:

1. Identify a problem.
2. Isolate the factors that appear to interact to create the observed symptoms.
3. Trace the cause-and-effect information feedback loops that link decisions to action to resulting information changes and to new decisions.
4. Formulate acceptable formal decision policies that describe how decisions result from the available information streams.
5. Construct a mathematical model of the decision policies, information sources, and interactions of the system components.
6. Generate the behavior through time of the system as described by the model (usually with a digital computer to execute the lengthy calculations).
7. Compare results against all pertinent available knowledge about the actual system.
8. Revise the model until it is acceptable as a representation of the actual system.
9. Redesign, within the model, the organizational relationships and policies which can be altered in the actual system to find the changes which improve system behavior.
10. Alter the real system in the directions that model experimentation has shown will lead to improved performance.

This methodology covers the identification (items 1, 2, 3, 4), analysis (items 5, 6), validation (items 7, 8), and design (items 9, 10) stages to be covered in addressing problems associated with complex systems in general. A step-by-step elaboration of this methodology with respect to the specific research at hand is in order.

The problem at hand is one of explaining successional modes of behavior as they arise from ecosystem structure under normal environmental conditions. More specifically, it is desired to achieve an ecological understanding of secondary succession processes in ecosystems, since proper manipulation of these processes is required for their preservation and improvement under utilization conditions. We shall review in the next chapter the various patterns of dynamic behavior that ecosystems exhibit during succession as well as the ecosystem factors or variables that appear to interact to generate succession. Structuring these interactions as closed-loop influence diagrams is the most crucial aspect of feedback dynamics as a research methodology. It involves the tracing of feedback influence loops among the identified system variables, the coupling of these loops within a closed system boundary, and the identification of the mechanisms governing the gains and delays within each loop, as well as their polarity. In the context of the investigation at hand, it involved tracing the feedback loops coupling organic matter, inorganic nutrients, species diversity, and other internal variables of grassland ecosystems, as well as identifying the mechanisms to account for both the positive feedbacks dominant during successional development and the negative feedbacks which become dominant as the climax ecosystem is reached. A verbal and/or diagrammatic statement describing the feedback relationships that are believed to cause the system behavior of interest constitutes a dynamic hypothesis, a theory of how system behavior results from its internal feedback structure. We shall be concerned with developing a dynamic hypothesis to integrate ecosystem structure and successional dynamics.

Putting forth a hypothesis to explain dynamic phenomena such as ecological succession immediately creates the need for testing it. In feedback dynamics research, model building is undertaken in order to permit simulated experimentation leading to either outright rejection or tentative acceptance of the dynamic hypothesis. The mechanics involved in constructing a detailed mathematical model to quantify the feedback relationships outlined in the dynamic hypothesis are well developed (Forrester, 1961). According to Forrester (1968b), the feedback structure of a system possesses four significant hierarchies:

The Closed Boundary

The Feedback Loops

Levels and Rates

Goal State
Observed State
Discrepancy Between Goal and Observed Conditions
Corrective Action

The system boundary is chosen so as to entertain a closed system, one whose behavior is dominated by internal structure rather than external events, with perhaps one or more exogenous inputs influencing particular modes of behavior. In the context at hand, the closed boundary is of course the natural boundaries of the subject ecosystem. Exogenous inputs to a grassland ecosystem, for example, are solar light, precipitation, and introduction of domestic animals.

The feedback loop is the basic system component, and the identification of the loop or set of interconnected loops believed to structure the system constitutes the dynamic hypothesis to be tested.

To formulate the substructure within each loop, ecosystem variables are to be classified as either levels or rates. Mathematically speaking, levels and rates are formulated as first- and zero-order difference equations, respectively. Whether a given ecological variable should be formulated as a level or a rate can be ascertained by conceptually bringing the ecosystem to rest. Variables that remain measurable in an ecosystem at rest are properly classified as levels, such as weight of plant biomass per unit area. Formulating the substructure of rate variables (e.g., the growth rate of plant biomass) may consist of simple algebraic expressions or involve complex non-linearities (i.e., table functions) to express flow processes as a function of the current values of the levels. A mathematical model thus constructed will be indicative of the specific data and parameter values needed to quantify the various model relationships; in this research, data required to quantify the model and permit testing of the dynamic hypothesis were abstracted from the literature on grassland ecosystems to the extent of their availability, but otherwise reasonable numerical values were assumed. In closing the discussion on the model-building aspect of the methodology, it is interesting to note that structuring an ecosystem model in this manner is in complete consonance with the best knowledge available on ecological modeling. H. T. Odum (1971), for example, classifies ecosystem components as (1) energy storage compartments, (2) energy flow pathways, (3) energy sources and sinks, and (4) complex work functions, to couple the various energy storages and flows throughout the ecosystem.

Subdivisions (1), (2), and (4) of Odum's classification clearly correspond to the levels, rates, and table functions, respectively, of the previous discussion. Sources and sinks are also used in feedback dynamics model building, and for the same basic purpose, to explicitly delineate the boundaries of the system being modeled. As indicated by the sixth step of the methodology, the model thus constructed is to be exercised through time in a digital computer. Following generally accepted practice in feedback dynamics research, the test model for grassland succession has been developed in the DYNAMO (DYNAmic MOdels) language (Pugh, 1963).

Modeling work eventually leads to a need for model validation. It is important to discuss the validation philosophy to be adopted and the validation methodology to be followed in the research. The validation concept for a given model must be justified in terms of the nature of the model or, equivalently, in terms of the nature of the modeling objectives; validation methodology follows naturally from a well-founded validation philosophy. The validation philosophy of feedback dynamics has been stated by Forrester (1961) as follows:

The significance of a model depends on how well it serves its purpose. The purpose of industrial dynamics models is to aid in designing better management systems. The final test in satisfying this purpose must await the evaluation of the better management. In the meantime the significance of models should be judged by the importance of the objectives to which they are addressed and their ability to predict the results of system design changes. The effectiveness of a model will depend first on the system boundaries it encompasses, second on the pertinence of selected variables, and last on the numerical values of parameters. The defense of a model rests primarily on the individual defense of each detail of structure and policy, all confirmed when the total behavior of the model system shows the performance characteristics associated with the real system. The ability of a model to predict the state of the real system at some specific future time is not a sound test of model usefulness.

Feedback dynamics modeling of ecological succession is directed at the qualitative study of dynamic modes of behavior such as the growth-followed-by-equilibrium behavior exhibited by ecosystems during their successional transient. This is in contrast to modeling for the quantitative purpose of computing numbers in a predictive fashion. Modeling dynamic modes of behavior calls for a validation concept that is itself qualitative and dynamic. A dynamic validation concept appropriate for this research is presented in figure 1.1.

Development of simulation models of ecosystem succession will draw from the currently available reservoir of ecological knowledge and general dynamic system principles, themselves the result of previous experimentation with (real-world) systems (denoted by the dashed-line block at the right in figure 1.1.) The block of dashed lines at the left of the figure denotes simulation, that is, experimentation in the model world. The resulting simulation model must be validated with respect to the currently available knowledge from which it was developed.

From the viewpoint of methodology, it is convenient to distinguish between structural validation and performance validation. Both are mutually complementary. Both are highly qualitative in character, but each one merits separate attention. Structural validation verifies that the causal relationships between the variables are meaningful and realistic in terms of, and consistent with, all relevant information available on the structure of

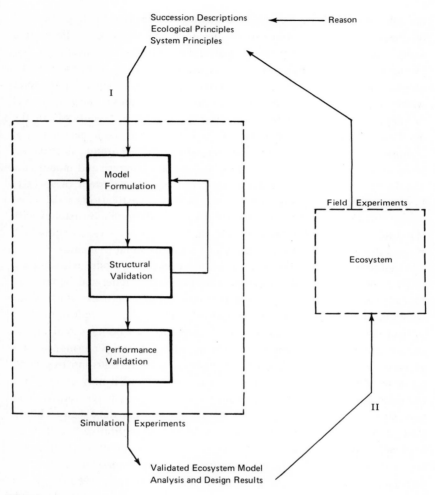

Figure 1.1
Dynamic validation concept.

the subject system. Performance validation verifies that the hypothesized feedback structure generates the same modes of behavior as the system under study, and that the quantification of the model has been accomplished properly. Properly does not necessarily mean accurately. When a structurally validated model reveals insensitivity to the value of a given parameter within its general order of magnitude, "properly" relates to the proper level of magnitude. Needless to say, "properly" means "accurate" in the opposite case; if model behavior is sensitive to a given parameter, it becomes desirable to estimate its numerical value as accurately as possible. In feedback dynamics, validation of both model structure and model data should be accomplished in the context of a specific system, a specific system model, and specific objectives. In this investigation, a validated ecosystem model will be one that displays no significant inconsistency with the full range of knowledge available on the subject ecosystem and which proves itself adequate for the study of its successional dynamics.

A point is reached, however, when the ecosystem model is exercised under conditions for which comparable ecosystem-generated behavioral data are not available. This stage will be reached in the process of using the validated ecosystem model for ecological policy design (or redesign). The subject ecosystem can then be altered according to policies that model experimentation has yielded as beneficial to successional performance for a given set of design criteria. The resulting response will contribute to expand the reservoir of available ecological knowledge, and it may or may not motivate a model revision to account for the new knowledge gained. The validation process for dynamic closed-loop models is thus seen as being itself dynamic and closed-loop. It is also highly qualitative because, as feedback systems increase in complexity (high order, involving both negative and positive feedback, nonlinearities, multiple-loops), their dynamic behavior changes in major qualitative ways (Forrester, 1968a); this is indeed the class of systems to which ecosystems belong, and the research objective is precisely the study of how successional dynamics arise from the complex feedback structure of ecosystems. This research traverses the dynamic validation loop from point I to II of figure 1.1, so as to produce an ecosystem model which is validated with respect to the available knowledge and which itself suggests further field experimentation to close the loop and start anew.

Successional Dynamics

2

Sweet flowers are slow and weeds make haste
—William Shakespeare (ca. 1600)

2.1 Successional Modes of Behavior

Ecological succession is the dynamic process whereby ecosystems evolve from extreme conditions to a state of equilibrium between the living community and its physical environment. A given succession, or sere, generally consists of an initial or pioneer stage, one or more intermediate or developmental stages, and a final or climax stage. Starting with the work of Cowles (1899, 1901, 1911) a wealth of descriptive information on successional modes of behavior under various conditions and in various ecosystems has gradually accumulated.

Successional behavior in grasslands was extensively described by Clements (1897, 1916) and other early investigators. For example, Shantz (1906, p. 190) offered the following account of successional behavior in a Colorado grassland:

Wherever short-grass land is broken and then abandoned, it is first covered by a growth of weeds, after which the type of vegetation that immediately preceded the short-grass in this particular place regains possession. If, for example, we break short-grass land which has been derived from the Gutierrezia-Artemisia association and consequently offers conditions favorable to that association, the land will become occupied by the latter association. The Gutierrezia-Artemisia vegetation will in turn gradually give way to the short-grasses, which will be fully reestablished within a period of 30 to 50 years. An area of short-grass land in which the physical conditions approach more nearly those of wire-grass land, if broken, will be possessed after the preliminary weed stage by plants of the wire-grass association, and will then gradually return to the short-grasses, the time required being 20 to 40 years.

Breaking done on wire-grass land will result in the establishment of a vegetation such as usually characterizes a still lighter type of soil. Many plants from the bunch-grass and the sand-hills mixed associations enter, and in the early stages of this succession bunch-grass itself quite generally occurs. The vegetation will ordinarily return to the wire-grass type in 15 to 30 years.

Wherever land characterized by the bunch-grass or the sand-hills mixed association is broken a blow-out may result. This, however, is unusual, although there is great danger if the land is plowed in the fall of the year. Usually the weed stage is most prominent the first year or so, but the native grasses soon regain possession and the succession is completed in a much shorter time than on the heavier types of land.

Shantz's observations are illustrative of the myriad of biotic and abiotic factors and symptoms associated with succession. What are the fundamental patterns or behavior modes underlying all seres? A problem with most of the available descriptions of succession is that overall behavior patterns are obscured by a multitude of instantaneous and/or localized symptoms and phenomena not really successional in character. It has been difficult for most observers and reporters of succession to isolate the smooth underlying patterns from the noise of nature. Another problem has been that, as Daubenmire (1968) has pointed out, "much of the earlier work was done with more enthusiasm than care, and if we become interested in explaining phenomena, the phenomena themselves must be accurately known." Significant advances have been made recently in reducing the myriad of available observations on succession to concise lists of well-defined behavior patterns. For example, Odum (1971, p. 262) has summarized successional behavior observed in grasslands by stating that "while the species vary geographically the same pattern everywhere holds." The pattern he outlines involves four successive stages: "(1) annual weed stage (2 to 5 years), (2) short-lived grass stage (3 to 10 years), (3) early perennial grass stage (10 to 20 years) and (4) climax grass stage (reached in 20 to 40 years). Thus, starting from bare or plowed ground, 20 to 40 years are required for nature to build a climax grassland, the time depending on the limiting effect of moisture, grazing, etc." More generally, both terrestrial and aquatic ecosystems exhibit certain modes of behavior during succession. Daubenmire (1968, pp. 216-217) has provided the following summary:

The progress of a sere commonly involves (1) change in dominance from small plants low on the phylogenetic scale to large plants high on this scale, (2) increasing longevity of the dominants, (3) conformity to a prevailing type of physiognomy that is characteristic of the region, (4) diversification of life form, (5) replacement of species with similar and broad ecologic amplitudes by groups having narrower and complementary requirements,

(6) increasing numbers of interspecific dependencies, (7) increase in the bulk of living tissue and dead organic matter per unit land area, (8) increasing regularity of floristic composition and structure among stands representing one association, (9) increase in the number of possible pathways along which matter circulates and energy flows, but a general slowing of circulation and flow, (10) a higher proportion of nutrients tied up in living cells and organic debris, (11) an amelioration of micro-environmental extremes, (12) maturation of the soil profile, and (13) greater resistance of the ecosystem as a whole to disturbing forces. Finally, growth rates and the general health of the dominants decline. Thus in a seral forest defective individuals are more common among late recruits than among those plants which became established when environmental resources were more plentiful. And in steppes too, the dominant grasses suffer loss of vigor and vitality in the absence of disturbance. Commonly, productivity increases during most of a sere, but it may decline somewhat as stability is approached.

Whittaker (1970, pp. 69-70) lists the general successional patterns:*

1. There is usually progressive development of the soil, with increasing depth, increasing organic content, and increasing differentiation of layers or horizons toward the mature soil of the final community.
2. The height, massiveness, and differentiation into strata of the plant community increase.
3. Productivity, the rate of formation of organic matter per unit area in the community, increases with increasing development of the soil and of community structure and increasing utilization by the community of environmental resources.
4. As height and density of above ground plant cover increase, the microclimate within the community is increasingly determined by characteristics of the community itself.
5. Species-diversity increases from the simple communities of early succession to the richer communities of late succession.
6. Populations rise and fall and replace one another along the time gradient in a manner much like that in stable communities along environmental gradients . . . The rate of this replacement in many cases slows through the course of succession as smaller and shorter-lived species are replaced by larger and longer-lived ones.
7. Relative stability of the communities consequently increases. Early stages are in some cases of evident instability, with populations rapidly replacing one another; the final community is usually stable, dominated by longer-lived plants, which maintain their populations with community composition no longer changing directionally.

*Reprinted with permission of Macmillan Publishing Co., Inc., from *Communities and Ecosystems* by Robert H. Whittaker. Copyright © 1970, Robert H. Whittaker.

In brief, the general pattern of ecosystem succession is for biomass to accumulate in time and space until a stabilized ecosystem is achieved in which maximum structure (biomass and diversity) consistent with the local physical environment is maintained per unit of energy flow. The energy flow itself increases rapidly during succession in order to satisfy energy requirements for growth, but eventually decreases as the growth rate approaches zero and the total energy flow through the ecosystem becomes allocated to maintenance functions. Thus the overall successional mode of behavior can be characterized as growth followed by equilibrium, with possibly biomass and diversity temporarily overshooting their climax values before settling down to their equilibrium levels in the long run. This overall successional pattern is shared by ecosystems whose variables display quite different numerical values.

Numerical time histories of successional variables for whole seres are difficult to obtain due to the length of time periods involved. Figures 2.1 to 2.5 reproduce some of the time histories available in the literature. Figure 2.1 is based on experimental data on microcosm succession (Cooke, 1967). It shows the patterns of production, respiration, and biomass accumulation observed following inoculation of samples of stock laboratory microcosm into fresh solutions contained in flasks. Light was the only external input allowed into the flasks. Production and respiration rates increase very rapidly during the first few days, peak after about 20 days, and then decline toward an equilibrium level. The level of biomass increases slowly at the beginning, then builds up more rapidly, but after 80 or 90 days further growth is inhibited as biomass approaches the maximum level that can be sustained by the physical environment of the microcosm community. Cooke (1967) reports that biochemical diversity was low in the immature system, high in the intermediate stages of succession, and again low in the mature microecosystem.

Figure 2.2 and 2.3 display time histories of forest succession. Figure 2.2 is due to Whittaker (1970) and is based on data of Whittaker and Woodwell (1968, 1969). It shows patterns of forest succession following fire on Long Island, New York. Notice that curve A represents net production or the difference between gross production and respiration. Figure 2.3 is taken from Horn (1975) and exhibits patterns of forest succession on Princeton, New Jersey, in plots farmed and then abandoned 35 to 150 years ago. The time axis in this figure is given logarithmically. The numerical magnitudes of the forest succession variables are of course many times those of microcosm succession. However, observe the recurrence of the basic behavior

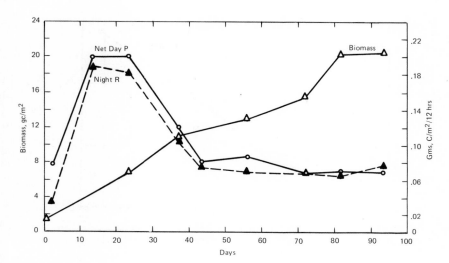

Figure 2.1
Patterns of aquatic laboratory microecosystem succession (From G. D. Cooke.
Reprinted, with permission, from the October 1967 *BioScience* published by the
American Institute of Biological Sciences.)

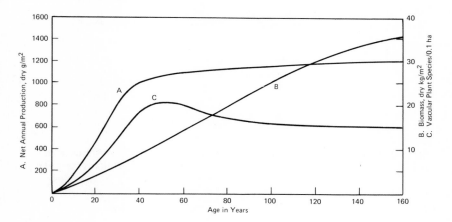

Figure 2.2
Patterns of forest succession following fire on Long Island, New York (Reprinted with
permission of Macmillan Publishing Co., Inc., from *Communities and Ecosystems* by
Robert H. Whittaker. Copyright © 1970, Robert H. Whittaker.)

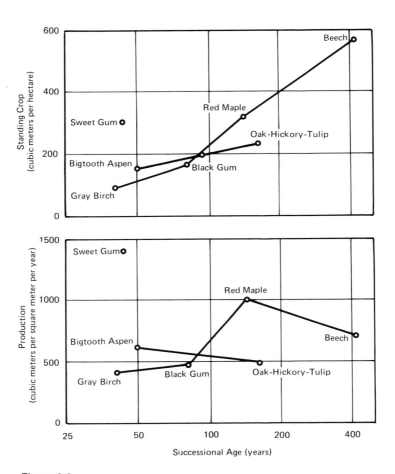

Figure 2.3
Patterns of forest succession in Princeton, New Jersey (From "Forest Succession"
by H.S. Horn. Copyright © 1975 by Scientific American, Inc. All rights reserved.)

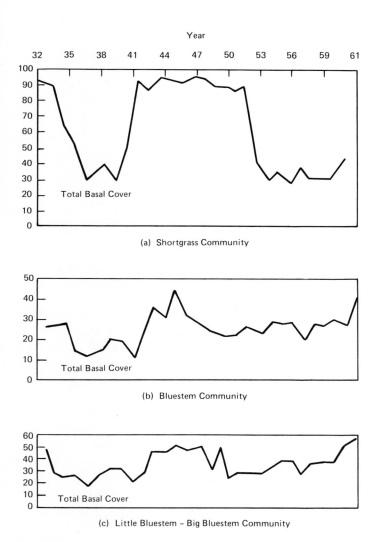

(a) Shortgrass Community

(b) Bluestem Community

(c) Little Bluestem – Big Bluestem Community

Figure 2.4
Patterns of basal cover during grassland succession in western Kansas (From F. W. Albertson and G. W. Tomanek, 1965, in *Ecology 46*:714-720. Copyright 1965 by the Ecological Society of America.)

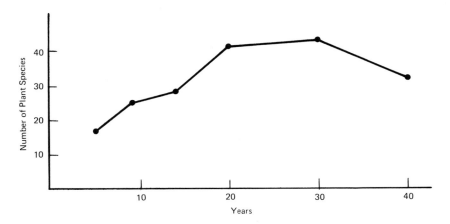

Figure 2.5
Patterns of species diversity during grassland succession in northeastern Colorado
(Based on data in Costello, 1944.)

patterns. Production, diversity, and biomass exhibit time-phased patterns of S-shape growth during succession, with each of these variables possibly reaching a peak value before declining slightly toward their long-term equilibrium levels. It is remarkable that ecosystems of such different size and appearance as an aquatic microecosystem and a temperate forest exhibit similar modes of successional behavior.

Similar behavior patterns are observable during grassland succession. Albertson and Tomanek (1965) have put together long-term time histories of basal cover for shortgrass and other grassland communities of western Kansas. Basal cover is defined as the percentage of area ground surface occupied by vegetation and should be closely correlated with biomass accumulation. Figure 2.4 reproduces Albertson and Tomanek's time histories. Notice how basal cover grows back toward the equilibrium level following the drought period of 1933 to 1939. The level of basal cover seems to overshoot slightly but remains at a high level until depleted again by the drought of the 1950s. Costello (1944) has presented data on changes in the number of plant species during grassland succession in northeastern Colorado. Costello's data is aggregated to total number of plant species (including grasses, forbs, and shrubs) and plotted against time in figure 2.5. The number of species present increases during the first 20 years or so, peaks about 30 years into the sere and then declines toward the number of species that the mature grassland can support in the long run.

The data are fragmentary, but some basic successional modes of behavior emerge from figures 2.1 to 2.5. It is important to clarify the meaning attached here to the phrase "successional modes of behavior." The variables in dynamic systems exhibit modes of behavior such as equilibrium, growth, decline, damped or sustained oscillation, or some combination of these. A certain combination of these is associated with successional dynamics, as illustrated in figures 2.1 to 2.5. The point to be stressed immediately is that, while these successional modes of behavior are quantitative in the sense that they are generated as time histories of numbers through time, it is not the numbers themselves that matter (from the viewpoint of the present investigation) but the behavioral time patterns. It will be shown that this observation follows naturally from the character of ecological succession and the modeling philosophy of feedback dynamics.

Odum (1969, 1971) has presented a tabular model of ecological succession that summarizes those ecosystem attributes closely related to the successional process. It also indicates the general levels of magnitude characteristic of each factor during the developmental and mature stages of succession. Odum's tabular model is reproduced in table 2.1. Observe that both the process of soil formation and the influence of exogenous processes are absent because the table refers to secondary autogenic succession and does not take into account primary or allogenic succession phenomena. The difference between primary and secondary succession was referred to in chapter 1, but the difference between autogenic and allogenic succession was not. Odum (1971, chapter 9) defines these terms as follows:

If development begins on an area that has not been previously occupied by a community (such as a newly exposed rock or sand surface, or a lava flow), the process is known as *primary succession*. If community development is proceeding in an area from which a community was removed (such as an abandoned crop field or a cut-over forest), the process is appropriately called *secondary succession*. Secondary succession is usually more rapid because some organisms or their disseminules are already present, and previously occupied territory is more receptive to community development than sterile areas.

Thus primary succession includes the process of soil formation out of bare rock, while secondary succession does not. Furthermore, Odum points out that "it is important to distinguish between autogenic processes (i.e., biotic processes within the system) and allogenic processes (geochemical forces acting from without)." While both allogenic factors and soil formation processes influence all seres, we shall for the time being restrict our attention to pure secondary autogenic succession. Once we have developed

Table 2.1
Odum's tabular model of ecological succession

Ecosystem attributes	Developmental stages	Mature stages
Community energetics		
1. Gross production/community respiration (P/R ratio)	greater or less than 1	approaches 1
2. Gross production/standing crop biomass (P/B ratio)	high	low
3. Biomass supported/unit energy flow (B/E ratio)	low	high
4. Net community production (yield)	high	low
5. Food chains	linear, predominantly grazing	weblike, predominantly detritus
Community structure		
6. Total organic matter	small	large
7. Inorganic nutrients	extrabiotic	intrabiotic
8. Species diversity—variety component	low	high
9. Species diversity—equitability component	low	high
10. Biochemical diversity	low	high
11. Stratification and spatial heterogeneity (pattern diversity)	poorly organized	well organized
Life history		
12. Niche specialization	broad	narrow
13. Size of organism	small	large
14. Life cycles	short, simple	long, complex
Nutrient cycling		
15. Mineral cycles	open	closed
16. Nutrient exchange rate, between organisms and environment	rapid	slow
17. Role of detritus in nutrient regeneration	unimportant	important

Selection pressure

18. Growth form

for rapid growth
("r-selection")

for feedback control
("K-selection")

19. Production

quantity

quality

Overall homeostasis

20. Internal symbiosis

undeveloped

developed

21. Nutrient conservation

poor

good

22. Stability (resistance to
external perturbations)

poor

good

23. Entropy

high

low

24. Information

low

high

Source: From E. P. Odum, 1969, in *Science 164*:262–270. Copyright 1969 by the
American Association for the Advancement of Science. Reprinted with permission.

Table 2.2
Summary of quantitative successional factors and trends

	Pioneer stage	Intermediate stages	Climax stage
Secondary succession			
1. Gross production	low	increasing and peaking	high
2. Net production	low	high	low
3. Biomass	small	increasing and peaking	large
4. Dead organic matter	small	increasing	large
5. Intrabiotic nutrients	small	increasing	large
6. Extrabiotic nutrients	large	decreasing	small
7. Species diversity	low	increasing and peaking	high
8. Size of organisms	small	increasing	large
9. Life cycles	short	increasing	long
10. Soil-carrying capacity	small	increasing	large
Primary succession			
11. Soil depth	thin	increasing	deep

a model, we shall generalize its structure to account for both primary succession and the influence of allogenic factors. The immediate task is then to explain how successional dynamics arise from ecosystem structure in a secondary area under constant climate and stable physiography.

A difficulty with the previously quoted summaries by Daubenmire and Whittaker, and with Odum's tabular model as well, is that both qualitative (conceptual) and quantitative (measurable) factors are included as ecosystem attributes. Qualitative attributes such as the "role of detritus in nutrient regeneration" and "resistance to external perturbations" (items 17 and 22 of Odum's table) would seem to be more the result of succession than factors actually interacting to produce the phenomenon. Further, for those factors that are measurable, Odum's table does not explicitly show the differences some factors exhibit during the initial, intermediate, and final stages of succession. For example, species diversity does not increase monotonically from a low pioneer level to a high climax level. It increases rapidly and peaks during succession, then declines toward the climax level.

In table 2.2 we present a summary of quantitative successional factors and trends. This table is also restricted to autogenic succession. However, it includes both primary and secondary successional patterns, and highlights peaks frequently observed during succession. Since many variations of these basic patterns have been observed, the table must serve as a guide rather than a rigid rule. Biomass may approach the maximum climax level without overshooting it. Biomass and other ecosystem variables may exhibit damped oscillations rather than smooth transient patterns as succession unfolds toward the climax. Furthermore, sustained oscillations around climax levels (rather than constant equilibrium values) may characterize the mature ecosystem due to weather and other environmental fluctuations. The time scale may expand or compress, and the values of production, respiration, standing crop, species diversity, and other variables may be greater or smaller for different ecosystems, but as far as is known the overall dynamics are the same. These are then the characteristic modes of successional behavior and the factors which appear to be involved. The important question is, how do these variables interact in order to generate succession?

2.2 The Classical Hypothesis

The early attempts to formulate a general hypothesis for successional dynamics approached succession as an ecosystem-level phenomenon. Succession was viewed as the unfolding of mutual interactions between the biotic community and the physical environment. The classical theory evolved out of the need to reconcile observed temporal and spatial changes in vegetation with the floristic, static analyses of plant formations predominant in ecology until the turn of this century.

Although recognition of vegetative changes in time and space can be traced back to Theophrastus in the year 300 B.C. (Drury and Nisbet, 1973), the concept of succession was articulated for the first time by Cowles (1899, 1901, 1911) on the basis of his observations of the sand dunes on the shores of Lake Michigan (1899) and other studies. He classified successions as regional, topographic, or biotic based on whether the climatic, topographic, or biological factor is the dominant causative agent. The following excerpts from ''The Causes of Vegetative Cycles'' document his thinking:*

In regional successions it would seem that secular changes in climate, that is, changes which are too slow to be attested in a human lifetime, and which perhaps are too slow to be attested in a dozen or a hundred lifetimes, are the dominating factors. Regional successions are so slow in their development that they can be studied almost alone by the use of fossils. It is to be pointed out that great earth-movements, either of elevation or subsidence, that is, the far-reaching and long-enduring epeirogenic movements, as contrasted with the oscillations of coastlines, must be considered in accounting for regional successions; the elevation of the Permian and the base-leveling of the Cretaceous must have played a stupendous part in instituting vegetative change. (p. 170)

In striking contrast to secular successions, which move so slowly that we are in doubt even as to their present trend, are those successions which are associated with the topographic changes which result from the activities of such agents as running water, wind, ice, gravity, and vulcanism. In general, these agencies occasion erosion and deposition, which necessarily must have a profound influence upon vegetation. As might be expected, the influence of erosion generally is destructive to vegetation, or at least retrogressive, while the influence of deposition is constructive or progressive. (p. 170)

Of less interest, perhaps, to the physiographer than are the vegetative changes hitherto considered, but of far greater import to the plant geographer, are the vegetative changes that are due to plant and animal agencies. These are found to have an influence that is more diversified than is the case with physiographic agencies; furthermore, their influence can be more exactly studied, since they are somewhat readily amenable to experimental control, but particularly because they operate with sufficient rapidity to be investigated with some exactness within the range of an ordinary lifetime. If, in their operation, regional agencies are matters of eons, and topographic agencies matters of centuries, biotic agencies may be expressed in terms of decades. (p. 171)

At first thought, it seems somewhat striking that far-reaching vegetative changes take place without any obvious climatic change and without any marked activity on the part of ordinary erosive factors. Indeed, it is probably true that the character of the present vegetative covering is due far more to the influence of biotic factors than to the more obvious factors previously considered. So rapid is the action of biotic factors that not only the climate, but even the topography may be regarded as static over large areas for a considerable length of time. It has been said that many of our Pleistocene deposits exhibit almost the identical form which characterized them at the time of their deposition, in other words, the influence of thousands of years of weathering has been insufficient to cause them to lose their original appearance. These thousands of years would have sufficed for dozens and perhaps for hundreds of biotic vegetative cycles. Many a sand dune on the shores of Lake Michigan is clothed with the culminating mesophytic forests of the eastern United States, and yet the sand dunes are products of the present epoch; furthermore, sand is regarded generally as a poor type of soil in which to observe rapid succession. If a clay upland were denuded of its forest and its humus, it is believed that only a few centuries would suffice for the mesophytic forest to return. (p. 172)

Although they grade into one another as do all phenomena of nature, we may recognize climatic agencies, which institute vegetative cycles whose duration is so long that the stages in succession are revealed only by a study of the record of the rocks. Within one climatic cycle there may be many cycles of erosion, each with its vegetative cycle. The trend of such a cycle can be seen by a study of erosive processes as they are taking place today, but the duration of the cycle is so long that its stages can be understood only by a comparison of one district with another; by visiting the parts of a river from its source to its mouth, we can imagine what its history at a given point has been or is to be. Within a cycle of erosion there may be many vegetative cycles, and among these there are some whose duration is so short that exact study year by year at a given point makes it possible to determine not only the trend of succession, but the exact way it comes about. It is clear therefore that vegetative cycles are not of equal value. Each climatic cycle has its vegetative cycle; each erosive cycle within the climatic cycle in turn has its vegetative cycle; and biotic factors institute other cycles, quite independently of climatic or topographic changes. (p. 181)

The biotic succession of Cowles clearly corresponds to an autogenic sere as discussed in the previous section. He recognized that physiographic and biotic agents interact during succession. However, his approach of classifying successions by cause and his focus on unidirectional rather than mutual causalities prevented him from recognizing that biotic successions may be caused by physiographic factors and vice versa. It was Clements (1916) who put the classical theory on a truly dynamic or developmental basis where "formation and habitat are regarded as the two inseparable phases of a development which terminates in a climax controlled by climate." (p. iii). According to Clements (1916, pp. 3–6):*

Succession is the universal process of formation development. It has occurred again and again in the history of every climax formation, and must recur whenever proper conditions arise. No climax area lacks frequent evidence of succession, and the greater number present it in bewildering abundance. The evidence is most obvious in active physiographic areas, dunes, strands, lakes, flood-plains, bad lands, etc., and in areas disturbed by man. But the most stable association is never in complete equilibrium, nor is it free from disturbed areas in which secondary succession is evident. (p. 3)

A sere is a unit succession. It comprises the development of a formation from the appearance of the first pioneers through the final or climax stage. Its normal course is from nudation to stabilization. All concrete successions are seres, though they may differ greatly in development and thus make it necessary to recognize various kinds, as is shown later. On the other hand, a unit succession or sere may recur two or more times on the same spot. Classical examples of this are found in moors and dunes, and in forest burns. A series of unit successions results, in which the units or seres are identical or related in development. They consist normally of the same stages and terminate in the same climax, and hence typify the reproductive process in the formation. (p. 4)

The development of a climax formation consists of several essential processes or functions. Every sere must be initiated, and its life-forms and species selected. It must progress from one stage to another, and finally must terminate in the highest stage possible under the climatic conditions present. (p. 4)

Since succession is a series of complex processes, it follows that there can be no single cause for a particular sere. One cause initiates succession by producing a bare area, another selects the population, a third determines the sequence of stages, and a fourth terminates the development. As already indicated, these four processes—initiating, selecting, continuing, and terminating—are essential to every example of succession. As a consequence, it is difficult to regard any one as paramount. Furthermore, it is hard to determine their relative importance, though their difference in role is obvious. It is especially necessary to recognize that the most evident or striking cause may not be the most important. In fact, while the cause or process which produces a bare habitat is the outstanding one to the eye, in any concrete case, it is rather less important if anything than the others. While the two existing classifications of successions (Clements, 1904; Cowles, 1911) have both used the initiating cause as a basis, it seems clear

*Reprinted with permission of The Carnegie Institute of Washington from Frederick E. Clements, *Plant Succession*, Washington, D.C.: The Carnegie Institute of Washington, 1916.

that this is less significant in the life-history of a climax formation than are the others. (p. 5)

The essential nature of succession is indicated by its name. It is a series of invasions, a sequence of plant communities marked by the change from lower to higher life-forms. The essence of succession lies in the interaction of three factors, namely, habitat, life-forms, and species, in the progressive development of a formation. In this development, habitat and population act and react upon each other, alternating as cause and effect until a state of equilibrium is reached. The factors of the habitat are the causes of the responses or functions of the community, and these are the causes of growth and development, and hence of structure, essentially as in the individual. Succession must then be regarded as the development or life-history of the climax formation. It is the basic organic process of vegetation, which results in the adult or final form of this complex organism. All the stages which precede the climax are stages of growth. They have the same essential relation to the final stable structure of the organism that seedling and growing plant have to the adult individual. Moreover, just as the adult plant repeats its development, i.e., reproduces itself, whenever conditions permit, so also does the climax formation. The parallel may be extended much further. The flowering plant may repeat itself completely, may undergo primary reproduction from an initial embryonic cell, or the reproduction may be secondary or partial from a shoot. In like fashion, a climax formation may repeat every one of its essential stages of growth in a primary area, or it may reproduce itself only in its later stages, as in secondary areas. In short, the process of organic development is essentially alike for the individual and the community. The correspondence is obvious when the necessary difference in the complexity of the two organisms is recognized. (p. 6)

Clements's formation concept "includes the whole group of relations between the basic unit of vegetation and its habitat" (1916, p. 116) and is therefore equivalent to the ecosystem concept. That Clements considered succession as a process emerging at the ecosystem level is also clear from the following account of habitat colonization and modification by the community (1916, p. 79):*

By the term *reaction* is understood the effect which a plant or a community exerts upon its habitat (Clements, 1904: 124; 1905: 256; 1907: 280). In connection with succession, the term is restricted to this special action alone. It is entirely distinct from the response of the plant or group, i.e., its adjustment and adaptation to the habitat. In short, the habitat causes the plant to function and grow, and the plant then reacts upon the habitat, changing one or more of its factors in decisive or appreciable degree. The

*Reprinted with permission of The Carnegie Institute of Washington from Frederick E. Clements, *Plant Succession,* Washington, D.C.: The Carnegie Institute of Washington, 1916.

two procedures are mutually complementary and often interact in most complex fashion. . .

The reaction of a community is usually more than the sum of the reactions of the component species and individuals. It is the individual plant which produces the reaction, though the latter usually becomes recognizable through the combined action of the group. In most cases the action of the group accumulates or emphasizes an effect which would otherwise be insignificant or temporary. A community of trees casts less shade than the same number of isolated individuals, but the shade is constant and continuous, and hence controlling. The significance of the community reaction is especially well known in the case of leaf-mold and duff. The leaf-litter is again only the total of the fallen leaves of all the individuals, but its formation is completely dependent upon the community. The reaction of plants upon wind-borne sand and salt-laden waters illustrates the same fact.

Note that Clements viewed the ecosystem as a closed deterministic system, a viewpoint we shall adhere to in developing our test model. Several investigators (Cooper, 1926; Phillips, 1931, 1934, 1935; Shelford, 1911; Tansley, 1920, 1929, 1935) elaborated upon the basic successional concepts developed by Cowles and Clements, but it was Lindeman (1942) who finally provided the ingredient still missing in Clements' work: he linked the open-loop flow of energy with the closed-loop cycling of matter and other community-habitat interactions, and he postulated this to be another important aspect (i.e., the trophic-dynamic aspect) of ecological succession. He summarized the role of energy flow in ecosystem succession as follows (1942, p. 415):*

1. Analyses of food-cycle relationships indicate that a biotic community cannot be clearly differentiated from its abiotic environment; the *ecosystem* is hence regarded as the more fundamental ecological unit.
2. The organisms within an ecosystem may be grouped into a series of more or less discrete trophic levels $(A_1, A_2, A_3, \ldots, A_n)$ as producers, primary consumers, secondary consumers, etc., each successively dependent upon the preceding level as a source of energy, with the producers (A_1) directly dependent upon the rate of incident solar radiation (productivity λ_0) as a source of energy.
3. The more remote an organism is from the initial source of energy (solar radiation), the less probable that it will be dependent solely upon the preceding trophic level as a source of energy.
4. The progressive energy relationships of the food levels of an "Eltonian Pyramid" may be epitomized in terms of the productivity symbol λ, as follows:

$$\lambda_0 > \lambda_1 > \lambda_2 > \ldots > \lambda_n.$$

*Reprinted with permission of Duke University Press from R. L. Lindeman, 1942, in *Ecology 23*, p. 415.

5. The percentage loss of energy due to respiration is progressively greater for higher levels in the food cycle. Respiration with respect to growth is about 33 per cent for producers, 62 per cent for primary consumers, and more than 100 per cent for secondary consumers.

6. The consumers at progressively higher levels in the food cycle appear to be progressively more efficient in the use of their food supply. This generalization can be reconciled with the preceding one by remembering that increased activity of predators considerably increases the chances of encountering suitable prey.

7. Productivity and efficiency increase during the early phases of successional development. In lake succession, productivity and photosynthetic efficiency increase from oligotrophy to a prolonged eutrophic stage-equilibrium and decline with lake senescence, rising again in the terrestrial stages of hydrarch succession.

8. The progressive efficiencies of consumer levels, on the basis of very meager data, apparently tend to increase throughout the aquatic phases of succession.

With Lindeman's work, the articulation of a general, self-contained hypothesis for ecological succession was essentially complete. Briefly stated, it consists of the following propositions:

1. Succession is an ecosystem-based and therefore an ecosystem-controlled phenomenon.

2. Succession arises from the interaction of mutual causalities between the living community and the physical environment.

3. Solar radiation captured by the green plants provides the source of energy flow necessary for the community to do both production work and habitat colonization and modification work during succession, as well as maintenance work, both during succession and after the climax equilibrium has been reached.

4. Succession is a deterministic process, with a myriad of details becoming "lost-in-the-blur," so to speak, as the basic successional patterns unfold toward the climax whatever the nature (physiographic, human, etc.) of the exogenous agent triggering the process.

We shall hereafter refer to these propositions as the classical hypothesis. It seeks an explanation of succession in properties emerging at the ecosystem level, and therefore is formulated at that level of aggregation. It is a holistic hypothesis, one which recognizes that ecosystem dynamics in general, and successional dynamics in particular, involves more than the sum of the actions and reactions of the individual biotic and abiotic components. But whereas Lindeman still regarded the ecosystem as "the more fundamental ecological unit" and succession as an ecosystem-controlled process, his work on community energetics may have paved the way for the contemporary concept of succession as a community-controlled process.

2.3 The Contemporary Hypothesis

Contemporary ecologists continue to regard succession as the general process of ecosystem development (see Odum, 1969). However, while recognizing that the physical environment influences and is influenced by succession, the contemporary approach has been to look at succession as a community-level and community-controlled process. The distinction is clearly stated by Watt (1973, p. 5):

Communities undergo a cycle of birth, growth, and senescence, like that in an individual organism. The difference is that communities do not die; rather one group of plants and animals replaces another. A community comes into being when some barren habitat, such as a lava flow, sand dune, bare rock, mud flat, or volcanic island is first invaded by a group of pioneer species. These species modify the habitat so that other species can invade and persist. Finally, the site is occupied by species that dominate the community and replace themselves, rather than being replaced by other species. Now we have a climax community. This whole process of replacement of groups of species, one by another, through habitat modification is called succession.

An even higher level of organization than the community is the ecosystem. Now we consider not only the total array of plant and animal species in an environment, but also the matter which cycles through the system and the energy which is used to power the system. Sunlight and warmth provide plants with energy to manufacture tissue out of carbon dioxide, water, and a host of minerals obtained from the soil. Some of this tissue is then eaten by animals, which then may be eaten by other animals. Ultimately, all living tissue is broken down by an immense variety of decomposers, and once again it becomes soil, available to be used again by the ecosystem.

The terminology is not uniform throughout the literature, however, and some contemporary accounts treat succession primarily as a community development process. The following account by Whittaker (1970, pp. 68–70) illustrates the point:*

As a lake fills with silt it changes gradually from a deep to a shallow lake or pond, then to a marsh, and beyond this, in some cases, to a dry-land forest. When in an area of forests a farm is abandoned, a series of plant com-

*Reprinted with permission of Macmillan Publishing Co., Inc., from *Communities and Ecosystems* by Robert H. Whittaker. Copyright © 1970, Robert H. Whittaker.

munities grow up and replace one another—first annual weeds, then perennial weeds and grasses, then shrubs, and trees—until a forest ends the development. If a landslide exposes a surface of rock in the mountains, the surface may be successively occupied by a sparse cover of lichens; a shrub thicket, which overtops and suppresses the grasses; a first forest stage of smaller trees, which seed into the shrub thicket, grow through it, and replace it; and a final stage of larger trees, which take dominance from the first trees and may form a larger and potentially permanent forest community.

Such processes of community development are called successions. In the first example the principal cause of the change in the community was a physical process—the filling of the lake with silt. In the second example, a principal cause was the growth of plants on an existing soil. In the third the succession proceeded by a back-and-forth interplay between organisms and environment: as one dominant species modified the soil and microclimate in ways that made possible the entry of a second species, which became dominant and modified environment in ways that suppressed the first and made possible the entry of a third dominant, which in turn altered its environment. Causes of successional changes are, to varying degrees, external to the community or internal to the community; many successions involve both kinds of causes and reciprocal influences. In any case a gradient of changing environment and a gradient of changing species populations and community characteristics parallel one another. A succession is an ecocline in time.

Whittaker's definition of succession as an ecocline (a gradient of ecosystems, i.e., a gradient of communities and environments) in time retains the holistic viewpoint and recognizes the mutual causalities between community and environment; yet an explanation for succession is primarily sought in the processes by which the community gradually modifies, and eventually achieves maximum homeostasis with, the physical environment (1970, p. 73):*

The variation in communities of a given area is generally affected by two or more environmental gradients and ecoclines, for example, elevation and topographic moisture gradient in mountains. The ecoclines can be used as axes in relation to which the communities of the area form a pattern, and in this pattern of communities and ecosystems we can relate to one another the patterns of (a) environmental gradients and habitats, (b) species distributions, which form together a complex population continuum, (c) characteristics of communities, and (d) the types of communities we choose to recognize. Community patterns of this sort are often used to analyze stable, mature, or climax communities only. In any particular habitat in the landscape, however, the climax community may have been destroyed or may not yet have developed. In this habitat the communities go through a progressive development of parallel and interacting changes in environments and communities, a succession. Through the course of succession community production, height, and mass, species-diversity, relative stability, and soil depth and differentiation all tend to increase (though there are exceptions). The end point of succession is a climax community of relatively stable species composition and steady-state function, adapted to its habitat and essentially permanent in its habitat if undisturbed.

Perhaps the most clearly articulated and comprehensive contemporary accounts of succession are those of Odum (1969; 1971, pp. 251–272). He summarizes the contemporary hypothesis on succession in the following propositions (1971, p. 251):*

(1) It is an orderly process of community development that involves changes in species structure and community processes with time; it is reasonably directional and, therefore, predictable. (2) It results from modification of the physical environment by the community; that is, succession is community-controlled even though the physical environment determines the pattern, the rate of change, and often sets limits as to how far development can go. (3) It culminates in a stabilized ecosystem in which maximum biomass (or high information content) and symbiotic function between organisms are maintained per unit of available energy flow.

We shall hereafter refer to these propositions as the contemporary hypothesis. It differs from the classical hypothesis, albeit only in emphasis, with regard to the role of the community during succession. Item (2) is the key statement of hypothesis: succession is a community-controlled process although it is an ecosystem-level phenomenon. In other words, the availability of physical resources such as space, water, and nutrients establishes limits on how far ecosystem development can proceed, but these availabilities by themselves do not generate succession. Given a light input source, a climax autotrophic community succeeds when inoculated into fresh media under laboratory conditions where the microecosystem remains completely closed to other external influences (Cooke, 1967). Given the presence of solar energy input and the presence of levels of precipitation, temperature, and so on, which remain approximately constant in the long run, terrestrial ecosystems succeed to become deserts, tundras, grasslands,

*Reprinted with permission of the Arnold Arboretum from W. H. Drury and I. C. T. Nisbet, 1973, in *Journal of the Aboretum 54*:331-368. Copyright 1973 by the Arnold Arboretum.

forests, and other stable formations (Odum, 1971). In both cases, the contemporary hypothesis postulates that the successional process is internally generated and controlled by the biotic community, not by external factors, although an exogenous perturbation may trigger a climax ecosystem into secondary succession toward either the same climax as before or a permanent disclimax.

2.4 The Drury-Nisbet Hypothesis

Five levels of biological organization are generally recognized: the cell, the individual organism, the population, the community, and the ecosystem. The classical and contemporary theories attempt to explain succession at the ecosystem and community levels of organization, respectively. Drury and Nisbet (1973) have recently offered an alternative hypothesis that attempts to account for succession as a process arising from the lower levels of biological organization: the cell and the individual organism.

After reviewing the classical and contemporary concepts of succession, Drury and Nisbet survey the field evidence available on secondary forest succession and point out behavior patterns that appear to be at variance with the classical and contemporary generalizations. In particular, they review cases where productivity and diversity do not necessarily reinforce each other during succession, or where mature communities grow in theoretically immature soils, or where the number of species is constant during succession with the only noticeable change being the relative dominance of the various species as succession unfolds. In addition, they make the following observations (1973, pp. 357–358):*

1. On sites which are cleared but initially free of seeds certain kinds of plant species (usually those of depressed life forms) tend to appear first; others (including those of successively larger and more complex life forms) appear later. Sites illustrating this sequence (''primary succession'') are rare in nature: examples include sandbanks, volcanic deposits, receding glaciers and mine tailings. Although many textbooks give hypothetical accounts of such successions, very few cases have been described. Evidence about later stages in primary succession is conflicting (e.g., Olson 1958) or lacking.
2. On sites which are cleared but not initially free of seeds, there is usually a similar vegetational sequence, often apparently involving the same kinds of plants, but usually taking place rapidly (''secondary succession''). Again most published studies are of the early stages in succession and accounts of the later stages are largely hypothetical. The evidence summarized in this paper suggests that the later stages of succession are not consistently unidirectional, and that forest succession is better represented by the lower half of Figure 1 [figure 2.1 in this book] than by the upper half.

3. Spatial gradients of several kinds of stress (climatic, chemical or radiological) give rise to similar sequences in space of life forms and vegetation. The congruence between sequences produced by different kinds of stress is reasonably well documented (see review by Woodwell 1970), although few detailed descriptions are available for any but climatic stresses.

On the basis of these observations, they suggest that "the main task in constructing a theory of forest succession is to explain the apparent congruence between the stress-induced sequences and the early and middle stages of primary and secondary succession" (1973, p. 358). With regard to stress gradients, they take a position based on the work of Raunkiaer and Woodwell (1973, p. 358):*

Vegetational sequences on stress gradients are reasonably well understood (Woodwell 1970). Each species appears to be specialized to a certain type of site and is competitively superior within a limited range of conditions, so that different species are dominant at different points along environmental gradients (MacIntosh 1967, Whittaker 1953). Plants of higher life form dominate under low stress conditions, but are unable to withstand higher stresses. The contrasting selection pressures have been considered by Raunkiaer (1934), who classified plants into life forms according to the location of their protected growing points. Those plants, geophytes, whose buds are well protected in the ground must grow their photosynthetic structures each year. They are readily overtopped. Tall, dominant plants, phanerophytes, have competitive advantages but their buds are vulnerable to drying winds, ice, fire, and radiation. Chamaephytes, whose buds are within a couple of meters of the ground, are intermediate in adaptations.
Woodwell (1970) emphasized that plants of higher life form usually have a larger ratio of supportive structures to productive structures: hence they have a smaller margin of reserve productive capacity to repair damage and are more susceptible to stress. Thus much of the observed correlation between stress gradients and vegetational sequences can be related to the problems of organization of a complex organism, together with the competitive pressure for plant species to evolve specializations to a limited range of environments.

With regard to the congruence of successional patterns in time and space, Drury and Nisbet develop the following argument (1973, p. 360):*

Species dominant in early stages of secondary or primary successions are those characteristic of high-stress sites (Woodwell 1970). According to the present interpretation, they achieve early dominance primarily because they grow faster than species adapted to lower-stress sites. A generalized explanation for the differential growth is given in the arguments of Raunkiaer and Woodwell summarized above. The early dominant species maintain dominance for as long as possible by suppressing competitors, but are replaced because in general they live less long and grow less tall than their successors. In primary successions (but to a much lesser extent in secondary successions) the establishment of the low-stress species may be delayed by delays in immigration and by physical stresses.

According to this highly generalized explanation, therefore, most of the phenomena of succession should be understood as resulting from the differential growth, differential survival, and perhaps differential dispersal of species adapted to grow at different points on stress gradients. The appearance of orderly replacement of ''communities'' of successively higher life forms results, at least in part, from the temporary dominance of certain species over their successors. Net productivity remains high throughout succession simply because the plants are growing, and it is reduced during the periods at which fullgrown plants suppress their potential successors. Net productivity rises when larger plants replace smaller plants, but this is a consequence of the growth of larger plants and is not a cause of the replacement (as the contemporary theories imply).

Under this interpretation, succession on a single site usually involves a sequence of species (rather than simply the growth of the ultimately dominant species) because no one species can dominate the vegetation throughout the period of growth. In other words the basic cause of the phenomenon of succession is the known correlation between stress tolerance, rapid growth, small size, short life and wide dispersal of seed. The few exceptions to this general correlation—mangroves, redwoods, coconut palms, douglas firs—are also exceptions to the generalization of succession: they are both 'early successional' and 'climax' species.

They conclude their discussion of succession with the following statement of hypothesis (hereafter referred to as the Drury-Nisbet hypothesis) and summary (1973, pp. 361–363):*

To place these arguments into a deductive framework, it is necessary to formulate the following hypotheses which differ at least in emphasis from those in contemporary theories of succession.
1. Gradients of soil conditions and exposure to stress exist continuously in essentially every geographic region, as a result of continuous geological processes of uplift and erosion.
2. Different species are specialized to grow under different site conditions, under the pressure of interspecific competition.

3. Individual plants already growing on a site generally have a competitive advantage over seedlings and immigrant individuals, but the advantage is often reduced by disturbance.

4. Dispersal mechanisms and tolerance of physical stress are correlated (together they constitute colonizing ability).

5. Colonizing ability and growth rate tend to be inversely correlated with size at maturity and with longevity.

Hypothesis (1) is geologically trivial, but it needs to be stated explicitly because it conflicts with the classical concept of landscape stability which underlay classical succession theory. Hypotheses (2) and (3) are biologically trivial, but represent the explicit introduction of natural selection into succession theory, in which it is customarily neglected.

Hypotheses (4) and (5) are the key statements underlying our explanation of succession. They amount to the assertion that certain adaptive strategies are mutually exclusive; species whose seeds travel far and grow fast in harsh conditions cannot also grow large and live long. There is a well-known correlation between size, longevity, and low growth-rate. We suggest that this correlation, together with the Raunkiaer-Woodwell argument, comprise a sufficient explanation of the broad features of succession.

An explanation of the correlation might be sought either in theories of senescence, or in theories of the organization of organisms. In any case, we suggest that a complete theory of vegetational succession should be sought at the organismic, physiological or cellular level, and not in emergent properties of populations or communities. The former approach seems more consistent with the theory of natural selection.

In contemporary usage the term succession refers to a sequence of changes in the species composition of a community, which is supposed to be associated with a sequence of changes in its structural and functional properties. The term succession is generally used for temporal sequences of vegetation on the same site, but only the early stages in the sequence can be observed and the later stages are usually inferred from observations on spatial sequences on adjacent sites. The term is customarily applied to sequences in many types of environment, although few detailed studies have been reported except for temperate forested regions. Contemporary theories of succession in general ascribe the observed phenomena to the action of the community itself in changing the environment.

This paper discusses a number of detailed studies of succession in forested regions, and shows that most of them do not conform to the contemporary generalization. The changes in structural and functional properties are not consistently associated with changes in species composition; the later stages in succession are not consistently unidirectional; and the effects of species already on the site appear frequently to delay rather than facilitate successional replacement.

An alternative explanation is outlined which is based on the observed congruence between temporal sequences of vegetation and spatial sequences along environmental gradients. According to this explanation, most of the phenomena of succession can be understood as consequences of differential survival (and perhaps also differential colonizing ability) of species adapted to growth at different points on environmental gradients. The appearance of successive replacement of one "community" or "association" by another results in part from interspecific competition which permits one group of plants temporarily to suppress more slowly growing successors. The structural and functional changes associated with successional change result primarily from the known correlations in plants between size, longevity, and slow growth. A comprehensive theory of succession should be sought at the organismic or cellular level, and not in emergent properties of communities.

The Drury-Nisbet hypothesis is inspired by observations of forest seres, but it has clear implications for the development of successional patterns in any ecosystem. Basically, Drury and Nisbet have abandoned the holistic viewpoint and extensive study methods in favor of a reductionist viewpoint and intensive study methods. In looking at succession, they attempt to use the microscope rather than the "macroscope." This seems strange in view of the fact that it is communities and ecosystems that exhibit successional behavior, not cells or organisms. It also seems strange because it is well known that the whole is more than the sum of the parts when it comes to explaining the dynamic behavior of complex systems. As Clements pointed out, "the reaction of the community is usually more than the sum of the reactions of the component species and individuals" (1916, p. 79). Yet it is also true that it is the individual organism that reacts, and the merit of Drury and Nisbet's important contribution is that it sheds light on the whys and hows of ecological succession at the lower levels of biological organization. Furthermore, they present field evidence which needs to be reconciled with the classical and contemporary theories.

2.5 Need for a Dynamic Hypothesis

Succession is a universal, exceedingly complex process that involves the ecosystem as a whole and that can and should be examined from many different points of view. The ecosystem can be viewed as an open system standing in interaction with other ecosystems and elements of the biosphere, or it can be viewed as a closed system with no exogenous inputs other than solar energy. Succession can be viewed as a stochastic process with a myriad of factors responsible for the variability of seral symptoms and climax characteristics, or it can be viewed as a deterministic process that follows certain basic underlying patterns uniquely directed toward a given climatic climax. The choice of viewpoint depends to a certain extent on whether one is inclined to follow a reductionist or holistic approach to the study of succession. In the former case, it would seem natural to focus attention on the behavior of individual organisms during succession, and this relatively microscopic emphasis naturally leads to assuming the ecosystem to be open to many external influences and succession to be a stochastic process with a variety of possible climax outcomes. If, on the contrary, one chooses to look at succession holistically, attention becomes focused on the successional behavior of factors or attributes that emerge at the higher levels of organization (the community and the ecosystem) and are more than the sum of the component organisms and populations; this macroscopic approach naturally leads to the view that the ecosystem is a closed, self-contained entity, and succession is a deterministic process entirely generated by the internal structure of communities and ecosystems.

The classical, contemporary and Drury-Nisbet hypotheses seek a general explanation of succession in attributes and relationships emerging at the ecosystem, community, and organism levels of organization, respectively. The classical and contemporary generalizations have evolved gradually, with contemporary work building upon the classical background. Both are holistic in nature, and differ from each other only in the emphasis placed by contemporary ecologists on community attributes and relationships. Thus Odum's definition of succession as "an orderly process of community development" (Odum, 1971, p. 251) is consistent with Clements definition of succession as "the universal process of formation development" (Clements, 1916, p. 3), except that for Odum succession "results from modification of the physical environment by the community" (Odum, 1971, p. 251) while for Clements "the habitat causes the plant to function and grow and the plant then reacts upon the habitat changing one or more of its factors in decisive or appreciable degree. The two processes are mutually complementary and often interact in most complex fashion . . ." (Clements, 1916, p. 79). The Drury-Nisbet hypothesis, on the other hand, is reductionist in nature and in our judgment differs rather substantially from the classical and contemporary theories. Indeed, Drury and Nisbet have endeavored to offer an explanation for successional symptoms apparently ignored by, or even in contradiction with, the classical and contemporary hypotheses. They contend that explanations of succession at the community and ecosystem levels are restricted to hypothesizing *why* the process happens in a very general sense but fade in power when confronted with specific situations and do not provide an adequate explanation for *how* it happens. They also present their hypothesis as an alternative explanation, one that cannot be reconciled with the others: "A comprehensive theory of succession should be sought at the organismic or cellular level, and not in emergent properties of communities" (Drury and Nisbet, 1973, pp. 362–363). This need not be so. We suggest that the differences and contradictions between the holistic and reductionist approaches should be resolved not in terms of elimination (of either one by the other) or duality but in terms of an integrated synthesis. Indeed, we shall not arrive at such a synthesis in this volume, but we shall attempt to integrate existing knowledge of ecological succession into a dynamic hypothesis, or model, of why and how successional behavior arises from ecosystem structure. We shall start down the holistic path, and the model to be presented will be entirely formulated at the ecosystem and community levels. However, there is no inherent methodological limitation as to how far down we could carry the formulation of ecological relationships.

The following difficulties appear to have hindered the development of a good model of succession to date: (1) Existing models of succession, such as those of Clements, Odum, and Drury and Nisbet, are articulated only verbally and are, therefore, both imprecise and inaccurate. (2) Existing models are too complex and tend to include too many variables and relationships relative to the available empirical succession data. Therefore accidental factors and symptoms cannot be separated clearly from critical ones. (3) Existing models are typically restricted to a single level of biological organization, such as the community or the organism, and therefore ignore the fact that behavior at a given level can be explained only partially by properties of the lower levels and only partially by properties emergent at that level. (4) Existing models fail to distinguish cause-and-effect relationships pertaining to autogenic succession from those pertaining to allogenic succession, and therefore confound open-loop and closed-loop relationships which call for different kinds of analyses. Thus we submit that what is required is a closed model, one that accounts for succession in as much as it is generated by the endogenous feedback structure of the ecosystem. Furthermore, we submit that, if a model is to be a valuable tool for integrating existing knowledge of and shedding new light on the process of succession, it must be precise, parsimonious, and hierarchical.

First, the model must be precisely formulated. It certainly must be formulated with greater precision than that allowed by the English language if the vagueness and ambiguities of the available models are to be avoided. On the other hand, we shall not attempt to formulate a model of ecosystem succession with the same degree of accuracy that would be appropriate for an engineering process. Precision refers to lack of ambiguity or sharp definition of concepts, while accuracy refers to the degree of conformity of a measure to a standard or true value. We shall endeavor to formulate our model precisely, but we shall have to relax somewhat the demand for a highly accurate prediction of the variables' magnitude at any specified point in time (event prediction) and settle for a moderately accurate prediction of the variables' behavior patterns (e.g., growth, decline, oscillations) through time (pattern prediction).

Second, the model must be parsimonious. It must include only fundamental ecological variables and how they interact to generate successional modes of behavior. It must include the smallest possible number of such variables consistent with adequate representation and required ecosystem-specific content.

Third, the model must be hierarchical. It must provide a framework where the influence on succession of properties and relationships arising at successive levels of biological organization can be incorporated. In attempting to develop this framework, we propose to follow a top-down approach, starting at the ecosystem level and successively incorporating in the model factors and relationships pertaining to lower levels of organization. The reasons for following a top-down rather than a bottom-up approach in developing a hierarchical model of succession are not difficult to see. Processes associated with lower levels of biological organization such as organisms and populations typically exhibit short cycle times. The time constants of the feedback loops involved become shorter and shorter for lower levels. At the cell or organism level, the time constants are very short in comparison with the time constants of succession. In general, many of the loops that operate at higher levels of organization are effectively open at lower levels. Therefore attempting to formulate a model of ecosystem succession at the cell or organism level of organization results in ignoring some of the critical higher level loops with long time constants. In developing our dynamic hypothesis and test model of secondary autogenic grassland succession, we shall focus on the relevant feedback loops at the highest levels of biological organization: the ecosystem and the community. As pointed out before, there is no inherent limitation in our model-building methodology as to how far down we can carry the formulation of ecological relationships, but the model we shall present is entirely formulated at the ecosystem and community levels.

Dynamic Hypothesis

Our discussion will be adequate if it has as much clearness as the subject matter admits of, for precision is not to be sought for alike in all discussions. . . . It is the mark of an educated man to look for precision in each class of things just so far as the nature of the subject admits.
—Aristotle (ca. 322 B.C.)

3.1 Fundamental Feedback Loops

In the present chapter we develop a hypothesis linking ecosystem structure to successional behavior. It has been pointed out (Watt, 1973) that energy, matter, diversity, space, and time are the fundamental ecological variables. Figure 3.1 exhibits a hypothesis on the feedback structuring of these fundamental variables. Solar energy is absorbed by the green plants and converted to fixed energy by the biochemical process of photosynthesis. The energy becoming available (i.e., being fixed) can be allocated to either growth or maintenance functions. By growth is meant the quantitative accumulation of living matter that results when energy is spent in fixing nutritive abiotic matter into biotic matter, or biomass. The energy expenditure necessary to accomplish this transition must come either from an internal source of stored energy or from the sun. In the early stages of development, the internal reservoir of stored energy is insignificant, and therefore the ecosystem is highly dependent on solar energy for its survival and development. Given a constant environment that includes the availability of incoming solar energy, vegetation builds up as long as soluble inorganic nutrients are available and the carrying capacity of the soil remains unsaturated.

In figure 3.1 and subsequent figures of this chapter we follow the familiar causal-loop diagramming conventions used in feedback dynamics. The links with arrows represent cause-and-effect relationship between variables, the variable at the tail of the link influences the variable at the head of the link. A positive sign in the link means that, when the variable at the tail of the link increases, the variable at the head of the link also increases. On the other hand, a negative sign means that, when the tail variable increases, the head variable decreases. The sequence of positive and negative signs around each loop determine the polarity of the loop. Specifically, an even number of negative signs implies that the loop is positive and an odd number of negative signs that the loop is negative. It is well known that positive loops act as deviation-amplifiers and therefore induce growth or decline, while negative loops act as regulators or deviation-reducers.

There are four feedback loops in the influence diagram of figure 3.1. The negative loop at the lower left-hand portion of the diagram is the production loop that regulates primary production as a function of the presence of soluble inorganic nutrients in the soil. It is well known (Lindeman, 1942; Borman and Likens, 1967, 1970) that it possesses negative polarity, returning the ecosystem to a state of trophic equilibrium after an exogenous perturbation. The positive loop in the lower portion of the diagram is the nutrient recycling loop that provides for sustained reproduction and growth of the standing crop year after year. Both loops in the upper portion of the diagram exhibit positive polarity and are postulated as the dominant forces behind the community-controlled growth dynamics associated with ecological succession. The upper inner loop is the biomass growth loop. Primary production results in increased biomass which in turn results in more primary production. The upper outer loop is the community diversification loop. When the carrying capacity of the soil becomes saturated, energy becoming available which can no longer be used for further quantitative growth is allocated to quality functions, such as building up community diversity. Exploitation of specialized niches by emerging species effectively results in increased carrying capacity, which in turn allows for further buildup of plant biomass, thus setting the stage for still further diversification, and so forth. This hypothesis is in consonance with Margalef's theory that ''succession is simply the exchange of an excess available energy in the present, for a future increase in biomass'' (Margalef, 1963). Eventually, however, a point is reached where further diversification does not result in increased carrying capacity either because (1) niche specialization cannot proceed any further or (2) because trophic equilibrium becomes limiting, or (3) because some environmental factor such as temperature or precipitation becomes limiting. As this point is approached, the gain of the positive feedbacks gradually vanish, and succession proceeds no further.

The coupled feedback loops of figure 3.1 provide a dynamic hypothesis

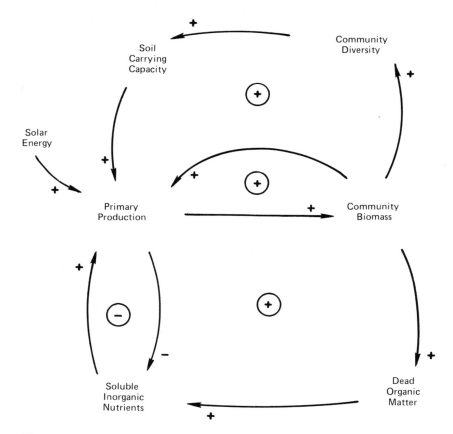

Figure 3.1
Basic dynamic hypothesis

of ecological succession which is highly parsimonious, that is, it accounts
for only the five fundamental ecological variables (energy, matter, diversity, time, and space) and the way they are postulated to interact in producing succession. The lower loops account for the circulation of matter. The
upper loops account for diversity and space, the latter expressed functionally in terms of carrying capacity. Energy flows into the ecosystem and is
either stored or gradually dissipated in the performance of work around the
loops. Finally, this structure generates successional behavior as a function
of time; each arrow in the diagram of figure 3.1 denotes a time delay.

It is illuminating to consider how all the factors listed by Odum in his
tabular model (table 2.1) are related to this hypothesis and, at the same time,

are indicative of how it should be further structured in developing a testable model. Gross production/community respiration, gross production/standing crop biomass, and biomass supported/unit energy flow (attributes 1, 2, and 3 of table 2.1) are quantitative indices of how the positive and negative feedbacks interact in allocating incoming energy for biomass production and other functions. Figure 3.1 explicitly recognizes that, given availability of nutrients and an unsaturated carrying capacity, incoming energy is to be primarily allocated to production of biomass. This is in consonance with the trends listed for net community production, or yield (attribute 4). Figure 3.1 also indicates that a buildup of biomass gradually has a positive influence on diversity but lacks content on the feedback structure which increasingly allocates energy to diversification and other quality functions as maturity is approached; this is, of course, a clear indication that further structuring of this aspect of the hypothesis is in order.

In the lower loops of figure 3.1, the values of the delays around the loop are not limiting during the early unfolding of the successional process, and they do not become limiting as long as the reservoir of soluble nutrients remains high in relation to the standing crop. Therefore functioning of the food chains (attribute 5) is effectively open and determined by grazing activity in the developmental stages; on the contrary, as trophic equilibrium is approached in the mature stages, the functioning of the food chain increasingly depends on the capacity for recycling of nutrients. A detritus food chain, however, is not explicitly incorporated. The lower loops of figure 3.1 also account for total organic matter (attribute 6) and inorganic nutrients (attribute 7), with the trends listed for these attributes being the consequence of these loops reaching trophic equilibrium. The dynamics of nutrient cycling as listed further down in the tabular model also arise from these loops. Thus mineral cycles (attribute 15) become effectively closed, nutrient exchange rate (attribute 16) slows down, and the rate of detritus in nutrient regeneration (attribute 17) becomes increasingly important to keep the whole ecosystem alive as the regulatory action of this loop becomes dominant at the climax.

Attributes 8 through 14 are certainly associated with the positive feedback mechanism behind succession, but the mutual causalities among these and other successional factors are for the most part unknown. For example, "the question of whether the seemingly direct relationship between organism size and stability is the result of positive feedback or is merely fortuitous remains unanswered" (Odum, 1969). Odum concludes that "whether or not species diversity continues to increase during succession will depend on whether the increase in potential niches resulting from increased biomass, stratification, and other consequences of biological organization exceeds the countereffects of increasing size and competition" (Odum, 1969). Therefore it appears reasonable to assume that different processes of diversification (attributes 8 through 11) proceed in parallel and reinforce each other, that the resulting niche specialization (attribute 12) has the net effect of increasing the carrying capacity of the soil up to certain limits, and that these developments reinforce, and are reinforced by, the ongoing buildup of biomass during succession; thus the upper loops of figure 3.1. With respect to size of organism and life cycles (attributes 13 and 14), Odum (1969) states:

In a mineral nutrient-rich environment, small size is of selective advantage, especially to autotrophs, because of the greater surface-to-volume ratio. As the ecosystem develops, however, inorganic nutrients tend to become more and more tied up in the biomass (that is, to become intrabiotic), so that the selective advantage shifts to larger organisms (either larger individuals of the same species or larger species, or both) which have greater storage capacities and more complex life histories, thus are adapted to exploiting seasonal or periodic releases of nutrients or other resources.

In that no mutual causalities appear to be discernible between these and other successional trends, they are not explicitly included in the tentative hypothesis of figure 3.1 Finally, attributes 18 through 24 are not themselves variables but rather consequences of the dynamic interaction between the positive and negative feedbacks hypothesized in figure 3.1 that become observable as succession unfolds. These positive and negative feedbacks are the force behind all these observables.

Thus the "simple" hypothesis of figure 3.1 establishes a framework that encompasses (either explicitly or implicitly) all attributes of Odum's tabular model (table 2.1) as well as all attributes listed under secondary succession in the revised tabular model presented in table 2.2. In order to construct a testable model, however, this hypothesis must be articulated in terms of quantifiable interloop and intraloop relationships. Taking the feedback structure of figure 3.1 as a point of departure, further articulation of the hypothesis will consist of (1) structuring the intraloop relationships of the nutrient-cycling process, (2) structuring the intraloop relationships of the community diversification process, and (3) structuring the energy flow relationships through which these processes stand in interaction.

3.2 Structure of the Plant Growth and Nutrients-Recycling Loops

The dynamics of ecosystem nutrient cycles have been extensively studied in ecology, although some of the specific processes involved are extremely complex and still poorly understood. The cycling of nutrients and the flow of energy are closely interconnected, and constitute the trophic-dynamic aspect of ecosystems (Lindeman, 1942). According to Lindeman's description, the trophic structure of an ecosystem is composed of four major sectors: abiota, producers, consumers, and decomposers. The feedback structuring of these sectors is traced in figure 3.2. This influence diagram accounts for the trophic dynamics of the ecosystem under the influx of solar energy and otherwise constant environmental conditions. It is composed of five levels: inorganic nutrients, producers biomass, consumers biomass, decomposers biomass, and organic nutrients. The inorganic nutrients level stands for the lumped sum of nutritive minerals available in soluble (i.e., absorbable) form in the soil of the grassland. The producer and consumer levels account for the sum total of grass and animal biomass, respectively. Similarly, the level of decomposers refer to the total amount of soil micro-organism biomass available to decompose dead biomass, plant and animal litter, and other soil organic matter back into soluble inorganic form. The organic nutrients·level lumps together all nutrients in organic form (i.e., organic debris) undergoing the process of decomposition.

The basic building block in the influence diagram of figure 3.2 is the (biotic or abiotic) level, together with its "inner" feedback loop structure. To illustrate, figure 3.3 isolates the basic building block for the producers: a biomass accumulation and the positive and negative feedback loops associated with biomass growth and regulation. The level of producers biomass increases or decreases dynamically depending on whether the gain of the positive growth loop is greater than the gain of the negative decay loop, or vice versa.

In the present discussion on the structure of figure 3.2, energy flow will be taken for granted; it will be formally accounted for later in this chapter. In figure 3.2, producers biomass is shown as growing under the influence of its own machinery and the availability of soluble inorganic nutrients in the soil. On the other hand, the standing crop of grasses is regulated by its own rate of decay and by consumption, namely, grazing by the primary consumers. Clearly, there must be other constraints on the growth of plant biomass besides nutrients availability. Even if nutrient resources do not become limiting, grasses will grow in a given grassland only to a certain saturation

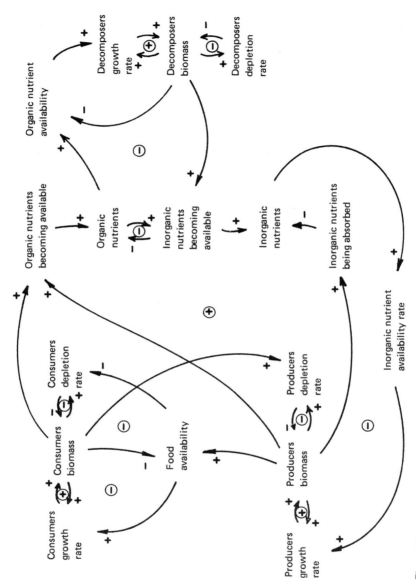

Figure 3.2
Nutrient cycling

Figure 3.3
Basic trophic structure

density which is a function of the local environment as reflected on soil-carrying capacity. Accordingly, the feedback structure of the producers sector is further detailed in figure 3.4. It shows producers growth rate as being the result of both replacement growth and new growth. This recognizes that grasses replace themselves from year to year and, in addition, generate new growth each year as succession unfolds. New growth rate vanishes when either the nutrients become limiting or the soil becomes saturated. Replacement growth rate, on the other hand, perpetuates biomass production year after year, so as to approximate each year the standing crop level of the previous year, as long as nutrients continue to be available. This is the meaning of the term ''indicated replacement growth rate.'' In this book, the term ''indicated'' is used to mean the value that one variable will induce in another after a certain period of time. Thus ''indicated replacement growth rate'' is the value that producers-depletion rate in a given year induces on replacement-growth rate the following year.

In the diagram of figure 3.4, inorganic nutrients, soil-carrying capacity, grazing pressure, and production efficiency appear as constants, where in fact they are not. Assuming for the moment a fixed, finite soil-carrying capacity, a continuous nonlimiting supply of nutrients, a constant production efficiency, and no grazing, let us consider the closed-loop dynamics of this feedback structure. This is best accomplished by first breaking it down into its component loops. The positive feedback loop which is hypothesized as generating new growth of plant biomass is isolated in figure 3.5. When the standing crop is below the level that can be carried by the soil of the grassland, gross new growth results as the plant machinery acts to take advantage of soil availability. Part of this new growth results in net new growth, the respiration loss depending on the production efficiency of the plants. There is, of course, a time delay elapsing before the new growth indicated by this production process actually impacts new growth rate (see figure 3.4), assuming that there exists a nutrient availability rate remaining for new growth after the nutrient absorption requirements for replacement growth have been satisfied. Thus in the new growth loop of figure 3.5

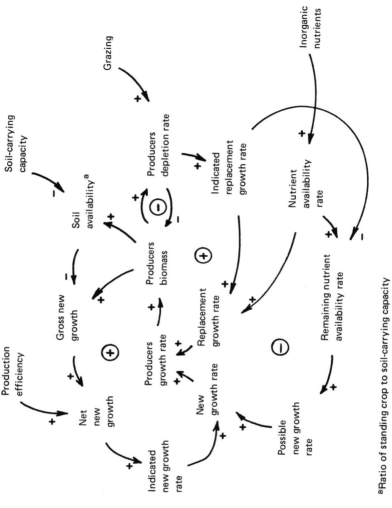

[a] Ratio of standing crop to soil-carrying capacity

Figure 3.4
Producers' sector

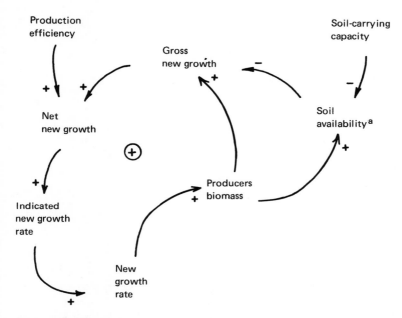

^aRatio of standing crop to soil-carrying capacity

Figure 3.5
New growth loop

growth of plant biomass results in still further growth of plant biomass as
long as soil-carrying capacity remains unsaturated. As the standing crop
approaches the level of soil saturation, the gain around this loop should
vanish.

In figure 3.6 an assumption is presented on how new plant biomass
production becomes limited by soil saturation. The figure shows a nonlinearity operative in the soil availability-to-gross new growth link of figure
3.5. Soil availability is measured as the ratio of standing crop over soil-
carrying capacity and represents the soil saturation and therefore the potential of a particular site to house new plants. When the ratio is close to zero,
physical crowding does not exert any suppressing effect on primary production and therefore the value of the production multiplier is unity, in other
words, the effect of soil saturation on new plant growth is neutral. In this
range the production of new plant biomass is limited only by the capacity of
the plant machinery to do the work (the producers biomass-to-gross new
growth link of figure 3.5). Furthermore, the suppressing effect of crowding
is not felt as long as plants are not growing too close to each other. This is

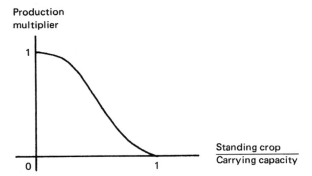

Figure 3.6
New production multiplier as a function of soil availability

why we postulate the nonlinearity as decreasing slowly at first, then decreasing more rapidly as the soil availability ratio approaches unity. The
curve approaches zero asymptotically rather than suddenly because plants
adapt to crowding and find ways to coexist in their microenvironment.
However, as the ratio approaches one, production for new growth gradually
vanishes under the pressures of a saturated environment, gross new production in figure 3.5 becomes inactive, and the gain around the loop vanishes.

The positive new growth loop of figure 3.5 stands in interaction with the
replacement growth loop, isolated in figure 3.7. While the new growth loop
is active only during succession, the replacement loop continues to work
after the standing crop has reached its climax level, to keep it there year after
year. The replacement loop also possesses positive polarity, that is, the
decay rate currently depleting plant biomass becomes the replacement
growth rate indicated for the following year, thus generating further growth
of plant biomass. As indicated in figure 3.4, the ability of this replacement
process to perform its function is constrained by the availability rate of
nutrients. Plants can continue to replace themselves only as long as inorganic nutrients continue to become available for absorption. Destroying the
positive feedback gain of this loop results in a gradual decay of standing
crop. Indeed, other factors besides limiting nutrients may constrain the
continued performance of this replacement process. It is interesting to note
that factors affecting the gain of the replacement growth loop in a detrimental fashion may be the dominant force behind senescence, the process
whereby mature ecosystems sometimes age and decay after a (possibly very
long) climax period. These considerations go, however, clearly beyond the
scope of the present hypothesis.

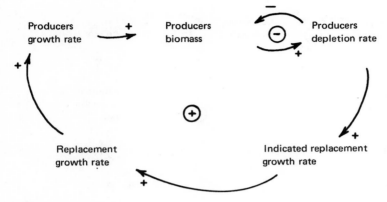

Figure 3.7
Replacement growth loop

At this point, the question arises as to whether development of the plant community is also influenced directly by natural consumers. Ellison (1960) conducted an extensive investigation on this matter. After reviewing all the available evidence, he concludes ''that the evidence of grazed plants' dependence on grazing animals is rather negative: the relation appears to be essentially one of parasitism by the animals.'' This conclusion implies that the growth of consumers lags behind the growth of producers during succession, and is, therefore, in consonance with the influence diagram of figure 3.2, which shows consumers influencing the depletion rate of producers but not their growth rate. The growth of consumers, on the other hand, is highly dependent on food availability, namely, the availability of abundant grass cover in the case of a grassland ecosystem.

The consumers biomass level in the diagram of figure 3.2 is also aggregated to include all kinds of consumers, both primary and secondary. The feedback structure of this sector is somewhat further detailed in figure 3.8. Under the benefit of a constant, presumably healthy environment, consumers biomass grows and decays in response to the relative availability of food, the ratio of food available over food required. When the grassland is in good condition and food is plentiful, consumers grow as a result of their ability to reproduce and multiply and the abundant food supply. Eventually, however, growth ceases either because the food supply becomes depleted due to the increase in consumption resulting from previous growth or as a consequence of interspecific competition, or both. These dynamics are accounted for by the positive and negative feedback loops to the left of figure 3.8. The negative feedback loops to the right-hand side of the

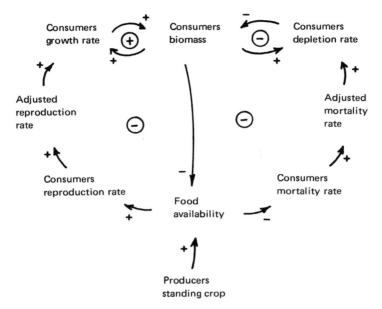

Figure 3.8
Consumers' sector

diagram are indicative of the fact that the total amount of living biomass in the consumers sector is regulated by both aging and food availability. There will be a time delay involved in adjusting either the reproduction rate or the mortality rate in response to changes in food availability. For a given level of food supply, an equilibrium level for consumers biomass will be approached in the long run, as graphically stated in figure 3.9.

According to the nonlinearities depicted in figure 3.9, both the reproduction rate and the mortality rate coincide at some steady-state "normal" value when the food availability index is equal to one. The food availability index is the ratio of standing crop over required standing crop to sustain a given consumer population. When this index is unity, the standing crop is just at the level required to sustain the population of consumers in the ecosystem. Therefore animals reproduce at their normal rate and die after a normal life span due to aging or reasons other than malnutrition. Let us consider each curve separately. The reproduction rate function rises monotonically from zero to some maximum value. When the food availability index is zero, the reproduction rate must be zero since there is absolutely no food available to the primary consumers. For very low values of the index

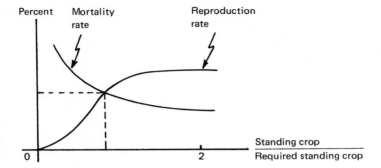

Figure 3.9
Consumers' reproduction and mortality rates as a function of food availability

the curve rises very slowly since the animals still have great difficulty in locating the scarce food available and therefore spend most of their energy just surviving. Then the curve rises more steeply up to the point where the food availability index equals one. The curve exhibits an inflection point here, indicating that after this point the reproduction rate continues to increase at a diminishing rate and only to a certain extent. If the standing crop of grass goes beyond (say) twice what is required to sustain the consumers, other factors such as crowding are assumed to become limiting on their further growth. Therefore the reproduction rate curve levels off at a certain percentage level which will not be exceeded even if food supply is plentiful. The mortality rate curve, on the other hand, also has a low constant value when food is plentiful and animals die of causes other than food scarcity. On the other hand, it rises sharply as food scarcity becomes acute.

As indicated in figure 3.2, dead plants and animals, as well as their litter, accumulate as organic matter available for decomposition. As this accumulation of organic matter to be decomposed builds up during succession, a corresponding increase in decomposers is indicated in order to break down the nutrients trapped in organic form back into soluble inorganic form. In the decomposers sector, the availability of decomposable biomass can play a role similar to the availability of plant biomass in the consumers sector. For the purposes at hand, an even more simplified hypothesis is suggested in figure 3.10. According to this influence diagram, a buildup in organic nutrients is indicative of the need for a proportional buildup in decomposers biomass; the latter reacts by gradually growing to the new required level. Naturally, a reduction in the level of organic nutrients would reverse the

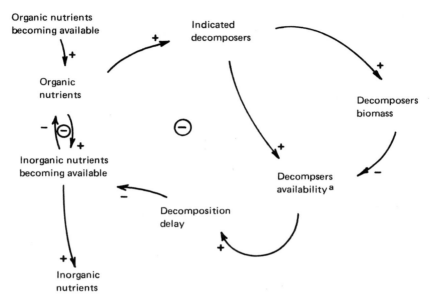

^aRatio of indicated decomposers biomass to decomposers biomass

Figure 3.10
Decomposers' sector

trend of the response. If decomposers availability is taken as the ratio of
decomposers indicated (i.e., needed to accomplish decomposition) over
decomposers available to do the work, then it seems reasonable to assume
that the decomposition delay will be some monotonically increasing function of decomposers availability. Figure 3.11 displays a linear approximation for this relationship. Decomposition delay is shown as a linear function
of the decomposers availability index. There is a minimum amount of time
that is needed to perform the decomposition work even at very low values of
the index, namely, when there is almost no dead organic matter to be
decomposed and therefore the needed or ''indicated'' decomposers approaches zero. This gives the ordinate intercept of the graph. This minimum
value of decomposition delay can be achieved if dead organic matter
becomes available and there is an abundance of decomposers present in the
ecosystem. Then there is an average or normal decomposition delay that is
obtained when decomposers match indicated decomposers, when the ratio
of the two approaches one, as shown by the dashed lines. If there is an
abundance of dead organic matter and insufficient decomposers to do the
work, the decomposition delay continues to increase in proportion to the

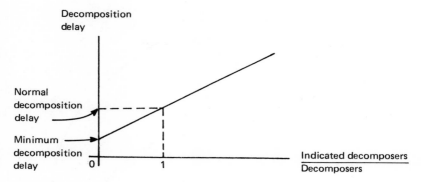

Figure 3.11
Decomposition delay as a function of decomposers availability

value of the ratio. In the limit, if there are no decomposers the decomposition delay would become infinity implying that the nutrients are not recycled at all; this would be the case in an ecosystem without any decomposers.

If this were to happen, succession would abort, and all life forms eventually would disappear from the ecosystem. What generally happens in the field is that during the successional transient the negative feedback loop of figure 3.10 will stimulate the growth of decomposers biomass so as to keep the recycling of nutrients going; as the ecosystem approaches maturity, it will regulate decomposers biomass about an equilibrium level such that the value of this ratio remains close to unity, thus yielding the "normal" decomposition delay when the ecosystem is in steady-state.

3.3 Structure of the Community Diversification Loops

A biotic community develops both by quantitative growth and by qualitative diversification. It modifies its physical environment so as to enhance its carrying capacity and pave the way for further community development, and it continues to do so until constrained by physical and biological limits such as unavailability of space, niches, and nutrients. This process is community controlled (Odum, 1969). As the limits of the environment are approached, a transition from growth to equilibrium is observed, eventually resulting in a stabilized climax community. These well-known observations constitute the basis for the upper loop of the dynamic hypothesis in figure 3.1, which shows the closed-loop interaction between species diversity, soil-carrying capacity and biomass production. A more explicit influence diagram for this aspect of the hypothesis is articulated in figure 3.12.

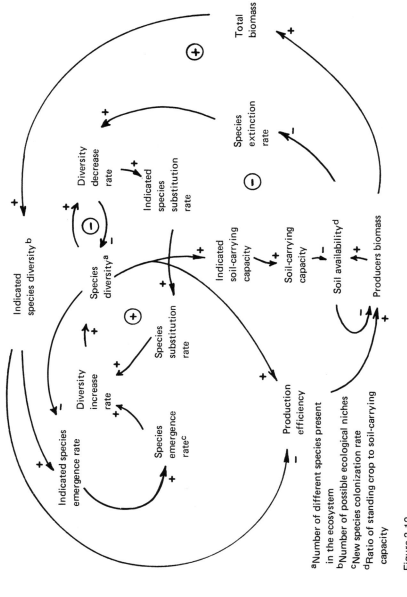

aNumber of different species present
 in the ecosystem
bNumber of possible ecological niches
cNew species colonization rate
dRatio of standing crop to soil-carrying
 capacity

Figure 3.12
Diversification

In discussing this feedback structure as an explanatory hypothesis for the successional modes of behavior discussed in section 2.1, it is first necessary to point out that successional patterns are not necessarily smooth. In fact, according to Lindeman (1942), smooth growth patterns are

seldom found in natural succession, except possibly in such cases as bare areas developing directly to the climax vegetation type in the wake of a retreating glacier. Most successional seres consist of a number of stages. . . . so that their productivity-growth curves will contain undulations corresponding in distinctness to the distinctness of the stages. The presence of stages in a successional sere apparently represents the persistent influence of some combination of limiting factors, which, until they are overcome by species-substitution, etc., tend to decrease the acceleration of productivity and maintain it at a more constant rate.

Thus it seems that at the beginning of succession soil-carrying capacity (refer to figure 3.12) would be typically modest, permitting only a correspondingly modest amount of further growth in biomass. As the current carrying capacity of the soil becomes saturated, two things happen: on the one hand, some species currently on the grassland may disappear under the pressures of competition and other factors arising from the current saturation of the physical environment; on the other hand, available energy that cannot be allocated any more to growth of more biomass will be allocated for diversification. While energy flow will not be formally accounted for until the next section, its presence is again assumed for the present discussion.

After a certain time delay, the allocation of energy to diversification gradually gives rise to a bloom in species diversity. This bloom is brought about both by recolonization of previously occupied niches and by colonization of new niches. These diversification activities are denoted in figure 3.12 as species substitution rate and species emergence rate, respectively. Now, a more diversified community is not only bound to exploit a greater number of available specialized niches but also to act on the soil, in effect, so as to increase its carrying capacity after some time has elapsed. Increased carrying capacity means, in turn, the ability of the soil to sustain a greater standing crop of the now more diversified community; after another period of time, the new growth in standing crop saturates once more the new carrying capacity of the soil, thus paving the way for still further diversification and the next successional stage. This stage-by-stage process eventually must come to an end, however, and the transition from growth to equilibrium arises from the intraloop relationships that govern the gain of the positive feedback.

There are four complex relationships in the structure of figure 3.12: indicated diversity as a function of total biomass, indicated soil-carrying capacity as a function of diversity, species extinction rate as a function of soil saturation, and production efficiency as a function of relative diversity, the ratio of species diversity to indicated species diversity. A fifth relationship, indicated species substitution rate as a function of diversity decrease rate, is clearly analogous to indicated replacement growth rate as a function of producers decay rate (see figures 3.4 and 3.7). As pointed out before, terms such as ''indicated species diversity'' refer to the value of the influenced variable (in this case species diversity) to be induced over a period of time by the influencing variable (total biomass). Among these relationships, the most crucial are the first two, because they provide the basic positive feedback mechanism. With regard to indicated diversity as a function of total biomass, Odum (1969) points out that

whether or not species diversity continues to increase during succession will depend on whether the increase in potential niches resulting from increased biomass, stratification [table 2.1, item 9] and other consequences of biological organization exceeds the countereffects of increasing size and competition.

A plausible functional relationship between total biomass and indicated diversity is hypothesized in figure 3.13. Total biomass is community biomass, including producers, consumers, and decomposers. Indicated diversity is the maximum community diversity induced by the increase in potential ecological niches that results from accumulation of biomass. It is evident that community diversity is zero if community biomass is zero; therefore the curve shows indicated diversity to be zero if total biomass is zero. The life history of organisms present at very low levels of biomass are characterized by broad niche specialization, small size, and short, simple life cycles. Under these conditions the number of new potential ecological niches increases very slowly in response to increases in biomass, thus the slow rising of indicated diversity for low values of total biomass shown in figure 3.13. However, further and further increases in biomass accumulation lead to the presence of organisms that exhibit narrow niche specialization, large size, and long, complex life cycles (see table 2.1). Under these conditions potential ecological niches proliferate at a much quicker pace. The curve of figure 3.13 reflects this by the steeper rise in indicated diversity for large biomass accumulations. But eventually a stage of development is reached in which (due to any one of many possible limiting factors, e.g., competition) further accumulation of biomass results in pro-

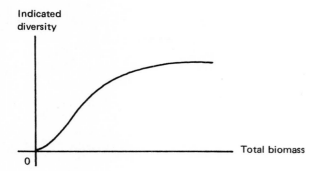

Figure 3.13
Indicated species diversity as a function of total biomass

gressively diminishing increases in the number of potential ecological niches. This is the reason for assuming in figure 3.13 that the indicated diversity curve approaches asymptotically some upper limit that depends on the biogeography of the ecosystem. Incorporation of this relationship immediately provides a mechanism for the transition from growth to equilibrium; that is, the gain of the positive feedback would gradually vanish as the horizontal asymptote of the nonlinearity in figure 3.13 is approached.

The causal relationship between total biomass and species diversity is not unidirectional, however. The mutual causality that exists is evident from Odum's statement. Elsewhere, DeVos (1969) also observes that ''production, both primary (by green plants) and secondary (by consumers) in an ecosystem is apparently increased by species variety because this permits the occupancy of more niches in the habitat.'' Consequently, it appears reasonable to assume that the effective carrying capacity per unit area of the soil increases as diversity increases, and that succession ends when further diversification does not result in increased soil-carrying capacity due to an exhaustion of specialized niches in which to pursue further growth. This assumption is expressed graphically in figure 3.14, which postulates that the actual carrying capacity of the soil ranges from a modest value when diversity is low to some upper bound for a highly diversified community. The rationale for this curve is as follows. Indicated soil-carrying capacity is the amount of biomass per unit area that is induced by the colonization of niches. This quantity would be zero if there is no soil; that would be the case at the onset of primary succession out of bare rock. For secondary succession the presence of a soil layer provides a potential of a modest carrying capacity even if the process starts out of bare land. As long as diversity is

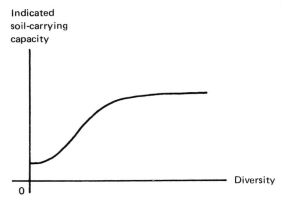

Figure 3.14
Indicated soil-carrying capacity as a function of diversity

low, soil-carrying capacity builds up slowly since only a few niches are being colonized. As the number of species present in the ecosystem increases, more niches are colonized and a greater amount of biomass per unit area is induced. Eventually, as all the niches become fully occupied, the carrying capacity of the soil approaches asymptotically some upper bound the value of which is ecosystem-specific. It follows then that the gain of the positive feedback loop of figure 3.16 will vanish as either the upper bound of figure 3.13, or the upper bound of figure 3.14, or both are approached.

Figure 3.15 displays the assumed nonlinear influence of denudation on species extinction rate. This curve is analogous to the production multiplier curve of figure 3.6. Note that according to the nonlinearity of figure 3.15 the species extinction rate is activated only when the standing crop is less than the carrying capacity. As standing crop approaches its equilibrium value with soil-carrying capacity in the undisturbed mature ecosystem, extinction of species continues at a very low rate or ceases altogether (i.e., a zero species extinction rate) as indicated by the right-hand end of the curve. If the standing crop is partially destroyed, some of the species on the range are bound to be driven away (at least temporarily) by the resulting scarcity of food, competition pressure, selective grazing, and so on. The right-hand end of the curve assumes that a slight destruction or removal of standing crop results in a negligible loss of species. For greater denudation (say, in the 25 to 75 percent range) the impact is proportional to the degree of denudation, thus the more rapid increase of the curve with constant slope from right to left. For very low levels of standing crop (almost complete denudation) the species extinction rate continues to increase though more

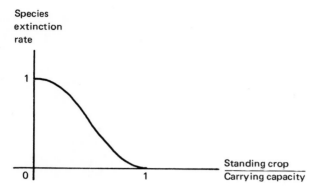

Figure 3.15
Species extinction rate as a function of soil availability

slowly, as under these conditions only the stronger and more resistant species (those that can survive the harshest competition for food) would remain present in the ecosystem. Obviously, all species would become extinct if the whole standing crop is destroyed.

In the hypothesis structured in figure 3.12, the biomass-diversity loop (isolated in figure 3.16) would be activated by the closed-loop interaction of the relationships previously discussed, even if production efficiency were to remain constant throughout the successional process. Production efficiency does change during succession, however, under the influence of a multitude of factors. Productivity will increase if diversity is suddenly destroyed in a mature ecosystem. This influence can be explicitly incorporated into the hypothesis by making production efficiency a function of relative diversity, actual diversity over indicated diversity, as stated graphically in figure 3.17. Following the same reasoning as before, the assumption implicit in figure 3.17 is that production efficiency would stabilize at some low value under undisturbed climax conditions but would rise to a much higher value were diversity to be destroyed completely (as in monocultures), with some intermediate values in between. The values of the upper and lower limits of production efficiency depend on the biology and microclimate of the producers and certainly may be quite different for different ecosystems such as a desert, a grassland, or a forest. The shape of the curve supports the hypothesis that the increase in production efficiency would be small if only a few species are removed from the ecosystem but would increase significantly if a large percentage of species are removed. These and other refinements can be incorporated to test the sensitivity of the hypothesis to various factors. It is emphasized, however, that the upper

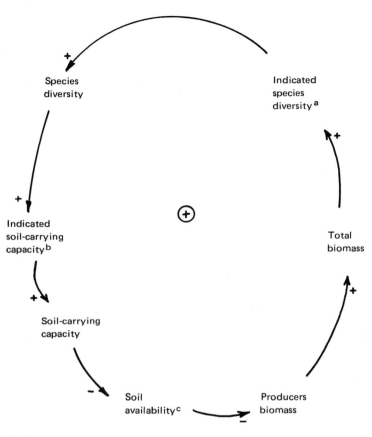

aNumber of possible ecological niches
bPossible accumulation of biomass in
  fully occupied niches
cRatio of standing crop to soil-carrying
  capacity

Figure 3.16
Positive feedback between biomass and diversity

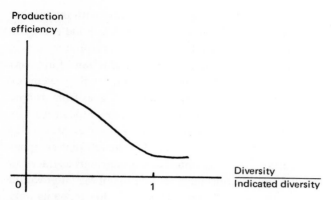

Figure 3.17
Production efficiency as a function of relative diversity

loop of figure 3.1 stands as the fundamental internal driving force behind the successional response of ecosystems to perturbation of their climax.

3.4 Open-Loop Energy Flow

In contrast with the closed-loop flow of nutrients, the flow of energy through an ecosystem is unidirectional (see Lindeman, 1942; Phillipson, 1966; Kormondy, 1969; Odum, 1971), thus the need for the sun as a continuous source of primary energy. In the context of the structure presented in figure 3.1, solar energy is fixed by the green plants of the grassland, and then it is either used (i.e., dissipated) for various purposes or stored in various forms as it flows through the ecosystem, providing the ability for the biotic community to do work. As it flows through the ecosystem, energy is conserved as it is successively transformed from one form to another, and at the same time it becomes successively degraded into increasingly dispersed forms that sooner or later become useless to the community. These facts follow from the first and second laws of thermodynamics. More specifically, energy flows through the nutrients recycling loop of figure 3.1 and is either temporarily stored as biomass or dissipated as heat; it also flows through the community diversification loop, and is dissipated in the performance of quality functions (e.g., diversification) and in the performance of work on the physical environment. Let us consider the flow of energy through each one of these processes as it relates to successional dynamics.

The successive transformation and degradation of energy around the nutrients cycling loop of figure 3.1 proceed concurrently with the trophic dynamics of the ecosystem, as diagrammed in figure 3.2. Food energy is successively fixed and transferred around the loop, with respiratory losses taking place at each trophic level. In other words, production of biomass plus respiration equals energy flow through each trophic level. The energy allocated for production is thus gradually dissipated as it goes from trophic level to trophic level around the loop. These are, of course, the energetics associated with the trophic-dynamic aspect of ecosystems as previously cited from the work of Lindeman (1942). In brief, it means that an open-loop flow of energy underlies the closed-loop flow of nutrients as traced in figure 3.2 and that, under any circumstances, activation of the latter would be impossible in the absence of the former. However, this accounts only partially for successional behavior, since trophic-dynamic interactions and the resulting growth in living matter would permit successional development to proceed only to a limited extent in the absence of diversification.

It seems clear that the qualitative work associated with diversification and other quality functions requires energy, just as the work associated with biomass production and maintenance requires energy. As succession unfolds, energy becoming available through photosynthesis must be allocated either for biomass production and maintenance or for qualitative functions such as diversification. In other words, it must be allocated for the performance of work around either the growth loops or the diversification loop of figure 3.1. Work performed around the diversification loop includes that required for maintaining the interactions among the species. For example, it is clear that energy is dissipated by both the predator and the prey as predator-prey interactions take place through time. In discussing the relationship between quantitative growth, qualitative change, and the energetics of succession, Margalef (1963) points out that it is necessary to distinguish between the energetics associated with biomass production and maintenance and those associated with the generation and maintenance of diversity and other aspects of structural complexity, and he concludes:

It seems safe to assume that maturity has a double measure: In its structural aspect, it can be measured in terms of diversity or of complexity over a certain number of levels. In the aspects relating to matter and energy, it can be measured as primary production per unit of total biomass. The connections between complementary aspects and measures require theoretical consideration.

What is needed is a tentative theoretical model, or hypothesis, to account for the structuring of these connections or, in other words, to account for the dynamic allocations of excess available energy to further either growth or diversification so as to bring about successive stages of development. The influence diagram of figure 3.18 displays a dynamic hypothesis for successional energetics. This hypothesis is based on admittedly sketchy descriptive information, such as Margalef's observations as quoted above. It exhibits the feedback structure that is assumed to determine the dynamic allocation of energy for storage and/or dissipation in the performance of work around the feedback loops of figure 3.1.

The net availability of energy to be allocated (i.e., the energy availability rate in excess of that required for biomass production and maintenance) depends on both the rate of solar energy fixation and the reservoir of internally stored energy, denoted in the diagram as "plant vigor." The rate of solar energy fixation depends, of course, on the availability of green plants machinery coupled with incoming solar radiation. It is assumed that this net energy availability rate will be allocated to further growth of biomass as long as such growth can continue without saturating the carrying capacity of the soil, as long as the new growth loop of figure 3.5 remains active for a given stage of successional development. Presumably, generation of new growth requires a consumption of energy in proportion to the amount of new biomass to be produced. The energy availability rate remaining after both replacement growth and new growth requirements have been satisfied is allocated to the performance of quality functions, primarily diversification. Some energy expenditure is required to maintain diversity at a given level, the level of necessary expenditure being proportional (as a first approximation) to the level of diversity. If the energy availability rate remaining from growth is inadequate for this maintenance function, diversity is bound to decrease. On the other hand, if energy is becoming available at a rate in excess of that required to sustain the present levels of both biomass and diversity (possibly as a result of no further growth currently being possible), such excess energy availability rate becomes available for further diversification. This energy provides the ability to perform all kinds of work associated with increasing the carrying capacity of the soil to a new level, so as to bring about the next stage of successional development; again as a first approximation, it may also be assumed that the energy thus dissipated will be in proportion to the intensity of diversification activity, as measured by the rate of increase in species diversity.

As the climax is approached, however, both total biomass and species diversity gradually approach steady-state levels, and the question arises as to the destination of energy availability rate in excess of that required for

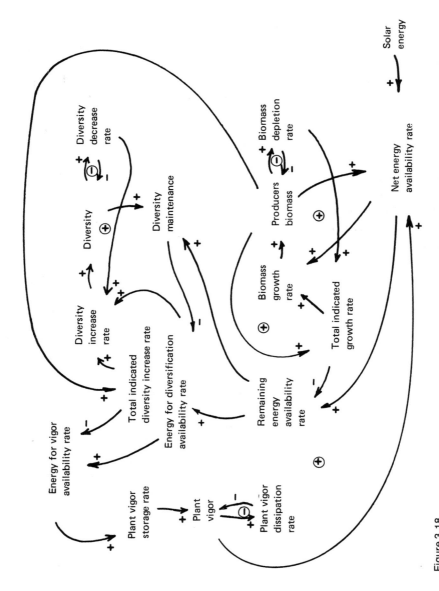

Figure 3.18
Successional energetics

continued maintenance of biomass and diversity at their steady-state levels. Presumably, as the ecosystem continues to mature such excess energy can be allocated to do further work on other quality functions such as biochemical and genetic diversification, which provide for higher resistance to disease and other external perturbations. Therefore this excess energy is assumed to be stored as potential energy in various forms which in the diagram of figure 3.18 are lumped together under a level of stored energy, or vigor. This hypothesis provides a rationale to explain the ability of grasslands, for example, to ''bounce back'' under grazing stress, at least to a certain extent. Energy stored under various forms of plant vigor is potentially available for biomass production work, as pointed out before. As indicated by the influence diagram, however, energy can be stored for a limited period of time; due to leaching, fossilization and other internal factors, plant vigor dissipates if it goes unused for too long. Thus the hypothesis accounts for the eventual disposition of all energy allocated for diversification and other quality work; although not explicitly shown in the diagram of figure 3.18, it is of course understood that energy allocated for growth is gradually dissipated as it is successively transferred from one trophic level to another throughout the food chain.

In consonance with the research methodology outlined in the first chapter, the basic dynamic hypothesis of figure 3.1 has been structured into a number of interconnected feedback loops, with each loop further structured in terms of levels and rates. The next step is the detailed analytical formulation of the hypothesis to permit its testing. Levels are to be formulated as first-order difference equations. The rates will be formulated as zero-order (i.e., algebraic) equations, with nonlinearities possibly involved in coupling rates of flow to the current values of the levels. The analytical formulation of the simulation model constructed to test the hypothesis is presented in the next chapter.

Model of Secondary Autogenic Grassland Succession

4

In the great chain of causes and effects no thing
and no activity should be regarded in isolation.
—Alexander von Humboldt (ca. 1807)

4.1 Overview of the Model

The hypothesis on ecological succession presented in the previous chapter
is, indeed, a provisional one. Nevertheless, in this chapter it is cast into
concise mathematical format and numerically quantified in order to (1)
permit its testing by means of simulation experiments, and (2) provide the
means for it to be fully exploited and/or easily revised as time or fuller
knowledge allows.

The simulation model was formulated in consonance with the notation
and conventions of the DYNAMO (DYNAmic MOdels) language (Pugh,
1963). DYNAMO is a special purpose compiler that was developed for the
digital simulation of feedback dynamics models, and is well established as
the standard simulation language in the field (Forrester, 1968).

According to the methodology outlined in section 1.3, dynamic models
are formulated in terms of albegraic and first-order difference equations.
Corresponding to these, DYNAMO programs are written in terms of rate
and level equations. Rate equations can have any appropriate algebraic
form. In the present context, they quantify the flow processes in the
ecosystem. Level equations, on the other hand, account for accumulations
(of information, biomass, nutrients, etc.) within the ecosystem, and they
have the form

$$\text{LEVEL.K} = \text{LEVEL.J} + (\text{DT}) (\text{INR.JK} - \text{OUTR.JK}) \tag{1}$$

where

LEVEL.K = value of LEVEL at time K,

LEVEL.J   = value of LEVEL at time J,
DT   = delta time (solution interval),
INR.JK   = input rate during time interval JK,
OUTR.JK   = output rate during time interval JK.

A graphical explanation of the time notation used in DYNAMO is given in figure 4.1. The main purpose of the time notation is to guide the formulation of equations in such a way that they are compatible with the procedure followed by the computer in calculating all equations at each iteration. Thus during the simulation runs levels will be computed at each point in time, say for example time $t = K$, based on the previous values of the levels at time $t = J$ and the values of the rates during the interval JK. This is, of course, a discrete time approximation of

$$LEVEL_t = LEVEL_{t=0} + \int_0^t \{INR(t) - OUTR(t)\}\, dt, \qquad (2)$$

that is, the theoretical formulation of levels in dynamic models when using an integral equation formulation. In that the formulation of the rates may involve complex interactions between two or more levels, auxiliary equations are sometimes used as intermediate analytical steps in computing levels and rates. At each iteration then the order of computation is first levels, then auxiliaries, and finally rates. In addition to levels and rates, DYNAMO programs include supplementary, constant and initial-value equations. Supplementary equations are used for ancillary computations related to printing and plotting of the results, but otherwise have no impact on the logic of the model. Constant and initial-value equations are convenient means for the numerical quantification of the model. DYNAMO also offers a number of special functions that are convenient for model building and/or simulated experimentation, such as step and ramp functions; maximum, minimum, and switching functions; and table functions. For further details on these and other features of the DYNAMO package, the reader is referred to the *DYNAMO User's Manual* (Pugh, 1963).

The following sections document the DYNAMO model that was employed to test the dynamic hypothesis of chapter 3, equation by equation. Standard DYNAMO notation and flow-diagramming conventions (as in Forrester, 1961) will be adhered to. Justification for the closed ecosystem boundary, the feedback loops included, the levels and rates included in each loop, and the main nonlinearities involved, follows from the dynamic hypothesis. Two tasks remain for the hypothesis to become testable by simulated experimentation: casting each relationship into precise mathematical format, and quantifying each relationship by means of ap-

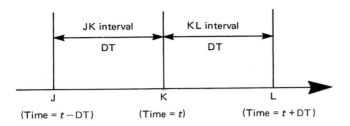

Figure 4.1
Time notation used in DYNAMO

propriate numerical values. With regard to the former, the approach will be
to use the simplest plausible mathematical formalization for each relationship, for example, as a linear function unless ecological considerations
clearly dictate a nonlinear one. With regard to numerical valuation of model
parameters, some data from the Pawnee grassland ecosystem in northeastern Colorado were available (Patten, 1971). Representative data from other
grasslands and reasonable hypothetical values were used to quantify
parameters not covered in the available sources. The basis for each analytical and numerical assumption is given in this chapter; implications on model
performance are discussed in the next chapter.

Figure 4.2 exhibits a flow diagram of the DYNAMO simulation model
constructed for the research. As customary in DYNAMO flow diagrams,
rectangles, valves, and circles represent level, rate, and auxiliary equations, respectively; solid lines represent physical flows (of biomass, nutrients, etc.) and dashed lines represent flows of information. Note that the
auxiliary equations are part of the formulation of the rates as functions of the
levels. Also note that there are levels in both the physical and information
flows. The physical levels are the measurable state variables of the system.
The information levels are introduced to take into account time delays in
causal relationships. The equations for each element of the diagram, as well
as the nominal numerical values for initial conditions and model parameters, are listed in table 4.1. The first column of the table provides the
equation number for easy cross-referencing with each element of the flow
diagram. The second column identifies the type of variable at the left-hand
side of each equation; represented are (L) level, (R) rate, (A) auxiliary, (S)
supplementary, (C) constant, and (N) initial condition.

The third column of the table provides the variable or parameter name and
the corresponding equation. The fourth column gives the units of measurement. Finally, the fifth column gives the equation numbers of the variables

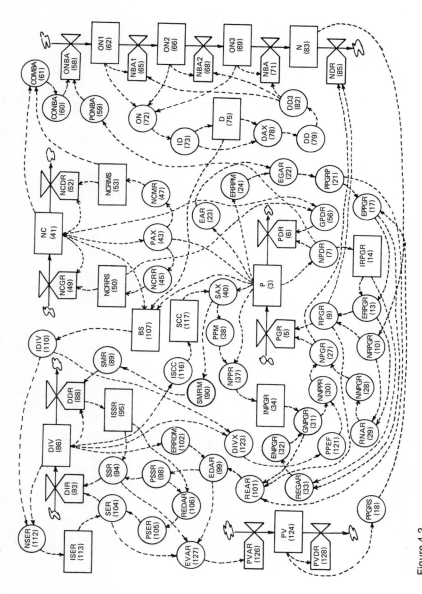

Figure 4.2
Flow diagram of DYNAMO simulation model

Table 4.1
Model summary

Equation number	Equation type	Name/equation	Units	Related equation number
3	L	Plant biomass: $\text{P.K.} = \text{P.J.} + (\text{DT})\,(\text{PGR.JK} - \text{PDR.JK})$	$g_p\text{m}^{-2}$	4, 5, 6
4	N	Plant biomass: $\text{P} = 1$	$g_p\text{m}^{-2}$	
5	R	Plant growth rate: $\text{PGR.KL} = \text{NPGR.K} + \text{RPGR.K}$	$g_p\text{m}^{-2}/\text{month}$	9, 27
6	R	Plant depletion rate: $\text{PDR.KL.} = \text{NPDR.K} + \text{GPDR.K}$	$g_p\text{m}^{-2}/\text{month}$	7, 56
7	A	Natural plant decay rate: $\text{NPDR.K} = \text{P.K} / \text{PDD}$	$g_p\text{m}^{-2}/\text{month}$	3, 8
8	C	Plant decay delay: $\text{PDD} = 6$	months	
9	A	Replacement plant growth rate: $\text{RPGR.K} = \text{MIN(NRPGR.K, ERPGR.K)}$	$g_p\text{m}^{-2}/\text{month}$	10, 13
10	A	Nutrient-limiting replacement growth rate: $\text{NRPGR.K} = \text{N.K.} / (\text{NPRC})\,(\text{NAD})$	$g_p\text{m}^{-2}/\text{month}$	11, 12, 83
11	C	Nutrient-to-plant requirement coefficient: $\text{NPRC} = 0.03$	$g_n g_p{}^{-1}$	
12	C	Nutrient absorption delay: $\text{NAD} = 3$	months	
13	A	Energy-limiting replacement plant growth rate: $\text{ERPGR.K} = \text{MIN(IRPGR.K, EPPGR.K)}$	$g_p\text{m}^{-2}/\text{month}$	14, 17

Table 4.1 (continued)

Equation number	Equation type	Name/equation	Units	Related equation number
14	L	Indicated replacement plant growth rate: IRPGR.K = IRPGR.J + (DT) (1 / PDRSD) (NPDR.J − IRPGR.J)	$g_p m^{-2}$/month	7, 15, 16
15	N	Indicated replacement plant growth rate: IRPGR = P / PDD	$g_p m^{-2}$/month	3, 8
16	C	Plant depletion rate smoothing delay: PDRSD = 12	months	
17	A	Energetically possible plant growth rate: EPPGR.K = PPGRP.K + PPGRS.K	$g_p m^{-2}$/month	18, 21
18	A	Possible plant growth rate—storage: PPGRS.K = PV.K / (EPRC) (PVDD)	$g_p m^{-2}$/month	19, 20, 124
19	C	Energy-to-plant requirement coefficient: EPRC = 1	$cal\,g_p^{-1}$	
20	C	Plant vigor dissipation delay: PVDD = 12	months	
21	A	Possible plant growth rate—photosynthesis: PPGRP.K = EGAR.K / EPRC	$g_p m^{-2}$/month	19, 22
22	A	Energy for growth availability rate: EGAR.K = EAR.K − ERRPM.K	$cal\,m^{-2}$/month	23, 24
23	A	Energy availability rate: EAR.K = (P.K) (EFR)	$cal\,m^{-2}$/month	3, 25
24	A	Energy rate required for plant maintenance: ERRPM.K = (P.K) (PMC)	$cal\,m^{-2}$/month	3, 26

Table 4.1 (continued)

Equation number	Equation type	Name/equation	Units	Related equation number
25	C	Energy fixation rate: EFR = 2	cal g_p^{-1}/month	
26	C	Plant maintenance coefficient: PMC = 0.1	cal g_p^{-1}/month	
27	A	New plant growth rate: NPGR.K = MIN (NNPGR.K, NNPPR.K)	$g_p m^{-1}$/month	28, 30
28	A	Nutrient-limiting new plant growth rate: NNPGR.K = MAX(0, RNAR.K)	$g_p m^{-2}$/month	29
29	A	Remaining nutrient availability rate: RNAR.K = NRPGR.K − ERPGR.K	$g_p m^{-2}$/month	10, 13
30	A	Net new plant growth rate: NNPPR.K = (PPEF.K) (GNPGR.K)	$g_p m^{-2}$/month	31, 121
31	A	Gross new plant growth rate: GNPGR.K = MIN (INPGR.K, ENPGR.K)	$g_p m^{-2}$/month	32, 34
32	A	Energetically possible new plant growth rate: ENPGR.K = MAX(0, REGAR.K)	$g_p m^{-2}$/month	33
33	A	Remaining-energy-for-growth availability rate: REGAR.K = EPPGR.K − IRPGR.K	$g_p m^{-2}$/month	14, 17
34	L	Indicated new plant growth rate: INPGR.K = INPGR.J + (DT) (1 / INGAD) (NPPR.J − INPGR.J)	$g_p m^{-2}$/month	35, 36, 37
35	N	Indicated new plant growth rate: INPGR = 0	$g_p m^{-2}$/month	

Table 4.1 (continued)

Equation number	Equation type	Name/equation	Units	Related equation number
36	C	Indicated new growth adjustment delay: INGAD = 6	months	
37	A	Production capacity for new plant growth rate: NPPR.K = (P.K) (PPM.K)	$g_P m^{-2}$/month	3, 38
38	A	Plant production multiplier: PPM.K = TABHL (PPMT, SAX.K, 0, 1, 0.1)	$month^{-1}$	39, 40
39	C	Plant production multiplier table: PPMT* = 1 / 0.96 / 0.88 / 0.70 / 0.50 / 0.34 / 0.20 / 0.10 / 0.04 / 0.01 / 0	$month^{-1}$	
40	A	Soil availability index: SAX.K = P.K./SCC.K	dimensionless	3, 117
41	L	Natural consumers biomass: NC.K = NC.J + (DT) (NCGR.JK − NCDR.JK)	$g_c m^{-2}$	49, 52
42	N	Natural consumers biomass: NC = 0.00625	$g_c m^{-2}$	
43	A	Plant biomass availability index: PAX.K = P.K / (PNCRC) (NC.K)	dimensionless	3, 42, 44
44	C	Plant-to-natural consumers requirement coefficient: PNCRC = 147.1	$g_P g_c^{-1}$	
45	A	Natural consumers reproduction rate: NCRR.K = TABHL (NCRT, PAX.K, 0, 2, 0.2)	$month^{-1}$	43, 46
46	C	Natural consumers reproduction table: NCRT* = 0 / 0.01 / 0.02 / 0.04 / 0.06 / 0.083 / 0.096 / 0.106 / 0.114 / 0.118 / 0.12	$month^{-1}$	

Table 4.1 (continued)

Equation number	Equation type	Name/equation	Units	Related equation number
47	A	Natural consumers mortality rate: NCMR.K = TABHL (NCMT, PAX.K, 0, 2, 0.2)	month^{-1}	43, 48
48	C	Natural consumers mortality table: NCMT* = 1 / 0.21 / 0.16 / 0.12 / 0.098 / 0.083 / 0.074 / 0.068 / 0.064 / 0.062 / 0.06	month^{-1}	
49	R	Natural consumers growth rate: NCGR.KL = (NC.K) (NCRRS.K)	g$_c$cm^{-2}/month	41, 50
50	L	Natural consumers reproduction rate smoothed: NCRRS.K = NCRRS.J + (DT) (1 / NCRD) (NCRR.J − NCRRS.J)	month^{-1}	45, 51, 55
51	N	Natural consumers reproduction rate smoothed: NCRRS = 0.096	month^{-1}	
52	R	Natural consumers depletion rate: NCDR.KL = (NC.K) (NCMRS.K)	g$_c$cm^{-2}/month	41, 53
53	L	Natural consumers mortality rate smoothed: NCMRS.K = NCMRS.J + (DT) (1 / NCRD) (NCMR.J − NCMRS.J)	month^{-1}	47, 54, 55
54	N	Natural consumers mortality rate smoothed: NCMRS = 0.074	month^{-1}	
55	C	Natural consumers response delay: NCRD = 6	months	
56	A	Grazing plant depletion rate: GPDR.K = (NC.K) (NCRRS.K) (NCPRC)	g$_p$m^{-2}/month	41, 50, 57
57	C	Natural consumers plant requirement coefficient: NCPRC = 14.71	g$_p$g$_c^{-1}$	

Table 4.1 (continued)

Equation number	Equation type	Name/equation	Units	Related equation number
58	R	Organic nutrients becoming available: ONBA.KL = PONBA.K + CONBA.K	$g_n m^{-2}$/month	59, 60
59	A	Plant organic nutrients becoming available: PONBA.K = (P.K.) (NPRC) / PDD	$g_n m^{-2}$/month	3, 8, 11
60	A	Consumer organic nutrients becoming available: CONBA.K = (COMBA.K) (NCPRC) (NPRC)	$g_n m^{-2}$/month	11, 57, 61
61	A	Consumer organic matter becoming available: COMBA.K = (NC.K) (NCMRS.K)	$g_c m^{-2}$	41, 53
62	L	Organic nutrients—stage one: ON1.K = ON1.J + (DT) (ONBA.JK − NBA1.JK)	$g_n m^{-2}$	58, 65
63	N	Organic nutrients—stage one: ON1 = (P) (DD3N) (NPRC) / PDD	$g_n m^{-2}$	3, 8, 11, 64
64	C	Decomposition delay three—normal: DD3N = 12	months	
65	N	Nutrients becoming available—stage one: NBA1.KL = ON1.K/DD3.K	$g_n m^{-2}$/month	62, 82
66	L	Organic nutrients—stage two: ON2.K = ON2.J + (DT) (NBA1.JK − NBA2.JK)	$g_n m^{-2}$	65, 68
67	N	Organic nutrients—stage two: ON2 = ON1	$g_n m^{-2}$	63
68	R	Nutrients becoming available—stage two: NBA2.KL = ON2.K / DD3.K	$g_n m^{-2}$/month	66, 82

Table 4.1 (continued)

Equation number	Equation type	Name/equation	Units	Related equation number
69	L	Organic nutrients—stage three: ON3.K = ON3.J + (DT) (NBA2.JK − NBA.JK)	$g_n m^{-2}$	68, 71
70	N	Organic nutrients—stage three: ON3 = ON2	$g_n m^{-2}$	67
71	R	Nutrients becoming available: NBA.KL = ON3.K / DD3.K	$g_n m^{-2}$/month	69, 82
72	A	Organic nutrients: ON.K = ON1.K + ON2.K + ON3.K	$g_n m^{-2}$	62, 66, 69
73	A	Indicated decomposer biomass: ID.K = ON.K /ONDRC	$g_d m^{-2}$	72, 74
74	C	Organic nutrients decomposers requirement coefficient: ONDRC = 0.5	$g_n g_d^{-1}$	
75	L	Decomposers biomass: D.K. = D.J. + (DT) (1 / DRD) (ID.J − D.J)	$g_d m^{-2}$	73, 76, 77
76	N	Decomposers biomass: D = (ON1 + ON2 + ON3) / ONDRC	$g_d m^{-2}$	63, 67, 70
77	C	Decomposers response delay: DRD = 3	months	
78	A	Decomposers availability index: DAX.K = ID.K / D.K.	dimensionless	73, 75
79	A	Decomposition delay: DD.K = DDMIN + (DDS) (DAX.K)	months	78, 80, 81

Table 4.1 (continued)

Equation number	Equation type	Name/equation	Units	Related equation number
80	C	Decomposition delay minimum: DDMIN = 6	months	
81	C	Decomposition delay slope: DDS = 6	months	
82	A	Decomposition delay three: DD3.K = DD.K / 3	months	79
83	L	Nutrients available: N.K. = N.J. + (DT) (NBA.JK − NDR.JK)	$g_n m^{-2}$	71, 85
84	N	Nutrients available: N = 14	$g_n m^{-2}$	
85	R	Nutrient depletion rate: NDR.KL = (NPRC) (RPGR.K + NPGR.K)	$g_n m^{-2}/month$	9, 11, 27
86	L	Species diversity: DIV.K = DIV.J + (DT) (DIR.JK − DDR.JK)	species	88, 93
87	N	Species diversity: DIV = 1	species	
88	R	Diversity decrease rate: DDR.KL = (DIV.K) (SMR.K)	species/month	86, 89
89	A	Species extinction rate: SMR.K = (SMRN) (SMRM.K)	$month^{-1}$	90, 92
90	A	Species extinction rate multiplier: SMRM.K = TABHL (SMRT, SAX.K, 0, 1, 0.1)	dimensionless	40, 91

Table 4.1 (continued)

Equation number	Equation type	Name/equation	Units	Related equation number
91	C	Species extinction rate table: SMRT* = 1 / 0.96 / 0.88 / 0.70 / 0.50 / 0.34 / 0.20 / 0.10 / 0.04 / 0.01 / 0	dimensionless	
92	C	Species extinction rate—normal: SMRN = 0.01	month^{-1}	
93	R	Diversity increase rate: DIR.KL = SER.K + SSR.K	species/month	94, 104
94	A	Species substitution rate: SSR.K = MIN(PSSR.K, ISSR.K)	species/month	95, 98
95	L	Indicated species substitution rate: ISSR.K = ISSR.J + (DT)(1 / SSD)(DDR.JK − ISSR.J)	species/month	88, 95, 97
96	N	Indicated species substitution rate: ISSR = (DIV)(SMRN)	species/month	87, 92
97	C	Species substitution delay: SSD = 60	months	
98	A	Possible species substitution rate: PSSR.K = MAX(0, EDAR.K)	species/month	99
99	A	Energy for diversification availability rate: EDAR.K = (1 / ESRC) (REAR.K − ERRDM.K)	species/month	100, 101, 102
100	C	Energy-to-species requirement coefficient: ESRC = 1	calm^{-2}/species	

Table 4.1 (continued)

Equation number	Equation type	Name/equation	Units	Related equation number
101	A	Remaining energy availability rate: REAR.K = (EPRC) (PPGRP) (PPGRP.K − GNPGR.K − RPGR.K)	calm^{-2}/month	9, 19, 21, 31
102	A	Energy rate required for diversity maintenance: ERRDM.K = (DIV.K) (DIVMC)	calm^{-2}/month	86, 103
103	C	Diversity maintenance coefficient: DIVMC = 0.1	calm^{-2}/month/ species	
104	A	Species emergence rate: SER.K = MIN(ISER.K, PSER.K)	species/month	105, 113
105	A	Possible species emergence rate: PSER.K = MAX(0, REDAR.K)	species/month	106
106	A	Remaining energy-for-diversification availability rate: REDAR.K = PSSR.K − ISSR.K	species/month	95, 98
107	L	Total biomass smoothed: BS.K = BS.J + (DT) (1 / BSD) (P.J + NC.J + D.J. − BS.J)	g$_m^{-2}$	3, 41, 75, 108, 109
108	N	Total biomass smoothed: BS = P + NC + D	g$_n^{-2}$	4, 42, 76
109	C	Total biomass smoothing delay: BSD = 12	months	
110	A	Indicated species diversity: IDIV.K = TABHL(DIVT, BS.K, 0, 100, 10)	species	107, 111

Table 4.1 (continued)

Equation number	Equation type	Name/equation	Units	Related equation number
111	C	Diversity table: DIVT* = 0 / 46 / 76 / 104 / 128 / 148 / 164 / 176 / 188 / 196 / 200	species	
112	A	New indicated species emergence rate: NSER.K = (1 / SED)(IDIV.K − DIV.K)	species/month	86, 110, 112a
112a	C	Species emergence delay: SED = 12	months	
113	L	Indicated species emergence rate: ISER.K = ISER.J + (DT)(1 / ISEAD)(NSER.J − ISER.J)	species/month	112, 114, 115
114	N	Indicated species emergence rate: ISER = 0	species/month	
115	C	Indicated species emergence adjustment delay: ISEAD = 60	months	
116	A	Indicated soil-carrying capacity: ISCC.K = TABHL(SCCT, DIV.K, 0, 100, 10)	$g_p m^{-2}$	86, 119
117	L	Soil-carrying capacity: SCC.K = SCC.J + (DT)(1 / SCCAD)(ISCC.J − SCC.J)	$g_p m^{-2}$	116, 118, 120
118	N	Soil-carrying capacity: SCC = TABHL(SCCT, DIV, 0, 100, 10)	$g_p m^{-2}$	87, 119
119	C	Soil-carrying capacity table: SCCT* = 20 / 23 / 32 / 57 / 94 / 102 / 112 / 116 / 118 / 119 / 120	$g_p m^{-2}$	
120	C	Soil-carrying capacity adjustment delay: SCCAD = 60	months	

Table 4.1 (continued)

Equation number	Equation type	Name/equation	Units	Related equation number
121	A	Plant production efficiency factor: PPEF.K = TABHL(PPET, DIVX.K, 0, 1, 0.1)	dimensionless	122, 123
122	C	Plant production efficiency table: PPET* = 0.5 / 0.49 / 0.46 / 0.43 / 0.39 / 0.35 / 0.25 / 0.18 / 0.13 / 0.11 / 0.10	dimensionless	
123	A	Diversity index: DIVX.K = DIV.K / IDIV.K	dimensionless	86, 110
124	L	Plant vigor: PV.K = PV.J + (DT)(PVAR.JK − PVDR.JK)	cal m^{-2}	126, 128
125	N	Plant vigor: PV = 0	cal m^{-2}	
126	R	Plant vigor accumulation rate: PVAR.KL = MAX(0, EVAR.K)	cal m^{-2}/month	127
127	A	Energy-for-vigor availability rate: EVAR.K = (ESRC)(EDAR.K − SSR.K − SER.K)	cal m^{-2}/month	94, 99, 100,
128	R	Plant vigor dissipation rate: PVDR.KL = PV.K / PVDD	cal m^{-2}/month	20, 124
129	S	Energy balance: EB.K = EAR.K − EUR.K	cal m^{-2}/month	23, 130
130	S	Energy utilization rate: EUR.K = EEP.K + ERRPM.K + ERRDM.K + EED.K + EEV.K	cal m^{-2}/month	102, 131, 132, 133,

Table 4.1 (continued)

Equation number	Equation type	Name/equation	Units	Related equation number
131	S	Energy expenditure rate for production: EEP.K= (EPRC) (GNPGR.K + RPGR.K)	$\text{cal}\,\text{m}^{-2}/\text{month}$	9, 19, 31
132	S	Energy expenditure rate for diversification: EED.K = (ESRC) (SER.K + SSR.K)	$\text{cal}\,\text{m}^{-2}/\text{month}$	94, 100, 104
133	S	Energy expenditure rate due to vigor dissipation: EEV.K = PV.K / PVDD	$\text{cal}\,\text{m}^{-2}/\text{month}$	20, 124
134	S	Gross plant growth rate: GPGR.K = GNPGR.K + RPGR.K	$\text{g}_p\text{m}^{-2}/\text{month}$	9, 31
135	S	Respiration rate: RESP.K = GPGR.K − NNPPR.K	$\text{g}_p\text{m}^{-2}/\text{month}$	30, 134

Table 4.2.
Program listing of DYNAMO simulation model

```
NOTE    SUCCESSIONAL DYNAMICS
NOTE
1L      P.K=P.J+(DT)(PGR.JK-PDR.JK)
1L      ON1.K=ON1.J+(DT)(ONBA.JK-NBA1.JK)
1L      ON2.K=ON2.J+(DT)(NBA1.JK-NBA2.JK)
1L      ON3.K=ON3.J+(DT)(NBA2.JK-NBA.JK)
1L      N.K=N.J+(DT)(NBA.JK-NDR.JK)
3L      IRPGR.K=IRPGR.J+(DT)(1/PDRSD)(NPDR.J-IRPGR.J)
3L      INPGR.K=INPGR.J+(DT)(1/INGAD)(NPPR.J-INPGR.J)
3L      D.K=D.J+(DT)(1/DRD)(ID.J-D.J)
1L      NC.K=NC.J+(DT)(NCGR.JK-NCDR.JK)
3L      NCRRS.K=NCRRS.J+(DT)(1/NCRD)(NCRR.J-NCRRS.J)
3L      NCMRS.K=NCMRS.J+(DT)(1/NCRD)(NCMR.J-NCMRS.J)
3L      ISSR.K=ISSR.J+(DT)(1/SSD)(DDR.JK-ISSR.J)
3L      ISER.K=ISER.J+(DT)(1/ISEAD)(NSER.J-ISER.J)
1L      DIV.K=DIV.J+(DT)(DIR.JK-DDR.JK)
3L      SCC.K=SCC.J+(DT)(1/SCCAD)(ISCC.J-SCC.J)
4L      BS.K=BS.J+(DT)(1/BSD)(P.J+NC.J+D.J-BS.J+0+0)
1L      PV.K=PV.J+(DT)(PVAR.JK-PVDR.JK)
NOTE
58A     PPEF.K=TABHL(PPET,DIVX.K,0,1,0.1)
20A     DIVX.K=DIV.K/IDIV.K
20A     SAX.K=P.K/SCC.K
58A     PPM.K=TABHL(PPMT,SAX.K,0,1,0.1)
20A     DD3.K=DD.K/3
14A     DD.K=DDMIN+(DDS)(DAX.K)
20A     DAX.K=ID.K/D.K
20A     ID.K=ON.K/ONDRC
58A     NCRR.K=TABHL(NCRT,PAX.K,0,2,0.2)
58A     NCMR.K=TABHL(NCMT,PAX.K,0,2,0.2)
42A     PAX.K=P.K/((PNCRC)(NC.K))
20A     NPDR.K=P.K/PDD
13A     GPDR.K=(NC.K)(NCRRS.K)(NCPRC)
44A     PONBA.K=(P.K)(NPRC)/PDD
13A     CONBA.K=(COMBA.K)(NCPRC)(NPRC)
12A     COMBA.K=(NC.K)(NCMRS.K)
8A      ON.K=ON1.K+ON2.K+ON3.K
58A     IDIV.K=TABHL(DIVT,BS.K,0,100,10)
12A     SMR.K=(SMRN)(PPM.K)
58A     ISCC.K=TABHL(SCCT,DIV.K,0,100,10)
54A     SSR.K=MIN(PSSR.K,ISSR.K)
7A      REDAR.K=PSSR.K-ISSR.K
56A     PSER.K=MAX(0,REDAR.K)
54A     SER.K=MIN(ISER.K,PSER.K)
7A      APGR.K=NPGR.K+RPGR.K
54A     RPGR.K=MIN(NRPGR.K,ERPGR.K)
42A     NRPGR.K=N.K/((NPRC)(NAD))
54A     ERPGR.K=MIN(IRPGR.K,EPPGR.K)
7A      EPPGR.K=PPGRP.K+PPGRS.K
7A      RNAR.K=NRPGR.K-ERPGR.K
7A      REGAR.K=EPPGR.K-IRPGR.K
54A     NPGR.K=MIN(NNPGR.K,NNPPR.K)
56A     NNPGR.K=MAX(0,RNAR.K)
12A     NNPPR.K=(PPEF.K)(GNPGR.K)
54A     GNPGR.K=MIN(INPGR.K,ENPGR.K)
56A     ENPGR.K=MAX(0,REGAR.K)
12A     NPPR.K=(P.K)(PPM.K)
19A     REAR.K=(EPRC)(PPGRP.K-GNPGR.K-RPGR.K+0)
42A     PPGRS.K=PV.K/((EPRC)(PVDD))
19A     EVAR.K=(ESRC)(EDAR.K-SSR.K-SER.K+0)
```

Table 4.2 (continued)

```
21A    NSER.K=(1/SED)(IDIV.K-DIV.K)
21A    EDAR.K=(1/ESRC)(REAR.K-ERRDM.K)
56A    PSSR.K=MAX(0,EDAR.K)
12A    ERRDM.K=(DIV.K)(DIVMC)
12A    EAR.K=(P.K)(EFR)
12A    ERRPM.K=(P.K)(PMC)
7A     EGAR.K=EAR.K-ERRPM.K
20A    PPGRP.K=EGAR.K/EPRC
NOTE
7R     PDR.KL=NPDR.K+GPDR.K
7R     ONBA.KL=PONBA.K+CONBA.K
20R    NBA1.KL=ON1.K/DD3.K
20R    NBA2.KL=ON2.K/DD3.K
20R    NBA.KL=ON3.K/DD3.K
18R    NDR.KL=(NPRC)(RPGR.K+NPGR.K)
12R    NCGR.KL=(NC.K)(NCRRS.K)
12R    NCDR.KL=(NC.K)(NCMRS.K)
12R    DDR.KL=(DIV.K)(SMR.K)
7R     DIR.KL=SER.K+SSR.K
6R     PGR.KL=APGR.K
56R    PVAR.KL=MAX(0,EVAR.K)
20R    PVDR.KL=PV.K/PVDD
NOTE
7S     GPGR.K=GNPGR.K+RPGR.K
7S     RESP.K=GPGR.K-NNPPR.K
NOTE
6N     N=14
6N     P=1
20N    IRPGR=P/PDD
6N     INPGR=0
46N    ON1=(P)(DD3N)(NPRC)/((PDD)(1)(1))
6N     ON2=ON1
6N     ON3=ON2
26N    D=(ON1+ON2+ON3)/(ONDRC+0+0)
6N     NC=0.00625
6N     NCRRS=0.096
6N     NCMRS=0.074
6N     ISER=0
12N    ISSR=(DIV)(SMRN)
6N     PV=0
8N     BS=P+NC+D
58N    DIV=TABHL(DIVT,BS,0,120,10)
58N    SCC=TABHL(SCCT,DIV,0,100,10)
NOTE
C      PDD=6
C      NAD=3
C      PDRSD=12
C      INGAD=60
C      DDMIN=6
C      DDS=6
C      DD3N=12
C      DRD=3
C      NCRD=6
C      NPRC=0.03
C      ONDRC=0.5
C      PNCRC=147.1
C      NCPRC=14.71
C      PPMT*=1/0.96/0.88/0.70/0.50/0.34/0.20/0.10/0.04/0.01/0
C      NCRT*=0/0.01/0.02/0.04/0.06/0.083/0.096/0.106/0.114/0.118/0.12
C      NCMT*=1/0.21/0.16/0.12/0.098/0.083/0.074/0.068/0.064/0.062/0.06
C      SED=12
C      SMRN=0.01
C      SSD=60
C      ISEAD=60
C      SCCAD=12
C      ESRC=1
C      EFR=2
```

Table 4.2 (continued)

```
C        EPRC=1
C        BSD=12
C        PVDD=12
C        DIVMC=0.1
C        PMC=0.1
C        SCCT*=20/23/32/57/84/102/112/116/118/119/120
C        DIVT*=0/46/76/104/128/148/164/176/188/196/200
C        PPET*=0.5/0.49/0.46/0.43/0.39/0.35/0.25/0.18/0.13/0.11/0.10
NOTE
PLOT     P=P/N=N,ON=O/GPGR=G,RESP=R/D=D/NC=C/DIV=Y/PV=V
SPEC     DT=1.0/LENGTH=720/PRTPER=6/PLTPER=6
RUN      MOD5A
C        DIVMC=0.5
RUN      MOD5B
C        PDD=3
RUN      MOD5C
C        ISEAD=120
RUN      MOD5D
C        SCCAD=120
RUN      MOD5E
C        PPET*=0.5/0.5/0.49/0.48/0.47/0.46/0.43/0.37/0.30/0.18/0.10
RUN      MOD5F
C        SCCT*=20/30/40/50/60/70/80/90/100/110/120
C        DIVT*=0/10/24/41/64/91/125/156/180/195/200
END
```

or parameters at the right-hand side of the equation. Therefore the reader can use this table in conjunction with the flow diagram to trace the cause-and-effect relationships assumed to be operative among the various variables of the ecosystem.

Table 4.2 provides a listing of the DYNAMO program used to implement the model. The alphanumeric symbols in the left-hand column of the list identify the form of each equation for the DYNAMO compiler. They are used internally by DYNAMO to establish the sequence of computations at initialization and subsequently at each time step during the simulation, but otherwise have no bearing on the ecological rationale underlying the model.

The sections that follow attempt to establish the ecological basis for each equation of the model. As the discussion unfolds, the reader may wish to refer back concurrently to the flow diagram of figure 4.2, the model summary of table 4.1, and the influence diagrams of the previous chapter.

4.2 Formulation of the Plant Growth and Nutrients-Recycling Loops

The nutrients-cycling loop is depicted in figure 3.2 as being composed of five major sectors: producers biomass, consumers biomass, decomposers biomass, organic nutrients (nutrients in dead organic matter), and inorganic nutrients (nutrients in soluble inorganic form). The growth loops within the producers sector are outlined in figure 3.4. In this section we proceed to quantify these loops and their interactions for the case of a grassland ecosystem. The rationale for each detail of the formulation will be presented with the equations and parameter values chosen.

In the presence of a constant physical environment (e.g., constant temperature, water supply, light intensity) grassland plants grow out of soluble inorganic nutrients by the process of photosynthesis. Thus plant biomass grows at a certain rate. It also declines at a certain rate, due to either natural decay or grazing by the consumers. Until such time as grasses die or are grazed away, plant biomass accumulates on the soil as standing crop. The stock of grasses standing at any given time is given by the level equation

$$P.K. = P.J + (DT) (PGR.JK - PDR.JK) \tag{3}$$

$$P = 1 \tag{4}$$

where

P   = plant biomass ($g_P m^{-2}$),
PGR = plant growth rate ($g_P m^{-2}$/month),
PDR = plant depletion rate ($g_P m^{-2}$/month),

and the initial value reflects what is presumably a modest standing crop at the beginning of secondary succession. Alternatively, the initial value could be set so as to assume the grassland is initially at its climax—approximately 100 gm^{-2} (grams per square meter) in the case of the Pawnee grassland (Patten, 1971, 1972). Initialization of the model for a particular simulation run depends, of course, on the purpose of the experiment: it may be to study the full successional process from youth to maturity, or it may be to study the successional response of the mature grassland to a moderate (either natural or man-made) perturbation. Both cases are covered in the next chapter. In this chapter, initial values will be indicative of a grassland that has been pushed back to the early stage of its successional development.

When the grassland ecosystem is in steady-state, or climax condition, grasses grow, mature, and either are eaten away or decay in (say) yearly cycles. They replace themselves from year to year, the standing crop for each year being approximately the same as the standing crop for the previous year. There may be fluctuations in biomass levels from year to year due to variations in climate and other short-term nonsuccessional factors, but in the long term the climax ecosystem remains stable. During succession, however, grasses not only replace themselves from year to year but in addition generate new growth each year as succession unfolds. Therefore

$$PGR.KL = NPGR.K + RPGR.K \qquad (5)$$

where

PGR = plant growth rate (g_pm^{-2}/month),
$NPGR$ = new plant growth rate (g_pm^{-2}/month),
$RPGR$ = replacement plant growth rate (g_pm^{-2}/month).

Plant depletion rate, on the other hand, depends not only on the natural decay rate of plant biomass, but also on consumption rate by the consumers; thus

$$PDR.KL = NPDR.K + GPDR.K \qquad (6)$$

where

PDR = plant depletion rate (g_pm^{-2}/month),
$NPDR$ = natural plant decay rate (g_pm^{-2}/month),
$GPDR$ = grazing plant depletion rate (g_pm^{-2}/month).

It will be assumed that the natural plant decay rate ($NPDR$) is inversely proportional to the average half-life of the grasses, that is,

$$NPDR.K = P.K / PDD \qquad (7)$$

$$PDD = 6 \qquad (8)$$

where
$NPDR$ = natural plant decay rate (g_pm^{-2}/month),
P = plant biomass (g_pm^{-2}),
PDD = plant decay delay (months).

Equation (7) assumes that the natural decay of plant biomass follows the pattern of exponential decay with an average delay of six months. Thus if P is the accumulation of biomass at time K, 0.606P will remain after three months, 0.368P after six months, 0.135P after one year, 0.018P after two years, and so on. The actual decay function may not be this simple but in the absence of specific data we are using this assumption as a first approximation.

The component of plant depletion rate that is due to grazing, GPDR, depends on the food requirements of the consumers and will be formulated later. At this time, let us consider the formulation of the "new growth" and "replacement growth" components of equation (5). Adequate availability rates of energy and absorbable nutrients are required (in addition, of course, to plant machinery) for replacement growth to continue; new growth requires, in addition, the availability of unsaturated soil-carrying capacity.

Let us consider first the replacement growth rate (RPGR). Since either nutrient availability rate or energy availability rate is limiting,

$$RPGR.K = MIN(NRPGR.K, ERPGR.K) \qquad (9)$$

where

RPGR   = replacement plant growth rate ($g_p m^{-2}$/month),
NRPGR= nutrient-limiting replacement plant growth rate ($g_p m^{-2}$/month),
ERPGR = energy-limiting replacement plant growth rate ($g_p m^{-2}$/month).

Equation (9) says that at any given time K the value of RPGR is the minimum of NRPGR or ERPGR at that time. Under the assumption of a constant water supply, it appears reasonable to assume that (as far as nutrients are concerned) the feasible limit to production of plant biomass is proportional to the reservoir of soluble inorganic nutrients in the soil, that is,

$$NRPGR.K = N.K / (NPRC) (NAD) \qquad (10)$$

$$NPRC = 0.03 \qquad (11)$$

$$NAD = 3 \qquad (12)$$

where

NRPGR = nutrient-limiting replacement growth rate ($g_p m^{-2}$/month),
N   = nutrients available ($g_n m^{-2}$),
NPRC   = nutrient-to-plant requirement coefficient (g_n/g_p),
NAD   = nutrient absorption delay (months).

The quotient N.K / NAD gives the nutrient availability rate, with NPRC providing the conversion from grams of abiotic matter, or nutrients (g_n) to grams of plant biomass (g_p). Thus, in words, equation (10) simply means that the production rate of plant biomass is limited in proportion to the availability rate of nutrients. As a first approximation the value of NPRC was abstracted from Pawnee data (Patten, 1971) by simply taking the quotient of the aggregate steady-state value of nitrogen compartments (3.51 $g_n m^{-2}$) over the aggregate steady-state value of plant biomass compartments (103.3 $g_p m^{-2}$) and taking the result (approximately 0.03) as indicative of mineral fixation requirement per unit of biomass production. A nominal value of three months was arbitrarily attached to NAD in the absence of specific data for this parameter. The approach used to quantify the parameters NPRC and NAD is illustrative of the approach consistently followed in the research: to construct a model which is theoretically (i.e., structurally) sound, to quantify the model relationships with reasonable or hypothetical numerical values, and to exerçise the model in order to detect sensitive parameters that merit more accurate field estimation.

The energy-limiting replacement growth rate (ERPGR) is formulated as follows:

$$ERPGR.K = MIN(IRPGR.K, EPPGR.K) \tag{13}$$

where

ERPGR = energy-limiting replacement plant growth rate (g_pm^{-2}/month),
IRPGR = indicated replacement plant growth rate (g_pm^{-2}/month),
EPPGR = energetically possible plant growth rate (g_pm^{-2}/month).

The indicated replacement plant growth rate (IRPGR) is simply the value of the natural plant decay rate (NPDR) delayed so as to account for the yearly replacement cycle of grasses, that is,

$$IRPGR.K = IRPGR.J + (DT) (1 / PDRSD) (NPDR.J - IRPGR.J) \tag{14}$$

$$IRPGR = P / PDD \tag{15}$$

$$PDRSD = 12 \tag{16}$$

where

IRPGR = indicated replacement plant growth rate (g_pm^{-2}/month),
PDRSD = plant depletion rate smoothing delay (months),
NPDR = natural plant decay rate (g_pm^{-2}/month),
P   = plant biomass (g_pm^{-2}),
PDD   = plant decay delay (months).

Note that according to equation (14) the replacement function is assumed to take care only of replacing grasses that matured and decayed according to their own life cycle; grasses grazed by consumers are to be replaced by new growth. The replacement loop would take care of both if this equation is reformulated with PDR in place of NPDR. The other limiting factor in equation (13), EPPGR, is equal to the plant growth rate which is possible using energy becoming available through photosynthesis, plus that which is possible by drawing from stored energy:

$$EPPGR.K = PPGRP.K + PPGRS.K \tag{17}$$

where

EPPGR = energetically possible plant growth rate (g_pm^{-2}/month),
PPGRP = possible plant growth rate—photosynthesis (g_pm^{-2}/month),

PPGRS = possible plant growth rate—storage ($g_p m^{-2}$/month).

The possible plant growth rate using stored energy (PPGRS) is proportional to the rate at which stored potential energy (i.e., "vigor") can be made available for production purposes:

$$PPGRS.K = PV.K / (EPRC) (PVDD) \tag{18}$$

$$EPRC = 1 \tag{19}$$

$$PVDD = 12 \tag{20}$$

where

PPGRS = possible plant growth rate—storage ($g_p m^{-2}$/month),
PV   = plant vigor ($calm^{-2}$),
EPRC = energy-to-plant requirement coefficient (cal/g_p),
PVDD = plant vigor dissipation delay (months).

On the other hand, the possible plant growth rate using photosynthetic energy (PPGRP) is to be computed at each point in time from the following set of equations:

$$PPGRP.K = EGAR.K / EPRC \tag{21}$$

$$EGAR.K = EAR.K - ERRPM.K \tag{22}$$

$$EAR.K = (P.K) (EFR) \tag{23}$$

$$ERRPM = (P.K) (PMC) \tag{24}$$

$$EFR = 2 \tag{25}$$

$$PMC = 0.1 \tag{26}$$

where

PPGRP = possible plant growth rate—photosynthesis ($g_p m^{-2}$/month),
EGAR   = energy for growth availability rate ($calm^{-2}$/month),
EPRC   = energy-to-plant requirement coefficient (cal/g_p),
EAR   = energy availability rate ($calm^{-2}$/month),
ERRPM = energy rate required for plant maintenance ($calm^{-2}$/month),
EFR   = energy fixation rate ($calg_p^{-1}$/month),
PMC   = plant maintenance coefficient ($calg_p^{-1}$/month),
P   = plant biomass ($g_p m^{-2}$).

The set of equations (10) to (26) account in a very simplified fashion for the initial disposition of photosynthetic energy, the maintenance and replacement of plant biomass, and the fixing of mineral nutrients as part of this production process. The photosynthetic machinery of plants fixes solar energy in a rate proportional to the standing crop (equation 23). Implicit to the formulation of equation (23) is the presence of solar radiation. The parameter EFR assumes that the sun rises every day over the grassland and that solar energy is available in a form that can be captured by the plants. If formulated explicitly, solar radiation would be the exogenous input or driving variable for the model.

Part of this energy is immediately dissipated in the performance of maintenance functions (equation 24), and the remaining energy becomes available for production functions (equation 22). Assuming that it takes so many calories to produce a gram of plant biomass, the production rate that is energetically possible (equation 17) is proportional to the energy becoming available from photosynthesis (equation 21) plus the energy becoming available from storage (equation 18). The plant community is assumed to attempt either this production rate (equation 17) or the production rate indicated for replacement purposes (equation 14), whichever is less (equation 13). The "attempt" is successful if the nutrient availability rate (equation 10) is not limiting; otherwise, the actual production rate accomplished is as limited by the availability rate of nutrients (equation 9). The values for EPRC, EFR, and PMC were deliberately chosen so as to ensure a nonlimiting availability of energy; no empirical basis for these numbers is claimed.

Let us consider now the new growth component of plant growth rate (NPGR). New growth, in addition to replacement growth, can be accomplished if there are excess availability rates of energy and nutrients and, in addition, available space or soil in which additional growth can be attempted. If all these resources are available, it is assumed that the plant community will attempt further growth before allocating excess energy to other functions. With these considerations in mind, the component NPGR of equation (5) can be formulated as

$$NPGR.K = MIN(NNPGR.K, NNPPR.K) \tag{27}$$

where

NPGR $\quad$ = new plant growth rate (g_pm^{-2}/month),
NNPGR = nutrient-limiting new plant growth rate (g_pm^{-2}/month),
NNPPR = net new plant growth rate (g_pm^{-2}/month).

The nutrient-limiting new plant growth rate is the nonnegative number

$$NNPGR.K = MAX(0, RNAR.K) \tag{28}$$

where

NNPGR = nutrient-limiting new plant growth rate ($g_p m^{-2}$/month),
RNAR = remaining nutrient availability rate ($g_p m^{-2}$/month).

Equation (28) says that at any given time K the value of NNPGR is the maximum of zero or RNAR at that time. The remaining nutrient availability rate is of course what is left unused after replacement growth requirements have been satisfied, that is,

$$RNAR.K = NRPGR.K - ERPGR.K \qquad (29)$$

where

RNAR = remaining nutrient availability ($g_p m^{-2}$/month),
NRPGR = nutrient-limited replacement plant growth rate ($g_p m^{-2}$/month),
ERPGR = energy-limited replacement plant growth rate ($g_p m^{-2}$/month).

The other limiting factor in equation (27) is NNPPR, the new net plant production rate; this is, of course, the percentage of the gross new plant rate that is not lost as respiration:

$$NNPPR.K = (PPEF.K)(GNPGR.K) \qquad (30)$$

where

NNPPR = net new plant growth rate ($g_p m^{-2}$/month),
PPEF = plant production efficiency factor (dimensionless),
GNPGR = gross new plant growth rate ($g_p m^{-2}$/month).

It is possible to assume that the efficiency factor PPEF is either a constant or a variable. A constant value in the range of 10 to 50 percent would be a reasonable approximation. In consonance with the discussion of figure 3.17, it will be formulated later as a function of relative diversity. Gross new plant growth rate (GNPGR) is the minimum of that which is energetically possible and that which is indicated by the availability of physical space in which to grow, thus

$$GNPGR.K = MIN(INPGR.K, ENPGR.K) \qquad (31)$$

where

GNPGR = gross new plant growth rate ($g_p m^{-2}$/month),
INPGR = indicated new plant growth rate ($g_p m^{-2}$/month),
ENPGR = energetically possible new plant growth rate ($g_p m^{-2}$/month).

Using the same technique employed before to compute the excess availability of nutrients, we can write

$$ENPGR.K = MAX (0, REGAR.K) \tag{32}$$

and

$$REGAR.K = EPPGR.K - IRPGR.K \tag{33}$$

where

ENPGR = energetically possible new plant growth rate ($g_p m^{-2}$/month),
REGAR = remaining-energy-for-growth availability rate ($g_p m^{-2}$/month),
EPPGR = energetically possible plant growth rate ($g_p m^{-2}$/month),
IRPGR = indicated replacement plant growth rate ($g_p m^{-2}$/month),
to compute the excess availability rate of energy for growth. The indicated new plant growth rate (INPGR) is computed as follows:

$$INPGR.K = INPGR.J + (DT) (1 /INGAD) (NPPR.J - INPGR.J) \tag{34}$$

$$INPGR \quad = 0 \tag{35}$$

$$INGAD \quad = 6 \tag{36}$$

$$NPPR.K \quad = (P.K) (PPM.K) \tag{37}$$

$$PPM.K \quad = TABHL(PPMT, SAX.K, 0, 1, 0.1) \tag{38}$$

$$PPMT^* \quad = 1 / 0.96 / 0.88 / 0.70 / 0.50 / 0.34 / 0.20 / 0.10 / \tag{39}$$
$$0.04 / 0.01 / 0$$

$$SAX.K \quad = P.K /SCC.K \tag{40}$$

where

INPGR = indicated new plant growth rate ($g_p m^{-2}$/month),
INGAD = indicated new growth adjustment delay (months),
NPPR = production capacity for new plant growth rate ($g_p m^{-2}$/month),
P = plant biomass ($g_p m^{-2}$),
PPM = plant production multiplier (month^{-1}),
SAX = soil availability index (dimensionless),
SCC = soil-carrying capacity ($g_p m^{-)}$,
PPMT = plant production multiplier table (month^{-1}).

Thus when the ratio P.K / SCC.K is small (i.e., when there is plenty of unutilized soil-carrying capacity), plant machinery responds by increasing its production activity beyond that required for replacement purposes; the result is new growth. Equation (38) gives the DYNAMO statement for the nonlinearity involved. The notation TABHL means that PPM.K is a table function of the independent variable SAX.K, that the range of SAX.K is between zero and one, and that the values of PPM.K as a function of

SAK.K are stored in table PPMT at 0.1 increments of the independent variable (equation 39). At each iteration, PPM.K is computed from the table by linear interpolation. Figure 4.3 shows alternative numerical valuations of PPMT. The shape of the curve is as hypothesized in chapter 3. The intensity of the new growth response to available space is, of course, proportional to the amount of plant machinery available in the grassland (equation 37). Furthermore, the new growth response is not instantaneous. In fact, it may take a significant amount of time (say, 5 years) for the plant community to adjust its production machinery to exploit a growth situation, thus the level of equation (34). It delays (i.e., smoothes) the value of new plant production rate, so that the current indicated value of new plant growth rate reflects the time delay involved in the adjustment process. This completes the feedback structure controlling the growth and decay of grasses. Several links with other sectors of the ecosystem, however, remain unformulated: soil carrying capacity (SCC), plant production efficiency factor (PPEF), and the plant depletion rate due to grazing (GPDR). Let us consider the last one first.

The rate at which grasses are eaten away from the soil depends on the density and growth rate of consumers. The biomass density of natural consumers is given by

$$NC.K = NC.J + (DT) (NCGR.JK - NCDR.JK) \tag{41}$$

$$NC = 0.00625 \tag{42}$$

where

NC = natural consumers biomass $(g_c m^{-2})$,
$NCGR$ = natural consumers growth rate $(g_c m^{-2}/month)$,
$NCDR$ = natural consumers depletion rate $(g_c m^{-2}/month)$.

NC is, of course, a highly aggregated level that lumps together all kinds of consumers, both primary and secondary. It might seem that this is an oversimplification in modeling the grassland ecosystem. But the purpose of the research, and therefore the purpose of the model, is not to account for specific dynamic processes such as, for example, predator-prey interactions; the objective at hand is to account for successional dynamics. From a successional-dynamic viewpoint, what matters is not so much the manyfold pathways followed by nutrients as they are transferred from trophic level to trophic level, as it is the overall time constants of the cycling process. The producers community is really the one that generates succession, and succession will proceed up to the limits imposed by the physical environment as long as the cycling of nutrients does not become limiting. In

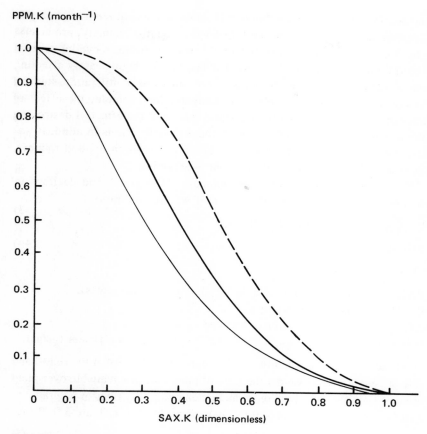

Figure 4.3
New production multiplier (PPM.K) as a function of soil availability (SAX.K)

accounting for nutrients cycling in this sense, it does not seem necessary to decompose trophic levels beyond the basic categories, namely, producers, consumers, and decomposers. In fact, the whole nutrients recycling process could be formulated as a high-order delay without significantly affecting the growth dynamics of the model. For subsequent utilization studies, however, it will be desirable to investigate, for example, the effect of augmenting consumers with domestic consumers, the effect of destroying the decomposers, and so forth. With these considerations in mind, it was decided to account for the various trophic levels in an explicit manner, though at the highest possible level of aggregation.

The level of natural consumers biomass (NC) grows and declines in response to the availability of grasses. If we take the ratio

$$PAX.K = P.K / (PNCRC) (NC.K) \tag{43}$$

$$PNCRC = 147.1 \tag{44}$$

where

PAX   = plant biomass availability index (dimensionless),
P   = plant biomass ($g_p m^{-2}$),
NC   = natural consumers biomass ($g_c m^{-2}$),
PNCRC   = plants-to-natural consumers requirement coefficient (g_p/g_c),

as an index of food availability for the consumers (note that the right-hand side of equation 43 is simply the ratio of plant biomass available over plant biomass required), then the reproduction and mortality rates of natural consumers would be functions of this index, as postulated in figure 3.9. Thus

$$NCRR.K = TABHL(NCRT, PAX.K, 0, 2, 0.2) \tag{45}$$

$$NCRT^* = 0 / 0.01 / 0.02 / 0.04 / 0.06 / 0.083 / 0.096 / 0.106 /$$
$$0.114 / 0.118 / 0.12 \tag{46}$$

$$NCMR.K = TABHL(NCMT, PAX.K, 0, 2, 0.2) \tag{47}$$

$$NCMT^* = 1 / 0.21 / 0.16 / 0.12 / 0.098 / 0.083 / 0.074 /$$
$$0.068 / 0.064 / 0.062 / 0.06 \tag{48}$$

where

NCRR   = natural consumers reproduction rate ($month^{-1}$),
NCMR   = natural consumers mortality rate ($month^{-1}$),
PAX   = plant biomass availability rate (dimensionless),
NCRT   = natural consumers reproduction table ($month^{-1}$),
NCMT   = natural consumers mortality table ($month^{-1}$).

According to Patten (1971) the steady-state values of aggregate consumers biomass and aggregate plant biomass are approximately 0.7 $g_c m^{-2}$ and 103 $g_p m^{-2}$, respectively; thus the value assigned to PNCRC ($103 \div 0.7 = 147.1$). The tables NCRT and NCMT used for the simulations are shown in figure 4.4 The superimposed graphs of NCRT and NCMT show that equilibrium occurs at PAX $= 1$, the situation where food available is equal to food required. According to the values assumed in figure 4.4, this equilibrium would result in reproduction and mortality rates of 0.083, which implies a yearly turnover of consumers biomass. If plant biomass exceeds the required value (PAX > 1), the reproduction rate will be greater than the mortality rate, and the level of natural consumers will increase; on the other hand, when food becomes scarce (PAX < 1) the mortality rate will be higher than the reproduction rate, and the level of natural consumers will decline. In the extremes, if the standing crop of plants is completely destroyed (PAX $= 0$), the reproduction rate of consumers will become zero, and mortality rate will increase dramatically. Consequently, the level of natural consumers will gradually vanish. On the other hand, an abundance of plant biomass generates further growth in natural consumers only to a certain extent. If there is an overabundance (e.g., PAX > 2) of grasses, other factors will become limiting, and both NCRR and NCMR level off at their maximum and minimum levels, respectively. It takes some time, however, for animals to adjust their numbers (either upward or downward) in response to the food supply; therefore, we chose to formulate the growth and death rates of natural consumers as follows:

$$\text{NCGR.KL} = (\text{NC.K}) \, (\text{NCRRS.K}) \tag{49}$$

$$\begin{aligned}\text{NCRRS.K} = {}& \text{NCRRS.J} + (\text{DT}) \, (1 \, / \, \text{NCRD}) \\ & (\text{NCRR.J} - \text{NCRRS.J})\end{aligned} \tag{50}$$

$$\text{NCRRS} = 0.096 \tag{51}$$

$$\text{NCDR.KL} = (\text{NC.K}) \, (\text{NCMRS.K}) \tag{52}$$

$$\begin{aligned}\text{NCMRS.K} = {}& \text{NCMRS.J} + (\text{DT}) \, (1 \, / \, \text{NCRD}) \\ & (\text{NCMR.J} - \text{NCMRS.J})\end{aligned} \tag{53}$$

$$\text{NCMRS} = 0.074 \tag{54}$$

$$\text{NCRD} = 6 \tag{55}$$

where

NCGR = natural consumers growth rate ($g_c m^{-2}$/month),
NC   = natural consumers biomass ($g_c m^{-2}$),

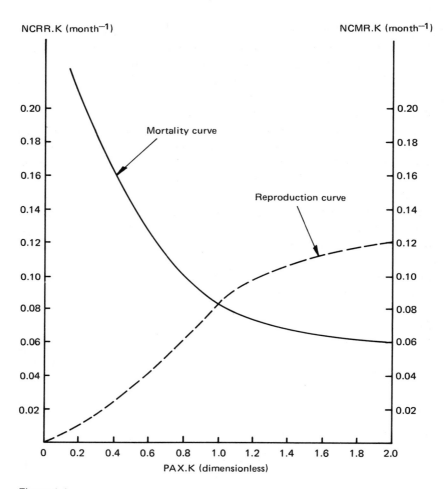

Figure 4.4
Natural consumers reproduction rate (NCRR.K) and mortality rate (NCMR.K) as a
function of plant availability index (PAX.K)

NCRRS = natural consumers reproduction rate smoothed (month^{-1}),
NCDR   = natural consumers depletion rate (g$_c$m$^-$/month),
NCMRS = natural consumers mortality rate smoothed (month^{-1}),
NCRD   = natural consumers response delay (months),
NCRR   = natural consumers reproduction rate (month^{-1}),
NCMR   = natural consumers mortality rate (month^{-1}).

As stated before, the rate at which grasses are consumed depends on the density and growth rate of animals. The formulation

$$GPDR.K = (NC.K) (NCRRS.K) (NCPRC) \tag{56}$$

$$NCPRC = 14.71 \tag{57}$$

where

GPDR   = grazing plant depletion rate (g$_p$m^{-2}/month),
NC   = natural consumers biomass (g$_c$m^{-2}),
NCRRS = natural consumers reproduction rate smoothed (month^{-1}),
NCPRC = natural consumers—plant requirement coefficient (g$_p$/g$_c$),

lumps together food intake rate requirements for both growth and maintenance, with NCPRC set at 10 percent of PNCRC. Admittedly, this is simplifying things quite a bit, but let us recall that the objective at hand is to account for the delays involved in the cycling of nutrients, rather than to account for specific processes within each trophic level.

As either plants or animals die, the dead organic matter must be broken down to complete the cycling of the nutrients back to soluble inorganic form. The delays involved in this process were modeled as follows. The rate of nutrients becoming available in organic form is formulated as the nutrient equivalent of decaying biomass:

$$ONBA.KL = PONBA.K + CONBA.K \tag{58}$$

$$PONBA.K = (P.K) (NPRC) / PDD \tag{59}$$

$$CONBA.K = (COMBA.K) (NCPRC) (NPRC) \tag{60}$$

$$COMBA.K = (NC.K) (NCMRS.K) \tag{61}$$

where

ONBA   = organic nutrients becoming available (g$_n$m^{-2}/month),
PONBA = plant organic nutrients becoming available (g$_n$m^{-2}/month),
CONBA = consumer organic nutrients becoming available (g$_n$m^{-2}/month),
COMBA = consumer organic matter becoming available (g$_c$m^{-2}/month),
P   = plant biomass (g$_p$m^{-2}).

NC   = natural consumers biomass $(g_c m^{-2})$,
NPRC   = nutrients-to-plant requirements coefficient (g_n/g_p),
NCPRC = natural consumers—plant requirement coefficient (g_p/g_c),
PDD   = plant decay delay (months),
NCMRS = natural consumers mortality rate smoothed $(g_c m^{-2}/month)$.

Decaying biomass accumulates in the soil, and is gradually broken down by the decomposers. The delay incurred in the process depends, of course, on the relative availability of decomposers to accomplish the breakdown. Due to the complex processes involved, the conversion of nutrients from organic to inorganic form is more gradual than would be implied by a first-order delay. In this model, this transition to complete the cycling of nutrients was formulated as a third-order delay, with the overall average delay being a function of the level of decomposers available. Experience has shown that a third-order delay is a good first approximation to account for high-order processes that respond only gradually to input changes (Forrester, 1961). The transient response of a first-order delay changes very fast as soon as the input changes. The response of a third-order delay, on the other hand, is S-shaped; it is initially zero and builds up only gradually following the input change. A third-order process can be formulated as a cascaded sequence of first-order process. Therefore the equations to account for the physical flow of nutrients undergoing the decomposition process are as follows:

$$ON1.K = ON1.J + (DT) (ONBA.JK - NBA1.JK) \qquad (62)$$

$$ON1 = (P) (DD3N) (NPRC) / PDD \qquad (63)$$

$$DD3N = 12 \qquad (64)$$

$$NBA1.KL = ON1.K / DD3.K \qquad (65)$$

$$ON2.K = ON2.J + (DT) (NBA1.JK - NBA2.JK) \qquad (66)$$

$$ON2 = ON1 \qquad (67)$$

$$NBA2.KL = ON2.K / DD3.K \qquad (68)$$

$$ON3.K = ON3.J + (DT) (NBA2.JK - NBA.JK) \qquad (69)$$

$$ON3 = ON2 \qquad (70)$$

$$NBA.KL = ON3.K / DD3.K \qquad (71)$$

where

ONBA = organic nutrients becoming available $(g_n m^{-2}/month)$,
ON1   = organic nutrients—stage one $(g_n m^{-2})$,

NBA1   = nutrients becoming available—stage one ($g_n m^{-2}$/month),
ON2   = organic nutrients—stage two ($g_n m^{-2}$),
NBA2   = nutrients becoming available—stage two ($g_n m^{-2}$/month),
ON3   = organic nutrients—stage three ($g_n m^{-2}$),
NBA   = nutrients becoming available ($g_n m^{-2}$/month),
P   = plant biomass ($g_p m^{-2}$),
DD3N   = decomposition delay three—normal (months),
NPRC   = nutrients-to-plants requirement coefficient (g_n/g_p),
PDD   = plant decay delay (months),
DD3   = decomposition delay three (months).

The delay DD3 varies as a function of the relative abundance of decomposers. In time, the level of decomposers depends on the level of organic matter available for decomposition. In order to see how the closed-loop interaction between organic matter and decomposers biomass arises, let us consider the total accumulation of organic nutrients.

$$ON.K = ON1.K + ON2.K + ON3.K \tag{72}$$

where

ON   = organic nutrients ($g_n m^{-2}$),
ON1 = organic nutrients—stage one ($g_n m^{-2}$),
ON2 = organic nutrients—stage two ($g_n m^{-2}$),
ON3 = organic nutrients—stage three ($g_n m^{-2}$).

It is assumed that, for decomposition to be accomplished in a normal amount of time, the indicated level of decomposers is proportional to the total amount of organic nutrients (ON). More specifically,

$$ID.K = ON.K / ONDRC \tag{73}$$

$$ONDRC = 0.5 \tag{74}$$

where

ID   = indicated decomposer biomass ($g_d m^{-2}$),
ON   = organic nutrients ($g_n m^{-2}$),
ONDRC = organic nutrients—decomposers requirement coefficient (g_n/g_d),

and the value of ONDRC was again abstracted from Patten's data (Patten, 1971) by taking the quotient of steady-state organics (computed to be approximately 6 $g_n m^{-2}$) over steady-state decomposers standing crop (approximately 12.4 $g_d m^{-2}$). Decomposers are simply assumed to react to a buildup in organic matter by growing to the indicated level, that is,

$$D.K = D.J + (DT) (1 / DRD) (ID.J - D.J) \tag{75}$$

$$D = (ON1 + ON2 + ON3) / ONDRC \tag{76}$$

$$DRD = 3 \tag{77}$$

where

D	= decomposers biomass ($g_d m^{-2}$),
ID	= indicated decomposers biomass ($g_d m^{-2}$),
DRD	= decomposers response delay (months),
ON1	= organic nutrients—stage one ($g_n m^{-2}$),
ON2	= organic nutrients—stage two ($g_n m^{-2}$),
ON3	= organic nutrients—stage three ($g_n m^{-2}$),
ONDRC	= organic nutrients—decomposers requirement coefficient (g_n/g_d).

The relative availability of decomposers is then given by the ratio

$$DAX.K = ID.K / D.K \tag{78}$$

where

DAX	= decomposers availability index (dimensionless),
ID	= indicated decomposers biomass ($g_d m^{-2}$),
D	= decomposers biomass ($g_d m^{-2}$),

and the decomposition delay which results from a given value of DAX was formulated (following the hypothesis of figure 3.11) as

$$DD.K = DDMIN + (DDS) (DAX.K) \tag{79}$$

$$DDMIN = 6 \tag{80}$$

$$DDS = 6 \tag{81}$$

$$DD3.K = DD.K / 3 \tag{82}$$

where

DD	= decomposition delay (months),
DDMIN	= decomposition delay minimum (months),
DDS	= decomposition delay slope (months),
DAX	= decomposers availability index (dimensionless),
DD3	= decomposition delay three (months).

The auxiliary variable DD3 is simply the prorating of the total decomposition delay DD to each stage in the third-order delay process (see equations 65, 68, and 71). Nutrients becoming available as a result of decomposition accumulate in the soil and are ready once more for utilization by the producers. It remains only to formulate this level to close the nutrients-cycling loop in the model; thus we can write

$$N.K = N.J + (DT) (NBA.JK - NDR.JK) \qquad (83)$$

$$N = 14 \qquad (84)$$

where

N = nutrients available ($g_n m^{-2}$),
NBA = nutrients becoming available ($g_n m^{-2}$/month),
NDR = nutrients depletion rate ($g_n m^{-2}$/month).

The rate of nutrients becoming available (NBA) was formulated in equation (71). As nutrients become available in the soil, however, they are consumed again by the producers at a rate that is proportional to both the replacement and new growth rates, that is

$$NDR.KL = (NPRC) (RPGR.K + NPGR.K) \qquad (85)$$

where

NDR = nutrients depletion rate ($g_n m^{-2}$/month),
$NPRC$ = nutrients-to-plants requirement coefficient (g_n/g_p),
$RPGR$ = replacement plant growth rate ($g_p m^{-2}$/month),
$NPGR$ = new plant growth rate ($g_p m^{-2}$/month).

In other words, nutrients depletion rate equals the rate at which they are absorbed by the plants, to start a new cycle. Thus in this model the rate of circulation of nutrients may change, as well as the distribution of the total amount of nutrients to the various trophic levels, but the total amount in circulation remains invariant with time; this is, of course, as it would be in a closed ecosystem. The model equations fully account for the closed-loop flow of nutrients. Energy flow, on the other hand, is open. Energy fixed as biomass is gradually dissipated as it is transferred from one trophic level to another, never to become usable again to the grassland community. Beyond the producers, biomass flow and energy flow are one and the same; only that, while nutrients are conserved, energy is not.

In brief, the nutrients-cycling loop is composed of five major sectors: producers, consumers, decomposers, dead organic matter, and soluble inorganic nutrients. Our mathematical formulation of this loop quantifies the aggregate dynamics of nutrient flow from abiotic to biotic and then back from biotic to abiotic form. The continued unfolding of secondary succession is contingent on the aggregate recycling of nutrients regardless of what pathways the nutrients follow around the loop. Therefore, we have not attempted to break down producers, consumers, or decomposers into sub-sectors. Breaking down consumers into primary consumer (herbivores) and secondary consumers (carnivores), for example, would result in more detailed information on nutrient distribution among trophic sectors but does not result in more or less total nutrients being recycled in a given period of time. For the same reason we did not attempt to break down the pool of nutrients into components such as nitrogen or carbon. However, we formulated the decomposition of dead organic matter as a third-order delay to recognize that decomposition is generally a slow, complex process with gradual, rather than sudden, transient response to input changes.

4.3 Formulation of the Community Diversification Loops

The model formulated thus far does not account for one critical aspect of succession, namely, the ability of the biotic community to increase the carrying capacity of the physical environment. In the case of a grassland ecosystem, the carrying capacity of the physical environment is basically the carrying capacity of the soil. In consonance with the hypothesis of chapter 3 (see figures 3.1 and 3.16), the model assumes that increments in soil-carrying capacity are effectively brought about by the diversification that follows a buildup in biomass and "permits the occupancy of more niches in the habitat" (DeVos, 1969). The enhanced soil-carrying capacity, in turn, encourages further growth. The analytical formulation of this positive feedback was accomplished as follows. Species diversity is the total number of species in the community and given by

$$DIV.K = DIV.J + (DT) (DIR.JK - DDR.JK) \qquad (86)$$

$$DIV = TABHL(DIVT, BS, 0, 120, 10) \qquad (87)$$

where

DIV = species diversity (species),
DIR = diversity increase rate (species/month),
DDR = diversity decrease rate (species/month),
BS = total biomass smoothed (gm^{-2}).

Total biomass smoothed is the total accumulation of biomass that has been present in the ecosystem. It is obtained in equation (107). Diversity decreases when species disappear. It increases with the emergence of new species and/or substitution of those that have vanished. During succession, species come and go in response to changes in total biomass accumulation. Those that go after each successional stage must be substituted by others, better adapted to the forthcoming stage; furthermore, completely new species emerge as succession unfolds, resulting in successive net diversity increments. As the climax is approached, however, both DIR and DDR should approach zero. The soil availability index of equation (40), SAX.K = P.K / SCC.K, provides valuable information on the benevolence of current conditions toward species currently on the grassland. Thus a value of SAX.K close to zero is indicative of a new successional stage being at hand; conditions are bound to change, competition is bound to increase, and as a result species will begin to disappear at some nominal rate. On the other hand, a value of SAX.K close to one is indicative of maturity and stability, and therefore indicative of zero species decrease rate. With these considerations in mind, the diversity decrease rate was formulated as

$$DDR.KL = (DIV.K) (SMR.K) \tag{88}$$

$$SMR.K = (SMRN) (SMRM.K) \tag{89}$$

$$SMRM.K = TABHL(SMRT, SAX.K, 0, 1, 0.1) \tag{90}$$

$$SMRT^* = 1 / 0.96 / 0.88 / 0.70 / 0.50 / 0.34 / 0.20 / 0.10 /$$
$$0.04 / 0.01 / 1 \tag{91}$$

$$SMRN = 0.01 \tag{92}$$

where

DDR = diversity decrease rate (species/month),
DIV   = species diversity (species),
SMR = species extinction rate (month^{-1}),
SMRN = species extinction rate—normal (month^{-1}),
SMRM = species extinction rate multiplier (dimensionless),
SAX = soil availability index (dimensionless),
SMRT = species extinction rate table (dimensionless),
PPMT = plant production multiplier table (dimensionless),

and SMRT is equated with PPMT, since a nonlinearity of the same shape (see figure 4.3) would apply. The reader will note that, in the model listing of table 4.2, equation (89) is written as SMR.K = (SMRN)(PPM.K), which eliminates the need for equations (90) and (91). Both versions are computationally equivalent, but the theoretically correct formulation is as written in equation (89).

The diversity increase rate, as stated before, is the result of both species substitution and the emergence of additional new species, that is

$$DIR.KL = SER.K + SSR.K \tag{93}$$

where

DIR = diversity increase rate (species/month),
SER = species emergence rate (species/month),
SSR = species substitution rate (species/month).

Given the potential for further niche specialization, two resources are required for diversification to take place: biomass and energy. These factors are limiting on the diversification process in a way similar to the limits imposed on the growth process by space, nutrients, and energy. Thus the species substitution rate (SSR) was formulated as

$$SSR.K = MIN(PSSR.K, ISSR.K) \tag{94}$$

where

SSR = species substitution rate (species/month),
PSSR = possible species substitution rate (species/month),
ISSR = indicated species substitution rate (species/month).

The rate of species substitution "indicated" is the rate necessary to replace species which have abandoned the ecosystem in the recent past (say, during the last few years) as a result of successional developments. Therefore the indicated species substitution rate is equal to the value of diversity decrease rate equation (88) after a substitution delay, that is,

$$ISSR.K = ISSR.J + (DT) (1 / SSD) (DDR.KJ - ISSR.J) \tag{95}$$

$$ISSR = (DIV) (SMRN) \tag{96}$$

$$SSD = 60 \tag{97}$$

where

ISSR = indicated species substitution rate (species/month),
SSD   = species substitution delay (months),
DDR   = diversity decrease rate (species/month),
DIV   = species diversity (species),
SMRN = species extinction rate—normal (month^{-1}).

The rate of species substitution actually possible, however, is a function of the availability of energy for diversification, which in turn depends on energy availability in excess of that required for growth work. In order to account for the limiting effect of energy on diversification, PSSR is computed at each point in time from the following set of equations:

$$PSSR.K = MAX(0, EDAR.K) \tag{98}$$

$$\text{EDAR.K} = (1 \text{ / ESRC}) \text{ (REAR.K} - \text{ERRDM.K)} \qquad (99)$$

$$\text{ESRC} = 1 \qquad (100)$$

$$\text{REAR.K} = (\text{EPRC}) \text{ (PPGRP.K} - \text{GNPGR.K} - \text{RPGR.K)} \qquad (101)$$

$$\text{ERRDM.K} = (\text{DIV.K}) \text{ (DIVMC)} \qquad (102)$$

$$\text{DIVMC} = 0.1 \qquad (103)$$

where

PSSR   = possible species substitution rate (species/month),
EDAR   = energy for diversification availability rate (species/month),
ESRC   = energy-to-species requirement coefficient (calm^{-2}/species),
REAR   = remaining energy availability rate (calm^{-2}/month),
EPRC   = energy-to-plants requirement coefficient (cal/g_p),
PPGRP   = possible plant growth rate—photosynthesis (g_pm^{-2}/month),
GNPGR   = gross new plant growth rate (g_pm^{-2}/month,
RPGR   = replacement plant growth rate (g_pm^{-2}/month),
ERRDM   = energy rate required for diversity maintenance (calm^{-2}/
          month),
DIV   = species diversity (species),
DIVMC   = diversity maintenance coefficient (calm^{-2}/month/species).

The set of equations (98) to (103) simply converts the energy availability rate remaining from growth (REAR, equation 101) to its equivalent in terms of further diversification potential (equation 99), taking into account that some energy is required just to maintain the current level of diversity (equation 102). Empirical data on the energetic coefficients associated with diversification work appear to be unavailable in the literature, so the values assumed above (equation 100 and 103) are purely hypothetical.

As succession unfolds, energetic limits to the emergence of additional new species follow from the previous accounting of energy availability rate and can be formulated as

$$\text{SER.K} = \text{MIN(ISER.K, PSER.K)} \qquad (104)$$

where

SER   = species emergence rate (species/month),
ISER = indicated species emergence rate (species/month),
PSER = possible species emergence rate (species/month),

and PSER is the species emergence rate which still is energetically possible after energy expenditures for diversity maintenance and species substitution have been accounted for, that is,

$$\text{PSER.K} = \text{MAX}(0, \text{REDAR.K}) \tag{105}$$

$$\text{REDAR.K} = \text{PSSR.K} - \text{ISSR.K} \tag{106}$$

where

PSER   = possible species emergence rate (species/month),
REDAR = remaining energy-for-diversification availability rate
             (species/month),
PSSR   = possible species substitution rate (species/month),
ISSR   = indicated species substitution rate (species/month).

The indicated species emergence rate, on the other hand, represents the appearance of additional new species brought about by the ongoing buildup of total biomass in the community. Grasses, of course, constitute the major portion of this buildup. However, the total amount of biomass as it accumulates in the ecosystem can be consolidated by means of the level equation

$$\text{BS.K} = \text{BS.K} + (\text{DT}) (1 / \text{BSD}) (\text{P.J} + \text{NC.J} + \text{D.J} - \text{BS.J}) \tag{107}$$

$$\text{BS} = \text{P} + \text{NC} + \text{D} \tag{108}$$

$$\text{BSD} = 12 \tag{109}$$

where

BS   = total biomass smoothed (gm^{-2}),
BSD = total biomass smoothing delay (months),
P   = plant biomass ($g_p\text{m}^{-2}$),
NC   = natural consumers biomass ($g_c\text{m}^{-2}$),
D   = decomposers biomass ($g_d\text{m}^{-2}$).

At any given successional stage, further accumulation of biomass in the ecosystem is indicative of increased species diversity in the near future. It is also indicative of previous increases in diversity that brought about the increased carrying capacity which in turn resulted in the present buildup of biomass. Let us consider first the former side of this mutual causality, the positive influence of community growth on community diversity. Following the hypothesis of figure 3.13, it can be assumed that the level of species diversity indicated at any given time is functionally related to current accumulation of total biomass,

$$\text{IDIV.K} = \text{TABHL (DIVT, BS.K, 0, 100, 10)} \tag{110}$$

$$\text{DIVT*} = 0 / 46 / 76 / 104 / 128 / 148 / 164 / 176 /$$
$$188 / 196 / 200 \tag{111}$$

where

IDIV = indicated species diversity (species),
DIVT = diversity table (species),
BS   = total biomass smoothed (gm^{-2}),

but empirical data on the graphical appearance of DIVT (i.e., the shape of
the functional relationship) does not appear to be available. On the basis of
descriptive evidence pointed out in chapter 3, it seems reasonable to assume
that increments in species diversity are roughly proportional to increments
in total biomass as succession goes on. Alternatively, it may be assumed
that the relationship is nonlinear, with biomass accumulation ceasing to
generate further diversification after a certain point, possibly due to an
increase in the size of organisms, the length and complexity of life histories,
and interspecific competition resulting in the elimination of some species.
Alternative assumptions for DIVT are shown explicitly in figure 4.5. The
rationale behind the numerical values attached to the horizontal and vertical
axis is simple enough. The maximum accumulation of total biomass at the
Pawnee grassland ecosystem appears to be approximately 120 gm^{-2} (Patten, 1971). The maximum number of species has never been counted for
this or, for that matter, for any large ecosystem. The maximum indicated
number of species shown in figure 4.5 is 200. The actual number may be
lower or higher. The important thing is that under natural conditions it has a
high value, and the influence of total biomass on community diversity
continues to be positive as long as the curve does not level off. Then, the
emergence rate of new species which is indicated in order to correct the
difference between indicated, or goal diversity and current diversity is

$$NSER.K = (1 / SED) (IDIV.K - DIV.K) \qquad (112)$$

$$SED = 12 \qquad (112a)$$

where

NSER = new indicated species emergence rate (species/month),
SED   = species emergence delay (months),
IDIV = indicated species diversity (species),
DIV   = species diversity (species),

assuming new species appear for the first time on the year after successional
development has reached the stage appropriate for their emergence. It does
not seem reasonable, however, to assume that all new species will appear as
soon as they potentially can do so. To take into account the gradual
character of diversification, the indicated species emergence rate ISER of

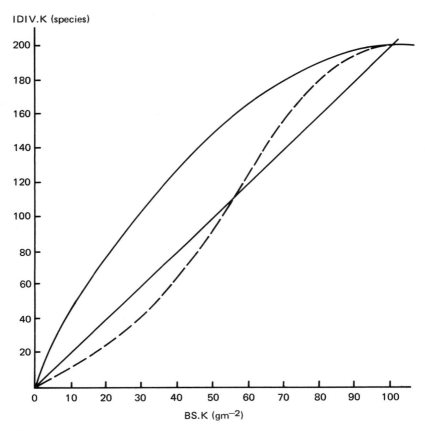

Figure 4.5
Indicated diversity (IDIV.K) as a function of total biomass (BS.K)

equation (104) was formulated as the value of NSER smoothed over a period of time (a few years, in the case of secondary succession) as follows:

$$ISER.K = ISER.J + (DT) (1 / ISEAD) (NSER.J - ISER.J) \qquad (113)$$

$$ISER = 0 \qquad (114)$$

$$ISEAD = 60 \qquad (115)$$

where

ISER   = indicated species emergence rate (species/month),
ISEAD = indicated species emergence adjustment delay (months),
NSER   = new indicated species emergence rate (species/month).

Having accounted for the influence of biomass on diversity, let us account for the influence of diversity on biomass. As pointed out in the statement of the dynamic hypothesis (chapter 3), when the biotic community diversifies, it is bound to exploit a greater number of specialized niches in the soil, and it is also bound to modify the soil so as to, effectively speaking, increase its carrying capacity after some time has elapsed. Two notions are subsumed in this statement: the notion that diversification implies further niche specialization and in turn greater soil-carrying capacity, and the notion that it takes a certain amount of time (again, a few years in the case of secondary succession) for the newly diversified community to exercise its influence on the soil. These two notions find analytical expression in the following manner:

$$ISCC.K = TABHL(SCCT, DIV.K, 0, 100, 10) \qquad (116)$$

$$SCC.K = SCC.J + (DT) (1 / SCCAD) (ISCC.J - SCC.J) \qquad (117)$$

$$SCC = TABHL(SCCT, DIV, 0, 100, 10) \qquad (118)$$

$$SCCT^* = 20 / 23 / 32 / 57 / 94 / 102 / 112 / 116 / 118 / 119 / 120 \qquad (119)$$

$$SCCAD = 60 \qquad (120)$$

where

ISCC   = indicated soil-carrying capacity ($g_p m^{-2}$),
SCCT   = soil-carrying capacity table ($g_p m^{-2}$),
DIV   = species diversity (species),
SCCAD = soil-carrying capacity adjustment delay (months),
SCC   = soil-carrying capacity ($g_p m^{-2}$).

Figure 4.6 exhibits alternative assumptions about the functional relationship SCCT. In either case, the positive influence of diversity on carrying

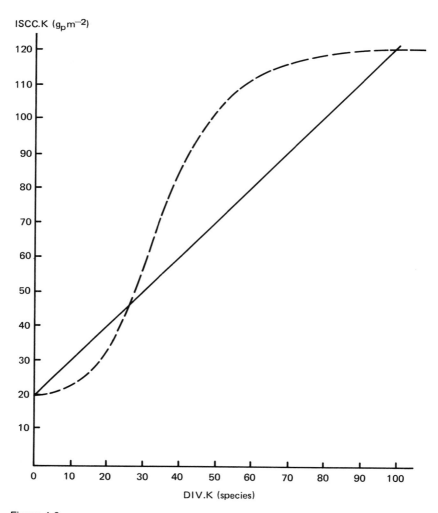

Figure 4.6
Indicated soil-carrying capacity (ISCC.K) as a function of species diversity (DIV.K)

capacity is assumed to level off as the potential for further niche specialization and further soil improvement is gradually exhausted. Again, the aggregate climax value (approximately 100 g_pm^{-2}) of vegetation at Pawnee (Patten, 1971) is taken as the ultimate limit for the process. As the physical environment becomes fully saturated, the capacity of the soil gradually vanishes. Therefore the gain of the positive feedback between biomass and diversity gradually vanishes as either the nonlinearity of figure 4.5 or the nonlinearity of figure 4.6, or both, become limiting.

Needless to say, community diversification impacts many other factors of the ecosystem in addition to soil-carrying capacity. One example, pointed out in the dynamic hypothesis of chapter 3, is the relationship between diversity and productivity. Within certain limits, productivity increases when diversity decreases, and vice versa. This notion can be used to formulate the plant production efficiency factor of equation (30) as a function of relative diversity, where the latter index is defined as the ratio of diversity over indicated diversity. The equations are

$$PPEF.K = TABHL(PPET, DIVX.K, 0, 1, 0.1) \tag{121}$$

$$PPET^* = 0.5 / 0.49 / 0.46 / 0.43 / 0.39 / 0.35 / 0.25 /$$
$$0.18 / 0.13 / 0.11 / 0.10 \tag{122}$$

$$DIVX.K = DIV.K / IDIV.K \tag{123}$$

where

PPEF = plant production efficiency factor (dimensionless),
PPET = plant production efficiency table (dimensionless),
DIVX = diversity index (dimensionless),
DIV   = species diversity (species),
IDIV = indicated species diversity (species).

Alternative assumptions can be made with respect to the nonlinearity PPET. Some possibilities are graphed in figure 4.7. The simplest possible alternative is, of course, to assume that production efficiency is constant. It would seem more realistic to assume, however, that production efficiency stabilizes at some modest value under undisturbed climax conditions but rises to much higher values when diversity is either partially or completely destroyed. The range of numerical values used to quantify the function are consistent with empirical evidence (see Lindeman, 1942) although the numerical values themselves are not the result of field measurement. As stated before, the sensitivity of the model to these and other parameter values is reported in chapter 5.

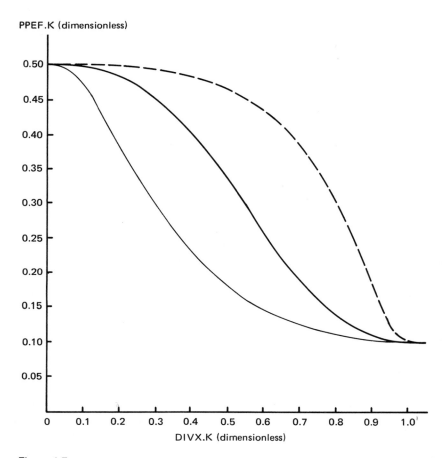

Figure 4.7
Plant production efficiency factor (PPEF.K) as a function of diversity index (DIVX.K)

4.4 Formulation of the Energy Flow

To complete the formulation of the model, it only remains to account for the disposition of energy flow through the producers which is neither used for growth nor for diversification. As pointed out before, the energetics of succession are controlled by the energy strategy of the producers. As energy becomes available to the plant community, it is allocated first for production work, then to diversification work. The basic question is, of course, what happens with any energy availability rate remaining after the current energy consumption rate requirements for production and diversification work have been satiated. The hypothesis suggested in chapter 3 (see figure 3.18) is that such excess energy is stored as potential energy in various forms (biochemical diversity, genetic diversity, etc.) that can be lumped together as a level of stored energy or, for lack of a better term, plant vigor. Energy can be stored for a limited period of time, however; eventually, it is either dissipated in the performance of other quality functions or becomes fossilized. In either case, after a certain amount of time, it is no longer available as a supplementary source of energy for production purposes (see equation 18). The formulation of this part of the model was accomplished as follows:

$$PV.K = PV.J + (DT) (PVAR.JK - PVDR.JK) \qquad (124)$$

$$PV = 0 \qquad (125)$$

$$PVAR.KL = MAX(0, EVAR.K) \qquad (126)$$

$$EVAR.K = (ESRC) (EDAR.K - SSR.K - SER.K) \qquad (127)$$

$$PVDR.KL = PV.K / PVDD \qquad (128)$$

where

PV   = plant vigor ($calm^{-2}$),
PVAR = plant vigor accumulation rate ($calm^{-2}$/month),
PVDR = plant vigor dissipation rate ($calm^{-2}$/month),
EVAR = energy-for-vigor availability rate ($calm^{-2}$/month),
ESRC = energy-to-species requirement coefficient ($calm^{-2}$/species),
EDAR = energy-for-diversification availability rate (species/month),
SSR   = species substitution rate (species/month),
SER   = species emergence rate (species/month),
PVDD = plant vigor dissipation delay (months).

It is important to verify whether the flow of energy through the producers is fully accounted for. When the ecosystem is in steady-state, the difference between the rates of energy flowing in and out of the ecosystem should tend to zero. The energy balance for the model is given by the equation

$$EB.K = EAR.K - EUR.K \tag{129}$$

where

EB = energy balance (calm^{-2}/month),
EAR = energy availability rate (calm^{-2}/month),
EUR = energy utilization rate (calm^{-2}/month).

Energy availability rate is the energy influx to the ecosystem, as given by equation (23). Energy utilization rate, on the other hand, is equal to the summation of energy expenditure rates associated with the various work functions of the community, that is,

$$EUR.K = EEP.K + ERRPM.K + EED.K +$$
$$ERRDM.K + EEV.K \tag{130}$$

$$EEP.K = (EPRC) (GNPGR.K + RPGR.K) \tag{131}$$

$$EED.K = (ESRC) (SER.K + SSR.K) \tag{132}$$

$$EEV.K = PV.K / PVDD \tag{133}$$

where

EUR = energy utilization rate (calm^{-2}/month),
EEP = energy expenditure rate for production (calm^{-2}/month),
$ERRPM$ = energy rate required for plant maintenance (calm^{-2}/month),
EED = energy expenditure rate for diversification (calm^{-2}/month),
$ERRDM$ = energy rate required for diversity maintenance (calm^{-2}/month),
EEV = energy expenditure rate due to vigor dissipation (calm^{-2}/month),
$EPRC$ = energy-to-plants requirement coefficient (cal/g_p),
$GNPGR$ = gross new plant growth rate (g_pm^{-2}/month),
$RPGR$ = replacement plant growth rate (g_pm^{-2}/month),
$ESRC$ = energy-to-species requirement coefficient (calm^{-2}/species),
SER = species emergence rate (species/month),
SSR = species substitution rate (species/month),
PV = plant vigor (calm^{-2}),
$PVDD$ = plant vigor dissipation delay (months),

and the terms $ERRPM$ and $ERRDM$ are given by equations (24) and (102), respectively. Simulation exercises with the model confirmed, in fact, that the difference of equation (129) vanishes in the steady-state. Another difference that should vanish, and in fact does, is the difference between gross production and community respiration. If respiration is defined as gross production minus net production, gross production and respiration are given by the equations

$$GPGR.K = GNPGR.K + RPGR.K \qquad (134)$$

and

$$RESP.K = GPGR.K - NNPPR.K \qquad (135)$$

where

GPGR   = gross plant growth rate ($g_p m^{-2}$/month),
GNPGR = gross new plant growth rate ($g_p m^{-2}$/month),
RPGR   = replacement plant growth rate ($g_p m^{-2}$/month),
NNPPR = net new plant growth rate ($g_p m^{-2}$/month),
RESP   = respiration rate ($g_p m^{-2}$/month).

The terms RPGR, NNPPR, and GNPGR are given by equations (9), (30), and (31), respectively. Equations (134) and (135) could be expressed in energetic units ($cal m^{-2}$/month) just as well by simply introducing the appropriate conversion factor, EPRC (cal/g_p). Equation (135) can be reformulated as community (rather than plant) respiration by adding the respiration terms for consumers and decomposers. While these supplementary equations (129 to 135) in no way influence the feedback structure of the model, they were useful in printing and plotting variables of interest for model verification.

For the simulation experiments discussed in chapter 5, it was also necessary to incorporate into the model the ability to introduce exogenous perturbations to test model performance under both natural and utilization conditions. Thus perturbation terms were added to plant depletion rate (equation 6) and diversity decrease rate (equation 88) to test model response to destructive natural perturbations such as fire and drought. Terms to account for the introduction of domestic consumers were added to grazing plant depletion rate (equation 56) and consumer organic nutrients becoming available (equation 60) to test model response to grazing pressure. The analytical formulation of these perturbation terms is straightforward, using simple pulse and step input functions of constant amplitude to simulate the effect of transitory and sustained perturbations, respectively.

Computer Simulations 5

All flesh is grass.
—Isaiah 40:6

5.1 Overview of the Simulations

The present chapter is devoted to the presentation of the simulation results obtained in testing the model. Simulations were conducted to test model performance under both ''natural'' (the grassland undisturbed) and ''utilization'' (the grassland subject to grazing) conditions. We have tested the sensitivity of model performance to parametric perturbations, the response to natural exogenous perturbations such as fire or drought, and the response to alternative intensities and frequencies of grazing stress by livestock. In this chapter we discuss the various behavior patterns generated by the model vis-a-vis those known to be associated with secondary succession in grasslands.

All the simulation runs were performed using a solution interval of one month. Table 5.1 provides a summary of the simulation runs to be discussed. The results of the base run using the nominal values for all parameters (those listed in table 4.1) are shown in figure 5.3. This and the other simulations show that the dominant modes of dynamic behavior generated by the model are determined by its internal feedback structure irrespective of the values of parameters or initial conditions. The numerical results approximate rather closely the climax value of standing crop, for which some grassland data is available. However, the model could be calibrated to approximate other values of standing crop and other variables if the values computed were proven to be wrong. Therefore, in examining the results of figures 5.1 to 5.18, the reader is encouraged to focus his attention on the behavior patterns over time rather than the specific numerical values at any given time.

The emphasis on qualitative behavior patterns as opposed to numerical accuracy is imposed by the lack of accurate field measurements of grassland variables for whole seres. Most of the available data on secondary grassland succession is descriptive data. A survey of these data was provided in chapter 2. On the basis of these descriptive data and the scarce numerical data at our disposal, we put together in section 2.1 a composite picture of successional dynamics in the form of time histories and a tabular model. Since numerical accuracy is clearly absent from the quantification of the test model, we do not attempt to make any form of numerical comparisons or inferences. However, we intend to show that the dynamic behavior generated by the test model is qualitatively in consonance with the full range of empirical evidence available on grassland succession.

Table 5.1
Summary of simulation experiments

Figure	Run	Conditions
5.1	Dynamics of the nutrient-cycling loop	IRPGR.K = IRPGR.K + (DT) (1 / PDRSD) (NPDR.J + GPDR.J − IRPGR.J), PPEF = 0.10 (constant), SCC = 103.3 (constant)
5.2	Dynamics of the nutrient-cycling loop with revised replacement subloop	IRPGR.K = IRPGR.K + (DT) (1 / PDRSD) (NPDR.J − IRPGR.J), PPEF = 0.10 (constant), SCC = 103.3 (constant)
5.3	Dynamics of the nutrient-cycling loop coupled with the community diversification loop	base run; model as listed in tables 4.1 and 4.2
5.4	Effect of reducing the lifetime of grasses by one-half	PDD = 3
5.5	Effect of increasing the species emergence delay by a factor of two	ISEAD = 120
5.6	Effect of increasing the soil-carrying capacity adjustment delay by a factor of ten	SCCAD = 120
5.7	Effect of increasing energy requirement for diversity maintenance by a factor of five	DIVMC = 0.5
5.8	Effect of higher-valued production efficiency curve	upper curve in figure 4.7
5.9	Joint effect of a lower-valued diversity curve and a linearized soil-carrying capacity curve	lower curve in figure 4.5 and piecewise linear curve in figure 4.6

Table 5.1 (continued)

Figure	Run	Conditions
5.10	Successional response to sudden partial destruction of standing crop	50 percent impulse increase of PDR
5.11	Response to sudden partial destruction of species diversity	50 percent impulse increase of DDR
5.12	Response to sustained partial destruction of standing crop	2 g_pm^{-2}/month step increase of PDR
5.13	Response to sustained partial destruction of standing crop and species diversity	2gm^{-2}/month step increase of PDR and 5 species/month step increase of DDR
5.14	Successional response to sustained harvesting of the standing crop with net loss of nutrients	60-year 1.5 g_pm^{-2}/month pulse increase of PDR without any increase in ONBA
5.15	Successional dynamics after an extended period of grazing pressure	60-year 0.5 g_pm^{-2}/month pulse increase of PDR with proportional increase in ONBA
5.16	Successional dynamics under a 10-year stocking cycle	5-year 1.5 g_pm^{-2}/month pulse increases of PDR starting at years 0, 10, 20, 30, 40, 50
5.17	Successional dynamics under a 20-year stocking cycle	10-year 1.5 g_pm^{-2}/month pulse increases of PDR starting at years 0, 20, 40
5.18	Successional dynamics under a 30-year stocking cycle	15-year 1.5 g_pm^{-2}/month pulse increases of PDR starting at years 0, 30

5.2 Model Testing under Natural Conditions

Let us consider first the behavior associated with the nutrients-cycling loop (i.e., the lower loop of figure 3.1) alone. Figure 5.1 exhibits a 60-year simulation of this loop, structured in accordance with the hypothesis elaborated in figures 3.2, 3.4, 3.5, 3.7, 3.8, and 3.10. Thus, in conducting the simulation run of figure 5.1, diversity was ignored, energy flow was taken for granted, and both production efficiency and soil-carrying capacity were assumed to possess constant values. The initial conditions were set so as to represent severe trophic disequilibrium, that is, a very small standing crop and a very large reservoir of nutrients available for absorption. For this particular run, the value of production efficiency was set at 10 percent and the value of soil-carrying capacity at 103.3 gm^{-2} of plant biomass. The latter corresponds to the climax value of soil-carrying capacity. Therefore

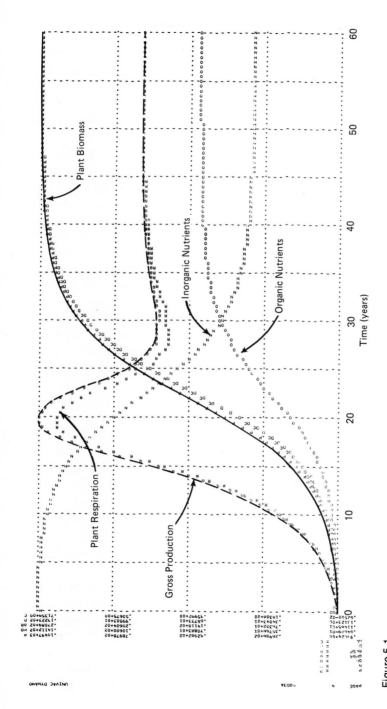

Figure 5.1
Dynamics of the nutrient-cycling loop

we are assuming that the community is already diversified and all potential niches already colonized as they would be in the climax ecosystem, and we are keeping that constant. This is, of course, a very strong assumption since we know that carrying capacity is typically very low at the onset of secondary succession. The assumption was made for the initial runs to test the trophic dynamics of the nutrient-cycling loop by itself but will be relaxed later.

Figure 5.1 displays the transients that arise in the process of approaching trophic equilibrium. The variables plotted are N = inorganic nutrients $(g_n m^{-2})$, O = organic nutrients in organic matter undergoing decomposition $(g_n m^{-2})$, G = gross production $(g_p m^{-2}/month)$, R = respiration $(g_p m^{-2}/month)$, P = producers biomass $(g_p m^{-2})$, C = consumers biomass $(g_c m^{-2})$, and D = decomposers biomass $(g_d m^{-2})$. These correspond to N, ON, GPGR, RESP, P, NC, and D, respectively, in the notation used for the formulation of the model in chapter 4. Note that gross production (G) and respiration (R) are rates measured in $g_p m^{-2}/month$ while the other variables are levels measured in grams per square meter. Also note that G and R, N and O, P, C, and D are plotted in their own scales. Gross production and respiration increase rapidly in response to the abundant supply of nutrients and uncolonized soil. A buildup of the standing crop gradually follows, and continues until the saturation value assumed for soil-carrying capacity is approached. Consumers and decomposers lag behind plants in the growth process. After reaching a peak during the most active years of production, both gross production and respiration decline and level off at the maintenance level. Toward the end of the simulation, the ecosystem is clearly approaching steady-state, with most of the nutrients now forming part of either living biomass (plants and animals) or organic matter in the process of decomposition. The biomass levels of producers, consumers, and decomposers approach maximum values of 104.97, 0.71, and 13.22 grams per square meter, respectively, which correspond approximately to the actual values at Pawnee, which are 103.3, 0.70, and 12.4 (Patten, 1971). Most of the growth has been accomplished after 30 to 40 years, with production activity peaking at about 20 years.

These results compare with the successional patterns of section 2.1 and are consistent with items 1, 2, 4, 6, 7, 16, and 17 of table 2.1 and with items 1, 2, 4, and 5 of table 2.2. The ratio of gross production over community respiration is greater than one during the first 30 to 40 years, but gradually approaches one in later years as production and respiration become equal. The ratio of gross production over standing crop biomass goes from a value greater than one at the beginning of the simulation to a value smaller than one as equilibrium is approached. Presumably, energy flow would be proportional to the level of production and respiration, so there is also implicit consistency with item 3 of table 2.1, that is, the ratio of biomass supported per unit energy flow goes from a low to a high value as the transients unfold through time. Net production (item 4 in table 2.1) is, of course, the difference between gross production and respiration losses; it gradually vanishes toward the end of the simulation. The food chain is grazing-oriented, with plants drawing from abundant nutrients and consumers drawing from abundant plants as rapidly as their own growth machinery allows. Total organic matter (item 6) accumulates to its maximum feasible value, and therefore most of the inorganic nutrients become intrabiotic (item 7). As the amount of dead organic matter accumulates, the nutrients-recycling role of decomposers becomes critical for continued survival of the biotic community (item 17), although nutrient exchange rate (item 16) slows down and nutrients recycling never becomes limiting in this case. Growth proceeds until limited by the saturation of soil-carrying capacity.

The dominant force behind the growth process shown in figure 5.1 is, of course, the new growth loop of figure 3.5. When the (constant) soil-carrying capacity level is approached, the gain of the positive feedback gradually vanishes (as a result of the nonlinearity of figure 3.6), and production activity becomes regulated solely by the replacement growth loop of figure 3.7. In brief, the standing crop builds up to the limit imposed by soil-carrying capacity, or to the limit imposed by the nutrients availability rate resulting from nutrient recycling, whichever is reached first. Changing the values of soil-carrying capacity and/or the delays involved in nutrient cycling will affect the limits of growth, but the modes of behavior shown in figure 5.1 would remain the same. Similarly, changing the value of production efficiency and/or the valuation of the nonlinearity of figure 3.6 (without changing the shape of the curve) would affect the gain of the loop, and therefore would result in slower or faster growth, as the case may be, but the overall dynamic patterns would still be the same.

Parametric sensitivities of the model will be explored in the next section. At this point, it is interesting to observe that the growth pattern for biomass in figure 5.1 approaches the limit asymptotically, in other words, there is no overshoot by the community before settling down to steady-state. In the model used for this run, the indicated replacement growth rate (refer to figure 3.4) was formulated as a delay of the total plant depletion rate, including both depletion due to natural decay and depletion due to grazing by the consumers. It was found that overshooting (as postulated by item 3 of table 2.2) occurs when the indicated replacement growth rate is reformulated as a delay of plant depletion due to natural decay only. The results are shown in figure 5.2. When the indicated replacement growth rate is reformulated in this manner, grasses eaten away by the consumers must be restored by new growth rather than replacement growth; a longer adjustment delay is involved, and overshooting results. The difference between gross production and community respiration for the producers no longer tends to zero, but rather to a positive steady-state value corresponding to the net yield required year after year by the consumers. The reformulation also results in a weakening of the new growth loop, due to the reduced rate of accumulation of standing crop which in turn results from the weakened replacement growth loop; as a result the steady-state is approached at a level that is below either the limit imposed by soil-carrying capacity or the limit imposed by the rate of recycling of nutrients. The revised formulation of indicated replacement growth rate may be realistic in that it introduces the tendency of the growth process to overshoot before approaching steady-state, and this is the formulation used in the balance of the simulations. Whether one formulation or the other is used, however, the nutrient-cycling loop alone does not explain how successional dynamics arise. The actual carrying capacity of the soil is usually very modest at the beginning of succession, and will not increase unless acted upon by the community. In order to account for ecological succession as a community-controlled process, the upper and lower loops of figure 3.1 must stand in interaction.

Figure 5.3 displays the result of testing the model for the full dynamic hypothesis, which integrates the dynamics of nutrient cycling, diversification, and energy flow. Soil-carrying capacity and production efficiency are now functions of diversity and relative diversity, respectively, as defined in the preceding chapter. Starting with a modest value of approximately 20 gm^{-2}, soil-carrying capacity built up during the simulation to 120 gm^{-2} in response to community development and diversification. Production efficiency assumed values ranging from 10 to 40 percent, depending on the stage of successional development. Starting with figure 5.3, two additional variables are plotted: Y = diversity (number of species) and V = vigor ($calm^{-2}$), corresponding to the levels denoted as DIV and PV, respectively, in chapter 4. The other plotted variables continue to have the same interpretation as before. It must be pointed out that, while the appearance of the P, C, D, G, R, N, and O curves resembles that of the previous runs, the controlling force now is the community (i.e., the upper loop of figure 3.1), whereas before it was simply the combined effect of assuming a high fixed value for soil-carrying capacity and setting the

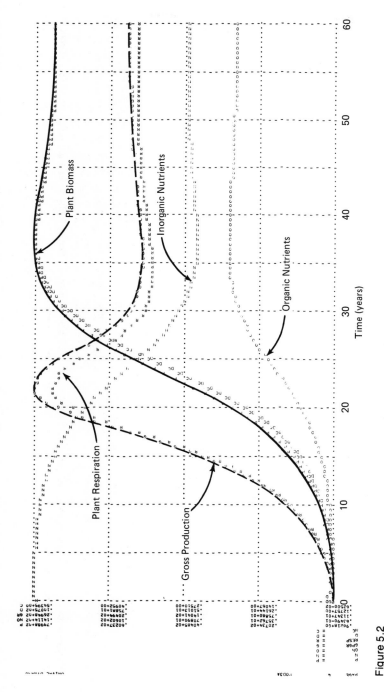

Figure 5.2
Dynamics of the nutrient-cycling loop with revised replacement subloop

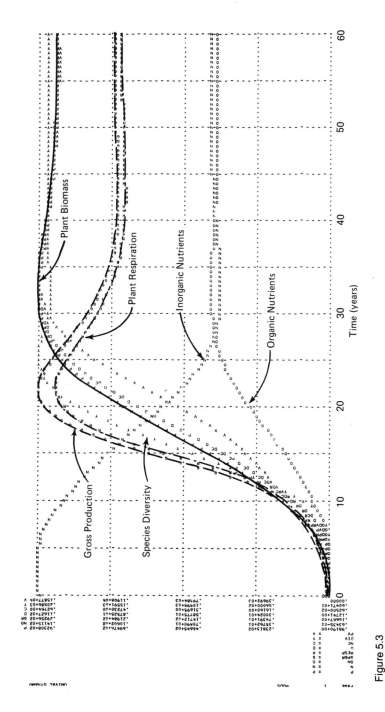

Figure 5.3
Dynamics of the nutrient-cycling loop coupled with the community diversification loop (From L. T. Gutierrez and W. R. Fey, 1975, in *Simulation* 24:113–125. Copyright 1975 by Simulation Councils, Inc. Reprinted with permission.)

initial conditions at nonsteady-state levels, together with the growth machinery of plants and the physical tendency toward equilibrium in the distribution of matter around the nutrient-cycling loop.

According to the results in figure 5.3, diversity increases and peaks first, then comes the peak in biomass, and lastly the buildup in energy stored, or vigor. The process of species diversification (item 8 of table 2.1) presumably results in increased niche specialization (item 12 of table 2.1) that in turn has a positive influence on soil-carrying capacity (figure 3.14) and allows for further growth of biomass (item 6 of table 2.1), which, of course, results in still further diversification (figure 3.13). As growth and diversification eventually become limited by space saturation, interspecific competition, and so on, energy flow increasingly becomes allocated to storage as vigor and, eventually, to dissipation in the performance of other quality functions. As the potential for both quantitative and qualitative growth becomes exhausted, the steady-state or climax condition is approached. The time histories of figure 5.3 are also in consonance with items 1 through 7 and item 10 of table 2.2. They display the energetically based dynamic behavior that arises in time from the feedback coupling of abiotic and biotic matter, the effects of community diversification, and the flow of energy. The simulation of figure 5.3 is used in the balance of this chapter as a base case for comparison with other simulations.

5.3 Sensitivity to Parametric Perturbations

The dynamic behavior discussed in the previous section arises from the feedback structure of the ecosystem. More specifically, the modes of behavior that appear in figure 5.3 arise from the feedback structure of the dynamic hypothesis in chapter 3. Parameter values determine, of course, such factors as the levels of magnitude associated with the various successional variables, the period and limits of succession, and the amplitude of oscillations. However, they determine neither the occurrence of succession nor the dynamic patterns associated with its unfolding. In order to verify that this is indeed the case, the simulation model was exercised repeatedly to test the sensitivity of successional behavior to changes in each one of the model parameters. Sensitivity analyses for each parameter were conducted on a one-at-a-time basis by perturbing its numerical value over a wide range and rerunning the model while keeping everything else constant. Additional simulations to test the effect of parameter variations on a several-at-a-time basis were conducted in a selective manner, with emphasis on those parameters that appear to have special relevance to ecological succession.

The parameters required to quantify the dynamic hypothesis under consideration are basically of three kinds: conversion coefficients, time delays, and table functions. Conversion coefficients include the amount of nutrients required to produce one unit of plant biomass (NPRC in the model), the amount of energy per unit time required to maintain one unit of plant biomass (EPRC), the amount of plant biomass required to sustain one unit of consumers biomass (PNCRC), the amount of energy per unit time required to maintain each one of the species in the community (DIVMC), and so forth. Time delays include such considerations as the average lifetimes of plants and animals (PDD and NCRD), the time required for the production machinery of plants to respond to favorable growth conditions (INGAD), the delay involved in the substitution of species (SSD), the average amount of time that energy can be stored before it becomes fossilized (PVDD). Table functions refer to the valuation of the complex ecological functions hypothesized in figures 3.6, 3.9, 3.11, 3.13, 3.14, 3.15, and 3.17. It would not seem necessary to display and discuss all the simulations conducted for sensitivity analysis purposes. However, a discussion of some selected cases is appropriate.

Let us consider first the effect of delays on succession dynamics. In the simulation of figure 5.3 (hereafter taken as the "standard run" for comparative discussion purposes), the average lifetime for the standing crop of grasses (denoted as PDD in the model) was assumed to be 6 months. The results of assuming a lifetime of only 3 months for grasses are shown in figure 5.4. The effect of shortening the lifetime of grasses by one-half is shown to be basically twofold: production activity peaks approximately 10 years *later*, and the standing crop of grasses levels off after succession at a *lower* steady-state level. Succession takes longer because shortening the life span of grasses reduces the accumulation of standing crop, which in turn reduces the production capacity of the plant community and results in a weakening of the new growth loop gain. It results in a lower climax level for plant biomass because the rate of availability of soluble inorganic nutrients becomes limiting as a result of the great quantity of nutrients that accumulate in organic form (i.e., trapped in organic matter in process of being decomposed). The effect of assuming that the average lifetime of grasses is longer than 6 months would be exactly the opposite: production activity would peak sooner, and the climax standing crop would be greater than in figure 5.3. In either case, however, the same modes of successional behavior occur; changing the numerical value of this delay changes the period of the successional patterns and their limits, but the patterns themselves do not change.

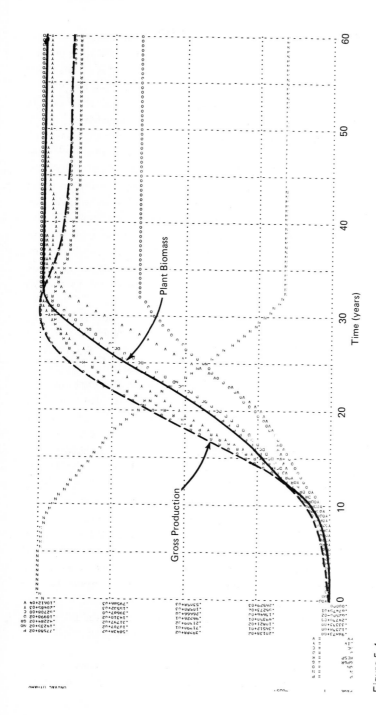

Figure 5.4
Effect of reducing the lifetime of grasses by one-half

With regard to figure 5.4, it is interesting to observe that while the climax accumulation of biomass is smaller than before, gross production peaks and then approaches steady-state at levels higher than before. This means that a greater amount of the energy flow is consumed in the long run for production purposes (as evidenced also by the reduced climax level of energy stored as vigor) and reveals that a plant community characterized by short-lived plants will tend toward a higher gross production over standing crop biomass ratio and a lower amount of biomass supported per unit energy flow than a community where long-lived plants predominate. Conversely, the longer the average life span of plants is, the lower the gross production over standing crop biomass ratio and the higher the biomass supported over unit energy flow ratio to be approached in the mature stages. The smaller climax accumulation of plant biomass and the greater accumulation of organic debris result in smaller and greater climax levels of consumers and decomposers biomass, respectively, when plants are short lived. Species diversity, on the other hand, does not seem to be affected in any significant way by the average lifetime of plants.

Delays also can affect successional transients by introducing oscillations. For example, figure 5.5 shows the effect of increasing the species colonization delay (ISEAD in the model) by a factor of two, from 5 to 10 years. Increasing the value of this delay means that it will take longer for new species to appear on the grassland in response to the ongoing buildup of biomass. The result is a slower takeoff of species diversity, followed by a diversification pattern that overshoots and then exhibits damped oscillations as it approaches its climax level. This behavior is intuitively appealing from the ecological viewpoint. The potential of the ecosystem as a site for colonization by new species increases as a result of the slow response to biomass accumulation. This potential eventually results in a diversification boom that brings to the grassland new species in numbers exceeding the natural niches available. Fierce interspecific competition results, and diversity declines. It declines too much, however, due to the severity of competition and/or the unsuitability of some of these species for the local niches. As a result some niches are left uncolonized, creating again the potential for the arrival of new species, which again compete for the remaining niches, and a new diversification cycle takes place. The gradual exhaustion of niches remains after each cycle brings about a gradual vanishing of the potential for further diversification and eventually leads to steady-state after several cycles of decreasing amplitude.

Since continued ecosystem growth and development is contingent on an expanding soil-carrying capacity, and this in turn depends on community

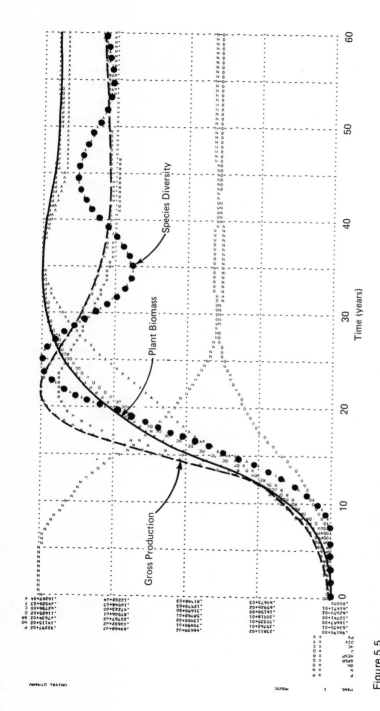

Figure 5.5
Effect of increasing the species emergence delay by a factor of two (From L. T. Gutierrez and W. R. Fey, 1975, in *Simulation* 24:113–125. Copyright 1975 by Simulation Councils, Inc. Reprinted with permission.)

diversity, the reader may wonder how it is possible that figure 5.5 shows diversity oscillating while the patterns of production and biomass are unaffected. This does not mean that changes in diversity do not have any significant effect on the rest of the system. Successional development appears to be insensitive to diversity in figure 5.5 because the oscillations occur after diversity has increased beyond the range within which soil-carrying capacity is sensitive to diversity. According to the nonlinearity assumed in figure 4.6, soil-carrying capacity becomes insensitive to further increases in diversity beyond 100 species. Increasing the species-colonization delay results in diversity overshooting up to approximately 245 species in figure 5.5. The subsequent damped oscillations occur in the 125 to 245 species range, well beyond the level at which soil-carrying capacity becomes insensitive to further diversification. Succession would have aborted if diversity had not increased from a low initial value of 6 to about 125 in the first 15 to 20 years. Furthermore, succession would be affected eventually if the delay under consideration continues to increase. If the length of the delay were to become infinite (meaning that diversification response to biomass growth never materializes), the carrying capacity of the soil would remain stagnant, and successional development would abort. The simulation of figure 5.5 illustrates how nonlinearities can generate counterintuitive behavior in complex systems.

There are three important delays in the positive feedback loop of figure 3.16. One is, of course, the delay associated with the production of plant biomass. Another is the delay involved in the appearance of new species in response to biomass accumulation, as discussed in the previous paragraph. The third one is the delay involved in the complex array of community activities that eventually results in increased soil-carrying capacity. In the simulation of figure 5.3, this delay (which is denoted as SCCAD in the model) was assumed to have a value of 12 months. In other words, it was assumed that the impact of new species on soil-carrying capacity becomes operative 1 year after the arrival of the new species. The effect of a tenfold increase in the value of this delay is shown by the simulation of figure 5.6. Successional modes of behavior remain invariant, as well as the climax levels eventually reached by the various variables, but the smoothness of the process is broken into distinct stages of development. Thus production activity and, therefore, plant biomass grow rapidly at the beginning, as before. After 10 years or so, however, biomass production and the accumulation of standing crop slow down due to the limiting effect of soil-carrying capacity, until this limit is relaxed by species substitution and the (now slower) activity of the increasingly diversified community.

Simulation runs conducted to test the effect of perturbing the value of other delays revealed a high degree of model insensitivity to wide variations in these parameter values. As expected, successional transients retained the same behavioral patterns in all cases. Sufficiently large values for some of the delays, however, have a limiting effect on succession. For example, the nutrient availability rate of figure 3.4 is directly proportional to the reservoir of soluble inorganic nutrients available in the soil and inversely proportional to the nutrient absorption delay (NAD in the model), which in turn depends on the availability of water and other factors. Thus, for a given reservoir of nutrients, increasing the nutrients absorption delay decreases the nutrient availability rate; the longer this delay is, the sooner nutrient availability becomes a limiting factor on succession. Similar remarks apply with regard to the delay involved in the decomposition of organic matter. This delay depends on the availability of decomposers to do the job (see figures 3.10 and 3.11), and decomposers grow in response to the accumulation of organic debris. If their response delay (DRD) is very large, decomposers will grow slowly, organic debris will accumulate at a rate faster than the decomposition rate in the meantime, the decomposition delay will increase, the reservoir of soluble inorganic nutrients in the soil will also decrease, and again the nutrient availability rate will become limiting sooner than if the decomposers grow quickly in response to the buildup in organic matter, with the limiting effect persisting at least until the actual level of decomposers catches up with the required level. Needless to say, if the length of the decomposers response delay were to become infinite, organic matter would accumulate without being decomposed, the recycling of nutrients would stagnate, and the growing standing crop would first level off and then eventually decline as nutrients continue to become unavailable for new growth or for replacement growth. In any of these cases, successional transients unfold as usual until suppressed by the limiting effect of the delay.

Let us consider next the sensitivity of successional behavior to the values of conversion coefficients. The gain of each feedback loop in the structure of the ecosystem depends on the numerical values of the parameters in that loop, whether they are time delays or conversion coefficients. When the gain in any one of the loops in the multiloop structure becomes limiting, succession is suppressed. This is the case whether a loop gain becomes limiting as a consequence of a coefficient or as a consequence of a delay. For example, consider again the possibility that the availability rate of nutrients (see figure 3.4) becomes limiting. It was pointed out that the nutrient availability rate is proportional to the amount of inorganic nutrients available in the soil and inversely proportional to the nutrient absorption delay. Therefore the maximum production rate of plant biomass that is feasible as far as nutrient availability is concerned (denoted NRPGR in the model) is equal to the nutrient availability rate divided by the quantity of nutrients necessary to produce one unit of plant biomass (i.e., the coefficient NPRC in the model). Evidently, the greater the value of this coefficient, the sooner nutrient availability effectively becomes a limiting factor of succession. It follows then that for a given inventory of nutrients, actual nutrient availability becomes limiting sooner if either the nutrient absorption delay or the nutrient conversion coefficient, or both, are increased. Whether it is the time delay or the conversion coefficient that causes nutrient availability to become limiting, successional transients continue their course until constrained by the limiting factor.

Similar remarks apply to other conversion coefficients in the various loops. Energy flow, of course, also can be made limiting by increasing one or more of the conversion coefficients involved. For example, the maximum production rate of plant biomass that is energetically feasible (EPPGR in the model) is equal to the rate of energy becoming available from photosynthesis plus the rate of energy becoming available from storage, all divided by the quantity of energy required to produce one unit of plant biomass (EPRC). Again, the greater the value of this coefficient, the sooner energy availability becomes limiting on succession. Short of becoming a limiting factor on growth and diversification, either decreasing energy flow or assuming that more of it must be used for production and/or diversification work results in weakened plant vigor during succession. An illustrative example is given by the simulation run of figure 5.7, which exhibits the effect of increasing the energy requirement coefficient for diversity maintenance (DIVMC) by a factor of five. According to the influence diagram of figure 3.18, this would affect the rate of energy remaining for storage, or vigor. The simulation shows that plant vigor, and therefore the ability of the plant community to draw from stored energy in order to sustain external perturbations (see item 22 of table 2.1), is detrimentally affected during succession, and also approaches a lower climax level. The same effect results from reducing, for example, the assumed energy fixation rate per unit of standing crop (EFR in the model). This is, of course, due to the higher priorities enjoyed in the hypothesis by production and diversification work, and the open-loop character of energy flow.

Finally, let us discuss the sensitivities associated with the nonlinearities of figures 3.6, 3.9, 3.11, 3.13, 3.14, 3.15, and 3.17. Structurally speaking, these functions are actually variable coefficients. They influence system behavior in ways similar to time delays and conversion coefficients, but in varying degrees depending on the value of the independent variable, which in each case is both an integral element of the feedback structure and an indicator of the stage of successional development. Thus the changes in the values of these variable coefficients are internally generated over time by the feedback structure of the ecosystem, and they both influence and are influenced by the unfolding of successional transients. In each case, sensitivities will depend on both the shape and the numerical valuation of the curve. The shape of each curve is as assumed in the dynamic hypothesis of chapter 3, and has remained invariant (except for some linearization trials) for the simulations we have conducted. The upper and lower limits of each function also remained constant for all simulations; in each case, the perturbation made for the sensitivity analysis runs consists of either inflating or deflating the numerical values of the curve within the hypothesized range. The interested reader may refer to figures 4.3 and 4.7 for the numerical values used.

As it was with regard to time delays and conversion coefficients, the most interesting sensitivities related to nonlinearities (table functions) were found to be associated with those belonging to the positive loop of figure 3.16. For example, the effect of inflating the values of the production efficiency curve (refer to figures 3.17 and 4.7) is shown in the simulation run of figure 5.8. The consequence of a higher-valued production efficiency curve is of course to increase the gain of the new growth loop of figure 3.5. As a result, the rate of production of plant biomass accelerates much faster and overshoots, generating oscillations of standing crop and species diversity before the ultimate climax is approached. A comparison with the time patterns of section 2.1 suggests that the production efficiency curve used for this simulation probably was too inflated.

Interesting results were also obtained by perturbing the indicated-diversity-as-a-function-of-total-biomass and the indicated-soil-carrying-capacity-as-a-function-of-diversity curves of figures 3.13 and 3.14, either one at a time or jointly. It was found that the distinctness between successive stages of ecosystem development becomes more apparent as a result of either increasing the delays around the loop (as in the simulation of figure 5.6) or perturbing the nonlinearities involved, or both. Figure 5.9 displays the effect of jointly deflating the diversity curve and linearizing the soil-carrying capacity curve (see figures 4.5 and 4.6 for the actual values used). It is illuminating to examine the results of figure 5.9 vis-a-vis the results

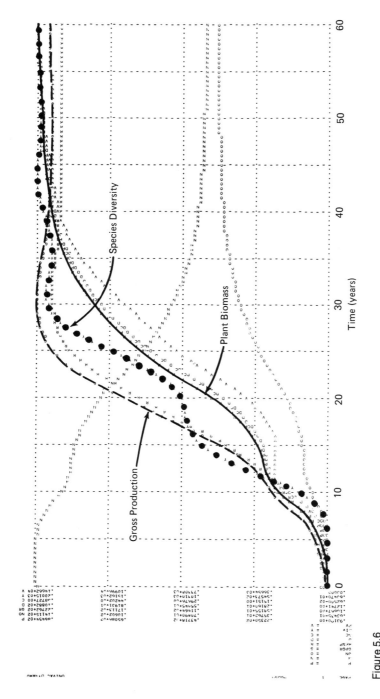

Figure 5.6
Effect of increasing the soil-carrying capacity adjustment delay by a factor of ten

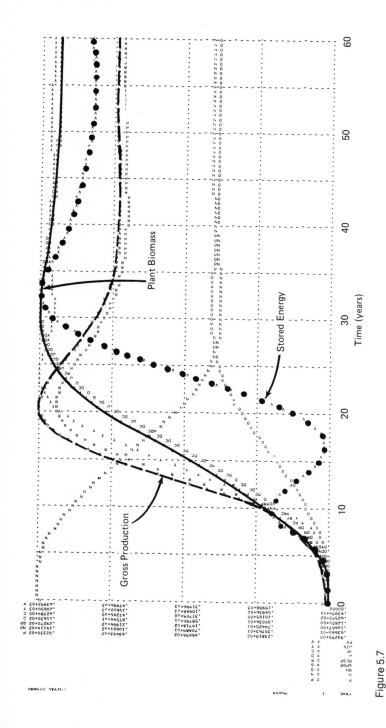

Figure 5.7
Effect of increasing energy requirement for diversity maintenance by a factor of five (From L. T. Gutierrez and W. R. Fey, 1975, in *Simulation* 24:113–125. Copyright 1975 by Simulation Councils, Inc. Reprinted with permission.)

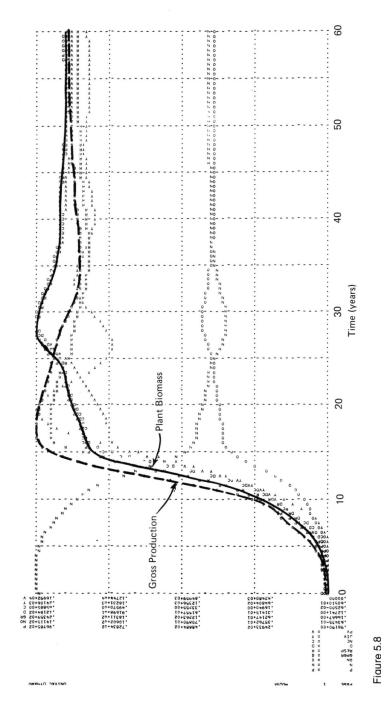

Figure 5.8
Effect of higher-valued production efficiency curve

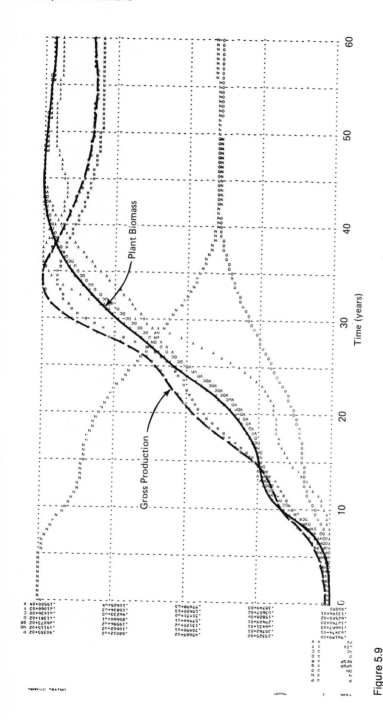

Figure 5.9
Joint effect of a lower-valued diversity curve and a linearized soil-carrying capacity curve (From L. T. Gutierrez and W. R. Fey, 1975, in *Simulation Councils Proceedings Series* 5:73–82. Copyright 1975 by Simulation Councils, Inc. Reprinted with permission.)

presented before in figure 5.6. While diversity leads biomass during most of the transient period in figure 5.6, the reverse is the case in figure 5.9. This is due to the different shape of the nonlinearities involved. In reference to figure 4.5, notice that using the slowest rising curve diminishes the multiplicative effect of biomass accumulation on diversity for modest values of biomass, namely, during the initial stages of succession. With regard to figure 4.6, using the piecewise linear curve increases the multiplicative effect of diversity on soil-carrying capacity for low values of diversity, which is again the situation at the onset of succession. Therefore the joint perturbation under which the simulation of figure 5.9 was conducted effectively shifts dominance during the early stages of succession to the gain associated with the soil-carrying capacity curve.

In figure 5.6, successive stages become distinct simply because of the delay involved in going from one to another; in figure 5.9, on the contrary, they become distinct because the more-growth versus more-diversity strategy of the early grassland community is assumed to shift in favor of increasing the carrying capacity of the soil, presumably to allow for faster growth. Nevertheless, the net result of assuming this change in community strategy is to reach the climax more or less at the same time as in figure 5.6 and approximately 10 to 15 years later than in the simulation of the standard run. Attempting to expand the carrying capacity of the ecosystem without (or even with less) species diversification results in oversaturation of the colonized niches, while leaving other niches unexploited. After a few years, growth must slow down to give time for a more diversified community to pursue a more comprehensive colonization of the grassland; then succession proceeds. With regard to the simulation of figure 5.9, it is also interesting to observe that it displays stages of grassland development that closely resemble (timewise) the four described in Odum's quotation in section 2.1 (Odum, 1971, p. 262).

The simulations reported in this section have shown that perturbing ecosystem parameters affect the limits of succession, the period of transient successional response, the period and amplitude of oscillations, and so forth. However, the dominant dynamic modes of successional behavior (as in figures 2.1 to 2.5 and tables 2.1 and 2.2) arise from the feedback structure of the ecosystem and are insensitive to parametric variations. In generating succession, all elements of the ecosystem interact according to the mutual causalities involved, with no one standing in isolation from the others. Precisely because of this, any factor that becomes limiting for the successional development of one element of the ecosystem structure becomes limiting for the whole ecosystem.

5.4 Response to Exogenous Perturbations

While the previous section explored sensitivities to ecological parameters as the ecosystem succeeds from youth to maturity, the present one describes the transient successional response of the climax grassland ecosystem to natural exogenous perturbations such as fire and drought. It has been shown how the positive feedback loop of figure 3.16 has a controlling influence on successional transients. Therefore it appears appropriate to test model performance under natural exogenous perturbations that periodically result in destruction of standing crop and/or species diversity. A set of simulation runs was conducted for this purpose, and the results are illustrated by figures 5.10 and 5.11. These simulations were accomplished by letting the model run during 60 years and then, with the ecosystem in steady-state (climax) condition, applying a severe pulse increment to the rates of depletion of plant biomass and species diversity (PDR and DDR in the model, respectively).

Figure 5.10 displays the successional response to a sudden destruction of approximately 50 percent of the standing crop of grasses. The net effect of the disturbance is to push the grassland back to a younger stage of successional development. Gross production (and therefore plant respiration also) declines during the year following the disturbance due to the destruction of plant biomass. As a result the standing crop for the year immediately following the perturbation is greatly reduced. The number of species in the community declines slightly, presumably the result of the weakest species abandoning the range under the pressure of increased competition brought about by the scarcity of food. Finally, plant vigor also declines in the aftermath, because the reduction in photosynthetic activity reduces energy flow below the level necessary for immediate replacement of energy being dissipated from storage. Beginning with the second year after the destruction, however, the grassland bounces back. Both gross and net production increase, plant biomass builds up, some of the abandoned niches are colonized anew, and the interplay between plant production and the still highly diversified community gradually drives the grassland back to its climax in approximately 10 to 15 years.

Figure 5.11, on the other hand, exhibits the successional transient which arises from suddenly forcing about 50 percent of the species in the biotic community out of the grassland. The initial reaction to the sudden decrease in diversity is an increase in gross production, and even greater increase in net production, and therefore a boom in the level of standing crop. Both the standing crop and its vigor flourish in the years immediately following the

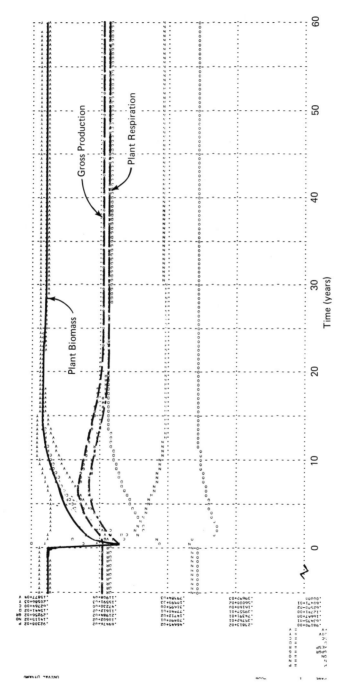

Figure 5.10
Successional response to sudden partial destruction of standing crop (From L. T. Gutierrez and W. R. Fey, 1975, in *Simulation* 24:113–125. Copyright 1975 by Simulation Councils, Inc. Reprinted with permission.

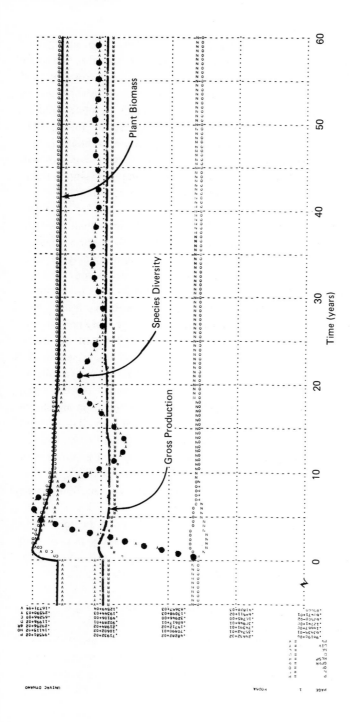

Figure 5.11
Response to sudden partial destruction of species diversity

disturbance. This is made possible by the reduced demand of energy for diversity maintenance work, which results in increased amounts of energy flow being allocated to production of biomass and the performance of quality functions other than diversification, with increased plant vigor as the net effect. Naturally, the bloom in productivity and the abundance of food which the accumulation of standing crop brings about immediately creates a high potential for community diversification. Too many species respond to the favorable conditions for colonization, and overshooting results, followed by damped oscillations since again the grassland is internally driven back to its climax by its own feedback mechanisms.

Other exogenous perturbations may be of some consequence in generating successional transients. For example, a disturbance causing a temporary destruction of decomposers would result in a slowdown of decomposition processes and, because of this, nutrient availability may become limiting and the standing crop (and even species diversity) may suffer a temporary decline until decomposers regenerate and an adequate rate of nutrients recycling is restored. On the other hand, a disturbance leading to a temporary extermination of consumers would relax the grazing pressure on grasses, and they would tend toward a new steady-state level involving no net new production until the animals come back. As discussed in the preceding section (in connection with sensitivity to nutrient availability delay, NAD), a disturbance causing water shortage may have the same limiting effect as destroying the decomposers. The concentration of soluble inorganic nutrients in the soil may be adequate, but nutrient availability still becomes limiting if they cannot be absorbed at the required rate. As was the case with parametric variations, external disturbances such as these may have an indirect (e.g., limiting) effect on successional transients, but the most interesting responses arise when perturbations are applied to the loop-coupling standing crop and species diversity.

With regard to the results of both figures 5.10 and 5.11, it is also interesting to note that the same feedback structure that generates and controls ecosystem succession is also responsible for its ability to bounce back from the destructive effect of external disturbances.

5.5 Model Testing under Utilization Conditions

Animal life, human life, and indeed all economic activity are ultimately based on the fact that grasses and other plants capture solar energy at a rate greater than that necessary for their own maintenance. The objective of the present section is to report the extent to which successional responses to a systematic exploitation of this surplus can be explained by the dynamic hypothesis of chapter 3.

Land may be used for urban development, for recreation, agriculture, forestry, grazing, and so on. Only the last mode of utilization will be considered here, as it is the typical mode of utilization for natural grasslands such as Pawnee. When a grassland is used as a range for livestock, the long-run consequences of the grazing stress may be either beneficial or detrimental to the range resource. It is well known that overgrazing sooner or later induces a depletion of palatable grasses and their substitution by undesirable species, as well as soil erosion and other harmful effects. On the other hand, it is also well known that field research conducted during the last few decades has resulted in grazing systems under which grasslands can endure sustained grazing pressure and even improve while being grazed. What is the basis for the (at least potentially) beneficial influence of grazing on grassland succession? The simulations reported in this chapter were directed at secondary succession as provoked by light or moderate grazing (as opposed to heavy grazing) in an attempt to establish to what extent grazing can be manipulated as a constructive ecological force. In so doing, we shall be testing the adequacy of the dynamic hypothesis to explain successional behavior under utilization conditions.

Needless to say, the crucial difference between natural exogenous disturbances, such as fire or drought and man-made or utilization perturbances is that while the former are momentary, the latter are usually sustained over long periods of time. When a severe conflagration takes place, the heat results in a sudden destruction of biomass and/or diversity, but then the community is left alone to reconstruct itself back to the climax. Let us examine now the effect of sustained stress on plant biomass and/or species diversity. The end result of an exogenous sustained grazing pressure is to push the ecosystem back to a younger successional stage and keep it there. Figure 5.12 shows this effect, as it would arise by introducing domestic consumers to harvest the standing crop of grasses on a continuous basis. The variables plotted in the simulations of this section are the same as before. In figure 5.12 the induced depletion of plant biomass brings about an increase in both gross and net production, which is sustained because of the sustained grazing pressure. The grazing activity of the domestic consumers also has a negative influence on the availability of food for natural consumers, which decline in proportion to the decline of plant biomass. The reduction of standing crop under grazing is then followed by declines in

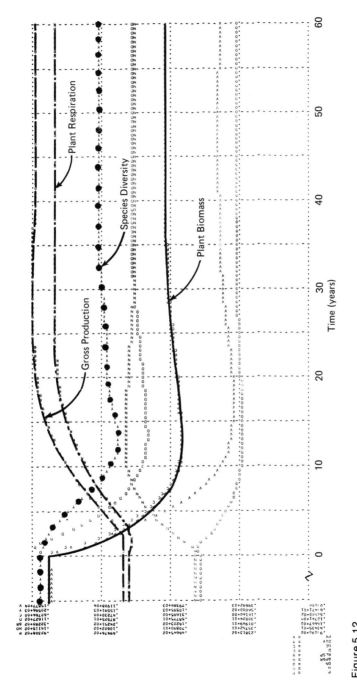

Figure 5.12
Response to sustained partial destruction of standing crop

vigor and diversity. The vigor of plants decreases because now they must spend a greater proportion of energy flow on production work. Diversity also suffers after a few years of continuous grazing because some of the species on the range are driven away (as postulated in figure 3.15) by the reduced supply of food, increased competition pressures, the cattle's preference for palatable grasses, for example, and also because the various activities of the domestic animals may force vacancy of some of the niches in the grassland (refer to figures 3.13 and 3.14).

It is also interesting to observe the patterns of organic and inorganic nutrients that arise in the simulation run of figure 5.12. In parallel with the pattern of standing crop, the accumulation of organic debris first increases a bit, then decreases toward a new equilibrium level. The pattern of decomposers reflects, of course, the pattern of organic matter available for decomposition; they increase when it increases, decrease when it decreases. The quantity of inorganic nutrients in the soil, on the other hand, increases to a new level that is higher than the climax level previously attained in the absence of the exogenous grazing stress. This is a consequence of the closed nature of the model and the law of conservation of matter, namely, since the system is closed, all nutrients in plant matter eaten away by either wild or domestic consumers are recycled. As the size of the standing crop declines, more inorganic nutrients are left unused in the soil, and thus the reservoir of nutrients accumulates to a higher level, as shown in figure 5.12. The implications of this assumption, as well as the result of an alternative assumption on the disposition of nutrients contained in harvested grasses, are discussed later in this section.

Let us consider now the simulation of figure 5.13, which shows the outcome of simultaneously applying a sustained stress on standing crop and community diversity. More specifically, exogenous step perturbations were applied to both plant depletion rate and diversity decrease rate (PDR and DDR in the model, respectively). This joint perturbation amounts to both introducing the cows and shooting the wolves, so to speak, and to keep doing so on a continuous basis, presumably in an attempt to keep undesirable species out of the range. As soon as the joint perturbation is applied, biomass and diversity start declining. However, as diversity continues to be destroyed, the resulting surplus of energy flow generates a dramatic increase in net production, and after 2 or 3 years the standing crop "bounces back" toward its climax level. The levels of wild consumers and decomposers, as well as the levels of organic and inorganic nutrients, follow the oscillations of standing crop. Artificial elimination of some species, how-

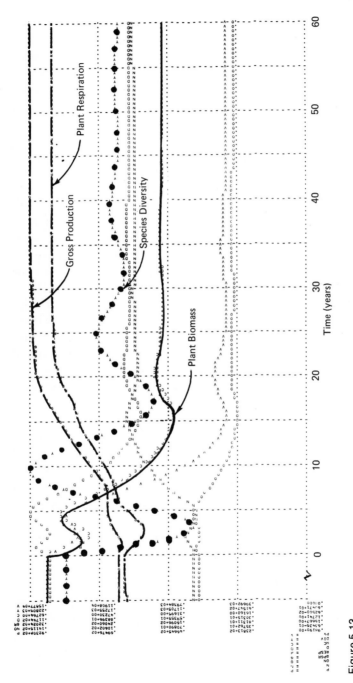

Figure 5.13
Response to sustained partial destruction of standing crop and species diversity

ever, has consequences that go beyond those species simply vanishing from the range. It also results in the species substitution mechanism (see figure 3.12) of the ecosystem being activated, and after a few years other species (presumably resistant to the perturbation technology being used) gradually start arriving to take their place. After about 5 years the new upsurge of diversification forces a decline in productivity, and both plant biomass and plant vigor start again on a downward pattern. From that point on, they both decrease with damped oscillations toward lower steady-state levels while interacting with oscillations in species diversity. The latter arise here for the same reasons as in the simulation of figure 5.11. After several decades of continuous stress, standing crop approaches the same lower level in figure 5.13 as it did in figure 5.12, while diversity and vigor approach even lower levels of equilibrium. Thus it is evident that destroying diversity in order to enhance the ability of the plant community to bounce back (production wise) in the short run is, at best, ineffective in the long run, and it may be that it actually causes more harm than good to the ecosystem. The more resistant species that replace the original ones may or may not be as desirable, but such a consideration is clearly beyond the scope of the model.

As pointed out before, another aspect of the model that is clearly oversimplified is the supply of nutrients. In the simulations of figures 5.12 and 5.13, as in those of the previous section, it is assumed that all nutrients contained in grasses eaten by either natural or domestic consumers are conserved. As long as nutrients are conserved while they flow around the nutrient-cycling loop (recall the lower loop of figure 3.1), the accumulation of nutrients in the soil depends on the level of the standing crop. The higher the proportion of nutrients in biotic form, the lower the proportion of nutrients remaining in abiotic form in the soil, and vice versa; thus the trends of O and N observed in the simulations. Actually, nutrients contained in plant biomass consumed by domestic animals may or may not be returned to the soil of the range. Figure 5.14 displays the effect of assuming that they are not returned. It shows the response to a sustained grazing pressure of light intensity, but assuming that all plant material which is eaten by the livestock, and therefore the nutrients contained therein, exit the system. The effect of assuming this net loss of nutrients is reflected in the trend of N, the concentration of inorganic nutrients in the soil. In less than 40 years, nutrients become limiting and the standing crop begins to decline from the level otherwise sustainable under this intensity of continuous grazing. After 60 years, the grazing stress is removed. However, since the reserve of nutrients in the ecosystem has been exhausted without replenish-

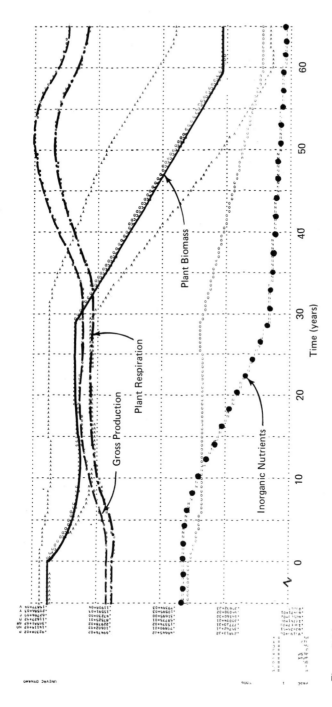

Figure 5.14
Successional response to sustained harvesting of the standing crop with net loss of nutrients (From L. T. Gutierrez and W. R. Fey, 1975, in *Simulation* 24: 113–125. Copyright 1975 by Simulation Councils, Inc. Reprinted with permission.)

ment, new growth is suppressed, and the standing crop never recuperates. What actually happens is, of course, somewhere in between the two extreme assumptions of either total conservation or total loss of nutrients under utilization conditions. There may also be net gains of nutrients coming into the ecosystem in diverse forms from external sources. This brings the discussion, however, to open-loop considerations which are outside the scope of the present research. Therefore, while bearing in mind the limitations involved, the rest of the simulations reported in this chapter were again conducted assuming the grassland ecosystem to be completely closed, or, equivalently, that it receives from external sources as much nutrients as are extracted from it through grazing.

The simulation results under consideration reflect the influence of grazing on grassland succession inasmuch as grazing activates some of the feedback mechanisms coupling the variables included in the dynamic hypothesis. It is by no means claimed that the present model accounts for the full spectrum of effects that grazing brings about. In addition to reducing the volume of herbage and therefore the area of photosynthetic surface, grazing animals may exert influence on the range by trampling, fertilizing the soil, disseminating plant seeds, shifting the species composition of plants, and so forth. According to Ellison (1960), whether these effects are actually beneficial or detrimental for the grassland is a matter for which conclusive experimental evidence is lacking. Thus it appears that as long as denudation does not result in soil erosion, which is irreversible and clearly not a successional phenomenon, the overall response to grazing is toward less vegetation with less diversity and vigor, and with the intensity of the successional transient being roughly proportional to grazing intensity. Ellison (1960) also points out, however, that "unless soil erosion is very active, denudation of vegetation is followed by an orderly succession," and Dyksterhuis (1958) reports that secondary succession is the dominant force underlying range dynamics, although successional patterns in the field may be obscured in time and space by climatic and edaphic factors of the physical environment, and their complex interactions and gradients. On this basis, it appears reasonable to conclude that the successional patterns of figure 5.12 are the dominant response to sustained grazing, other effects being "lost in the blur" so to speak. In figure 5.15, a constant grazing pressure was exogenously applied as before, and the simulation was extended to include the successional recovery of the range when the continuous grazing stress is removed after 60 years; indeed (since any consideration of soil erosion is absent from the model) orderly succession gradually brings the ecosystem back to climax condition.

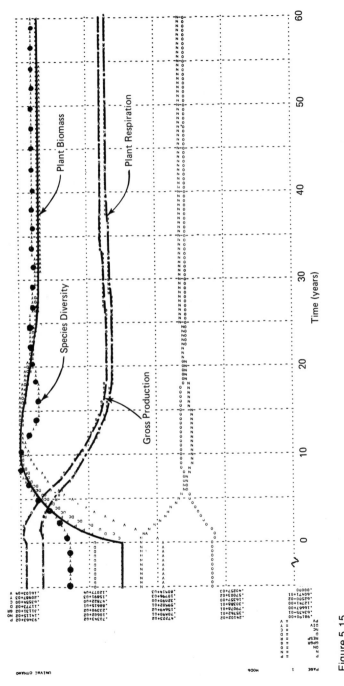

Figure 5.15
Successional dynamics after an extended period of grazing pressure

5.6 Response to Alternative Stocking Cycles

What are the implications of successional dynamics for range management? Needless to say, range preservation is an important consideration in the design of grazing policies, but not the only one. Grasses are the crop of the grassland, but they go to the market in the form of meat and other dairy products. As pointed out in the first chapter, grazing policy design must take into account both the successional dynamics of the grassland and the market dynamics associated with the commodity being produced. Let us restrict our attention here to grazing for meat production. The stockman has to be concerned with grass production inasmuch as it influences livestock gain, with preservation of the range resource, and with the dynamics of the economic system in which he operates. His objective is presumably to maximize profits. As he pursues this basic objective and adapts to pressures from the marketplace, he may or may not be looking for maximum grass and/or meat production. Economic considerations are outside the scope of the present work, however, and the following discussion will elaborate on the successional-dynamic aspect only, assuming the more simplistic objective of obtaining maximum yield consistent with range preservation.

Assuming that what really matters to the stockman is yield in the form of livestock gain, the problem is to determine what grazing system will extract the maximum of such gain from a particular pasture while preserving (or even improving) range condition. The key words here are "livestock gain," "range condition," and "grazing system." It is desirable to delve a bit on the meaning of these terms; then we shall be able to discern to what extent the model accounts for the factors involved and therefore to what extent it is relevant not only to range ecology, but also to range management.

All other things (grass palatability, nutritive value, etc.) being equal, it would seem that "livestock gain" depends on the abundance of herbage available for consumption, and it would seem that maximum yield should follow from maximum grass production. Actually, yield will depend on both the total amount of grass production and the efficiency of its utilization, the latter being defined as the proportion of herbage that is actually harvested by the animals. The matter of assessing utilization efficiency is by no means straightforward. Spedding (1971) points out that the amount of grass production harvested is a quantity that can be measured directly and otherwise presents no problems. Grass production, however, gives only the absolute level of utilization and must be supplemented by some indicator of utilization efficiency. He proposes the following ratios as indicators of utilization efficiency:

$$\frac{\text{amount harvested}}{\text{amount present at the beginning of the harvesting period}}, \tag{A}$$

$$\frac{\text{total amount harvested}}{\text{total actually grown over a period of time}}, \tag{B}$$

$$\frac{\text{total amount harvested}}{\text{potential growth}}. \tag{C}$$

Spedding's point is that both the level and the efficiency of utilization must be evaluated over time. Ratio (A) assesses utilization by a harvesting method (i.e., grazing by a given mix of animals at a given stocking density) on one harvesting period. It is simply the proportion of grass commodity present at one point in time that is actually harvested by the animals. Ratios (B) and (C), on the other hand, assess utilization by a harvesting pattern (i.e., a given sequence of frequency and severity in the application of a given harvesting method) over time in terms of actual and potential grass production, respectively. After discussing the relative merits and demerits of (A), (B), and (C) as indicators of utilization efficiency, Spedding concludes:

It seems obvious that what is required for agricultural purposes is both efficient utilization in sense (A), and very high crop production. Thus (C) would appear to be the most useful expression. To some extent this is so, and it is legitimate to ask at what percentage values for (A) and (B) is (C) maximized for different animals, pastures, and harvesting patterns.

It is clear then, that in order to be of value for range management, a dynamic model should account for the behavior that the ratios (A), (B), and (C) exhibit in response to alternative stocking policies. In particular, it should account for range condition, as implied by the denominator of (C), the utilization efficiency in terms of growth potential. While livestock gain may be the primary short-term consideration, in the long run it is also necessary to pay attention to the condition of the range.

Clawson et al. (1960) review the concept of "range condition" as "an attempt to estimate the productive potential of each range site, and then to rate the present condition of the range in relation to that potential." While it is true that the productive potential of a range depends to a certain extent upon external factors such as precipitation and temperature, it will be shown that its stage of successional development is the principal determinant. Indeed, range condition is a dynamic concept. A given range is generally improving or deteriorating in response to the grazing policies being applied. Thus it becomes necessary to measure range condition in a reliable manner. As pointed out by Clawson et al., there are many factors to be taken into account when assessing range condition, but the following are particularly significant: density of plant cover, its species composition, the vigor of individual plants, accumulations of plant litter, and soil stability. According to Dyksterhuis (1949), species composition provides the most reliable indicator of range condition. Our model is not of much help here, however, because, although it takes diversity into account, it does not take explicitly into account the relative proportion of decreasers, increasers, and invaders in the plant community. The matter of soil stability (or soil erosion) is also outside the scope of the model. On the other hand, the model does account (albeit in a very aggregated manner) for the other three indicators: density of plant cover, plant vigor, and the accumulation of organic debris. While species composition may in fact be an excellent measure, it is also true that the other indicators contain valuable information on range condition (Dyksterhuis, 1958). Therefore the model accounts for the dynamics of range conditions inasmuch as it is reflected by the levels of standing crop, plant vigor, and organic matter. More importantly, it accounts for the productive potential of the range inasmuch as it is determined by successional processes.

With regard to policy, there are three variables that are essential in the formulation of a "grazing system": stocking rate, livestock class, and grazing periodicity. According to Steger (1970), range managers attempt to use a stocking rate which fits the range, animals which are right for the forage, and grazing periods keyed to the major plant species. A given stocking rate, or stocking density per unit time, results in a given quantity of forage being harvested per unit time by the livestock. The model is of course testable in this sense, as illustrated in figures 5.12 to 5.15. As shown in these simulations, successional trends of the vegetation are roughly proportional to grazing intensity or, in other words, to stocking rate. What mix of animals is right for a given site is, however, a consideration that is clearly beyond the scope of this model, since standing crop is aggregated as a single accumulation of plant biomass, and it is therefore taken for granted that all forage is grazed uniformly. Whether the model is relevant for consideration of grazing periodicity depends on whether it is intrayear or interyear grazing periods that matter. The model developed in this research explains the successional dynamics of the range as they unfold from year to year, but without taking into account differences between the seasons of each year. The model would be inadequate, for example, to examine whether it is better to graze the range before or after seed maturity each year; continuous yearlong grazing is assumed. On the other hand, the model provides insight on the interplay between stocking cycles and secondary succession. The effect of grazing intensities associated with alternative stocking rates was discussed in the previous section. Assuming a fixed stocking rate and the right kind of livestock, let us consider now the interplay between stocking cycles and secondary succession, and how secondary succession can be manipulated to maximize grassland yield in the long run.

What is the best successional stage for grazing? Figures 5.16, 5.17, and 5.18 exhibit the successional trends associated with 10-, 20-, and 30-year stocking cycles, respectively. This means that the range was assumed to be continuously grazed, then continuously rested in successive periods of 5, 10, and 15 years, respectively, each cycle being composed of a period of uninterrupted grazing followed by a period of uninterrupted recovery. The simulations were accomplished by turning on and off the exogenous step perturbations on plant depletion rate at the indicated intervals. Let us consider the effect of these harvesting patterns from the viewpoint of grass production and utilization efficiency.

Under the 10-year stocking cycle policy, livestock is introduced to the range at a time of great net production. On the other hand, when the 20-year grazing cycle is used, livestock is brought in for grazing at the time when the standing crop of grasses is peaking. Deferring grazing over cycles longer than 30 years clearly results in the animals grazing at a time when the grasses are neither generating the highest possible yield nor covering the range in maximum quantity (recall that, after peaking, the standing crop will settle down to a lower climax level); conversely, succession-generated increases in either net production or standing crop would be negligible under grazing cycles shorter than 10 years. Thus, on the basis of grass abundance alone, the simulations suggest that a stocking cycle of approximately 20 years is optimal in the sense that, for this stocking density, it sets in motion successional processes that bring the standing crop to the highest possible level at the start of each grazing cycle. Other things being equal, this would be the stocking cycle to use if grass abundance makes grazing easier and results in maximum livestock gain. On the other hand, if maximization of net plant production were to be taken as the decision criterion, the 10-year cycle would seem better. This suggests that analysis and synthesis of grazing patterns in the successional time scale may be a

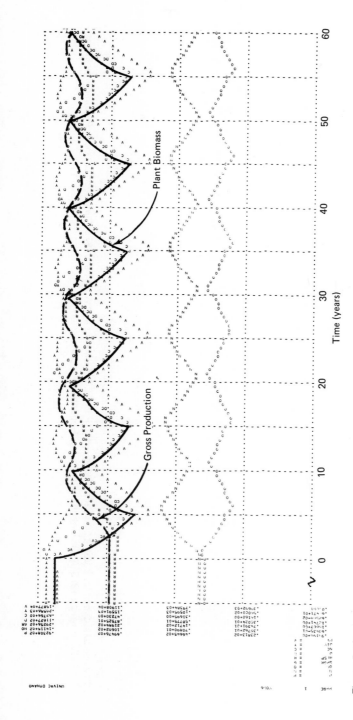

Figure 5.16
Successional dynamics under a 10-year stocking cycle (From L. T. Gutierrez and W. R. Fey, 1975, in *Simulation Councils Proceedings Series* 5:73–82. Copyright 1975 by Simulation Councils, Inc. Reprinted with permission.)

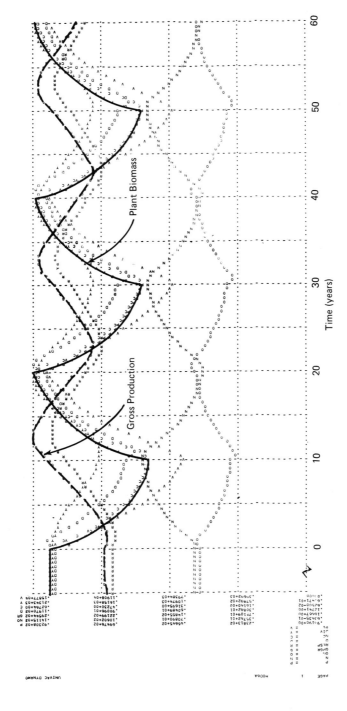

Figure 5.17
Successional dynamics under a 20-year stocking cycle (From L. T. Gutierrez and W. R. Fey, 1975, *Simulation Councils Proceedings Series* 5:73–82. Copyright 1975 by Simulation Councils, Inc. Reprinted with permission.)

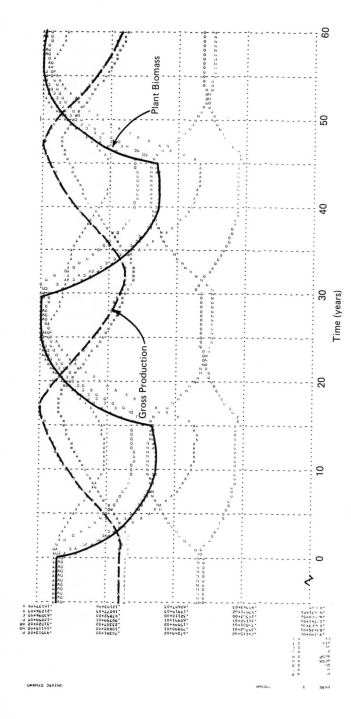

Figure 5.18
Successional dynamics under a 30-year stocking cycle (From L. T. Gutierrez and W. R. Fey, 1975, in *Simulation Councils Proceedings Series* 5:73–82. Copyright 1975 by Simulation Councils, Inc. Reprinted with permission.)

valuable complement to policies formulated under a shorter time resolution. Grazing systems such as seasonal, deferred, rotation, rest rotation, and deferred rotation manipulate the livestock from range to range on the basis of intrayear or, at the most, year to year considerations; thus, rotation grazing dictates that a given range should not be used at the same season every year, rest rotation implies that each range is periodically rested for one full year, and so on. Assuming yearlong grazing, the simulations suggest that, if secondary succession is to be manipulated for increased grass production (and, presumably, increased livestock gain), some sort of multiyear rotation may be desirable whereby a range is continuously grazed during several years, then rested for several years to allow secondary succession to either expand net production or generate a peak standing crop before using it again, depending on what criterion is relevant from the viewpoint of net production. It may be possible to integrate intrayear and interyear considerations into grazing systems that take both into account.

Let us reexamine the performance patterns of figures 5.16 to 5.18 in the light of the efficiencies (A), (B), and (C). Recall that the numerator of each ratio remains constant throughout each grazing period in the simulations. If this grazing pressure were to be sustained indefinitely, the reader will recall (refer back to figure 5.12) that the standing crop would decline gradually, then approach a lower steady-state level. Efficiency (A) is defined as the ratio of the amount harvested over the standing crop of each year, taking one year as the harvesting period. Since the amount harvested remains constant year after year while the standing crop declines, the ratio (A) would indicate that the efficiency of utilization is increasing from year to year as long as the standing crop continues to decline. In figures 5.16 and 5.17, it would continue to increase from year to year during the grazing period of each cycle, implying maximum efficiency in the last year of each period, when the standing crop is lowest. Thus, while the ratio (A) is a relevant measure of efficiency for a given year, it is meaningless for a multiyear planning horizon; a very high level of type (A) efficiency in a given year may render the range useless on the following year and, in cases of extreme defoliation, may induce detrimental effects such as soil erosion. It seems reasonable to assume that on the basis of empirical considerations, an experienced stockman knows the maximum efficiency of type (A) that he can obtain in a given year without harming the range in any significant way. Accordingly, let us assume that the amount of grass being harvested each year under the stocking rates of figures 5.16 to 5.18 maximizes efficiency in this sense. What about the efficiencies (B) and (C)?

As long as the grazing efficiency of the animals remains invariant, efficiency type (B) provides the same information as efficiency type (A) when computed on a yearly basis. The grazing efficiency of the animals may be affected by changes in crop growth rate and/or changes in species composition and sward structure, but such considerations would fall outside the scope of the present model. Thus in the present context (B) becomes meaningful when applied on a multiyear basis. A consideration of (B) and the simulated patterns on a multiyear basis does indicate, for example, that the 30-year grazing cycle is indeed too long. Clearly, the average value of (B) over the grazing cycle decreases due to several peak crops going ungrazed before cattle is brought back into the range. On the other hand, efficiency type (C) once again hints that stocking cycles shorter than 10 years, while increasing utilization efficiency in the sense of (B), may decrease the utilization of crop potential (C) by inhibiting the unfolding of secondary succession. If the total amount of herbage actually grown is less than the total amount that could have been grown, we would suspect that actual livestock gain is also less than could have been obtained. However, since the total amount harvested per year is always the same in the simulations regardless of the amount grown, it is not possible to arrive at more definitive conclusions. While the simulations indicate a range of stocking cycles (between 10 and 20 years) that should be approximately optimal with respect to both level and efficiency of utilization, more definitive and meaningful conclusions on efficiency will require a closed-loop coupling between standing crop and livestock gain.

Although detailed grazing policy design as such is beyond the scope of our present model, the preceding discussion is indicative of the relevance of successional dynamics to range management. The simulations confirm that secondary succession is the principal process to be taken into account in long-range planning of grazing patterns. While range productivity may be considerably influenced in the short run by variable climatic factors, successional processes are the dominant influence in the long run, thus the potential utility of a model which allows simulated experimentation in the successional time scale and under ideal management conditions. Simplicity and insensitivity are seen as the most attractive attributes of grazing patterns designed on a successional-dynamic basis, the assurance of success in the long run resting on the fact that, when following a grazing pattern so planned, the stockman would be working with nature, rather than against it. Successional-dynamic design of grazing patterns should result in yield performance insensitive to external disturbances and, at the same time, should provide simple schemes of operation which take into account the dominant factors in a process so exceedingly complex that trying to take all factors into account would result (if it results in anything) in recommendations that are difficult or even impossible to apply in practice. On the other hand, long-term grazing guidelines based on successional criteria—basically, that combination of stocking rate and stocking cycle which appears to give the best tradeoff between range yield and range condition—would be simple to follow, leaving short-term considerations to be worked out on an empirical basis. Due to the insensitivity of the design, the actual harvesting patterns that result from short-term adjustments should not differ significantly from the ideal one as far as yield and utilization efficiency are concerned.

These considerations are not to be regarded as a claim that anything but very tentative conclusions can be drawn from simulations of the present model. They merely illustrate the feasibility of designing ecosystem utilization policies on a successional-dynamic basis. Even under the simplistic assumption that maximum sustained yield is desirable, further elaboration of the ecosystem model itself may be necessary to account for the possibility of irreversible deterioration due to soil erosion, changes in the species composition of grasses, and hysteresis effects in the production efficiency curves, among other factors. As pointed out from the outset, mutual causalities between livestock gain and standing crop, and between livestock gain and the economic system into which the cattle are fed, should be taken into account in a realistic design model. In particular, the balance between nutrients lost via harvesting and nutrients gained via fertilization needs to be considered. The simulations assume 100 percent recycling of nutrients consumed by the livestock. This is certainly not true, but is equivalent to saying that the range is fertilized so as to exactly offset nutrient losses due to harvesting. Sustained loss of nutrients without replenishment by either natural or artificial means eventually would inhibit the ecosystem from bouncing back with new growth of plant biomass as we saw in the simulation of figure 5.14. The actual balance of nutrients coming into the ecosystem by natural means, plus nutrients becoming available through fertilization, minus nutrients leaving the ecosystem by natural means, minus nutrients being lost through harvesting can affect successional dynamics, and therefore should be estimated for a realistic analysis of stocking policies. Furthermore, the cost of artificial fertilization and other costs associated with intensive methods of range management would have to be compared with the gain experienced by the livestock under alternative stocking policies and their respective market values. Taking into account both the ecological and economic gains and losses and how they interact with each other provides a basis to address the complex issue of designing grazing policies that are both economically and ecologically sound.

Model Evaluation

6

In its early, naive stage, science . . . imagined that we could observe things in themselves, as they would behave in our absence. Naturalists . . . are now beginning to realize that even the most objective of their observations are steeped in the conventions they adopted at the outset . . . so that, when they reach the end of their analyses they cannot tell with any certainty whether the structure they have made is the essence of the matter they are studying or the reflection of their own thought.
—Pierre Teilhard de Chardin (ca. 1947)

6.1 Structural Validation

It was pointed out in section 1.3 that (short of empirical verification) the dynamic hypothesis under consideration can be validated on the grounds that (1) its structure is consistent with available knowledge on the structure and function of grassland ecosystems, and (2) it generates the same successional modes of behavior it is intended to account for when exercised as a simulation model. The consistency (or, at the very least, lack of inconsistency) between each structural element of the proposed dynamic hypothesis and the full range of knowledge available on ecological succession has been carefully documented in chapters 3 and 4. To a significant extent, the dynamic hypothesis under consideration is simply a formalization of existing empirical and conceptual information on ecological succession—thus far available in descriptive form only—into a closed feedback system which is mathematically realizable and therefore testable by means of simulation experiments. Where a search of the relevant literature proved unfruitful in yielding the desired information, plausible provisional assumptions necessary for the hypothesis to be self-contained were introduced, concurrently with consultations with professional ecologists. Let us briefly summarize the grounds on which each hierarchy of the hypothesis rests.

First, the closed boundary: the system boundary assumed by the hypothesis—the natural boundary of a grassland ecosystem—is consistent with the well-established concept that ecosystems are the basic units of study in ecology. Indeed, successional phenomena is but one class of ecosystem phenomena. By the assumed closeness of the boundary, the hypothesis qualifies itself as attempting to explain succession inasmuch as it is generated and controlled internally by the biotic community.

Second, the feedback structure: in chapters 3 and 4, the structuring of each loop or subloop of the hypothesis, as well as the interconnections among the loops, was paralleled by reference to and quotations from the information sources prompting its incorporation to the hypothesis. It does not seem necessary to refer back in detail to the evidence presented in support of each loop. In each case, it was pointed out whether the descriptive information available was sufficient to structure the entire loop, whether gaps had to be filled with plausible assumptions, and whether its relationship with the basic dynamic hypothesis of figure 3.1 is or is not widely recognized in modern ecological research. On balance, the feedback structures of figures 3.1, 3.2, 3.3, 3.4, 3.5, 3.7, 3.8, 3.10, 3.12, and 3.18 appear to be in agreement with the best information available in terrestrial ecology and, in particular grassland ecology.

Third, the relationships between levels and rates within each loop: of special interest are, of course, the functional relationships assumed in figures 3.6, 3.9, 3.11, 3.13, 3.14, 3.15, and 3.17. When looking at a grassland ecosystem through the "macroscope," as in this research, these relationships subsume complex webs of factors and interactions about which it is not useful to think in detail—even if this were possible. While each one of them seems consistent with either intuition or empirical evidence, or both, it is admitted that they may be simplistic and, perhaps, even naive. Still, they provide a rationale to develop a testable model, as mathematically formulated in chapter 4, and it is believed that the structure of the dynamic hypothesis does not exhibit any significant inconsistency with presently available information on ecosystem structure.

6.2 Performance Validation

According to Forrester (1961), "the defense of a model rests primarily on the individual defense of each detail of structure and policy, all confirmed when the total behavior of the model system shows the performance characteristics associated with the real system." Having discussed the structural validation aspect before, let us summarize the simulation results of chapter 5 insofar as they confirm the validity of the hypothesis.

The dynamic modes of behavior associated with ecological succession in real ecosystems were discussed in section 2.1. Figures 2.1 to 2.5 display examples of typical successional trends, and tables 2.1 and 2.2 provide a summary of successional patterns observed in nature. Therefore, for purposes of performance validation, the basic comparison to be made is between those performance patterns and the performance patterns of the model as documented in the previous chapter. For purposes of the present discussion, the simulation of figure 5.3 can be taken as the basic or nominal case. It depicts the basic modes of behavior generated by the model. These simulated successional patterns appear to be in consonance with those observed in nature. Production and respiration increase, reach a maximum value, and then decline toward their climax or steady-state values (compare with figures 2.1 and 2.3). In comparing figures 2.1 and 5.3 it is important to recall that while R stands for total community respiration in figure 2.1 it accounts for producers respiration only in figure 5.3; since a net yield is required year after year by the consumers, the difference between gross production and respiration does not tend to zero in the simulations. Biomass accumulates, overshoots, and decreases slightly toward its climax value. It is also important to recall that while total biomass approaches its climax level asymptotically in figures 2.1 and 2.2, it was considered more realistic to incorporate into the model the tendency of the biotic community to overshoot before settling down to its post-successional steady-state (as suggested by figure 2.4). Time-phased between the production and biomass curves of figure 5.3 is the curve depicting the increase in species diversity. This curve follows the same time pattern as those of figures 2.2 and 2.5. The time period of 20 to 40 years required for secondary grassland succession in abandoned plowed land (Shantz, 1906; Costello, 1944; Odum, 1971) is closely approximated by the simulated succession. In figure 2.4 it would seem that natural revegetation takes only about 10 or 15 years, but keep in mind that figure 2.4 refers to succession following drought. Since drought does not remove all the vegetation, the grassland can bounce back to climax levels much faster. In figure 2.5, which corresponds to the abandoned land case, species diversity increases and peaks after about 25 or 30 years. This is closely approximated by the simulated history of species diversity in figure 5.3.

The simulated time patterns of figure 5.3 are also consistent with other trends to be expected in ecological succession, as listed in Odum's tabular model (table 2.1). Comparative discussions of trends in tables 2.1 and 2.2 vis-à-vis simulated trends were provided in chapter 5 and will not be repeated here. These discussions showed that trend items 1, 2, 3, 4, 6, 7, and 8 of table 2.1, and therefore items 23 and 24 also, are reproduced by the simulations with a high degree of fidelity. While not directly measurable in terms of model variables, trend items 5, 15, 16, 17, 20, and 22 are descriptive of the way the model actually works. Item 21 is automatically implied by the choice of a closed boundary. Finally, it appears very reasonable to suppose that in real ecosystems the trends numbered 9 to 14, 18 and 19 unfold in parallel with those generated in the simulations. Although these factors were not explicitly included as separate variables in the hypothesis or the simulation model, their importance is recognized in some of the complex functions relating the other variables. For example, trend item 12, niche specialization, is an important element in the rationale underlying the relationship between diversity and carrying capacity. Model performance is also consistent with the patterns summarized in table 2.2 except for items 8 and 9 which are not part of the present closed-loop formulation.

In brief, then, the simulated patterns of figure 5.3 are consistent (or, at least, not inconsistent) with each one of the trends known to be associated with ecological succession. The simulations of figures 5.4 to 5.11 verify that the successional dynamics generated by the model remain well behaved under both parametric and exogenous perturbations, and further confirm the adequacy of the dynamic hypothesis. Furthermore, the simulation experiments of figures 5.12 to 5.18 appear to account for successional dynamics as they arise under sustained grazing pressure. The model appears to be well behaved under sustained stress. These results provide strong evidence that the dynamic hypothesis of chapter 3 does not generate the performance patterns associated with secondary succession, be it the result of either transitory or sustained perturbations to the climax grassland.

It must be pointed out that the basis for comparison here is nonquantitative and, for the most part, nonexperimental. Indeed, it would be very difficult to conduct field experiments to study successional trends under ideal management conditions and, in particular under moderate grazing pressure; most grazing experiments documented in the literature refer to extreme cases of overgrazing and therefore do not constitute a good basis for comparison (Ellison, 1960). Documented descriptions of the effects of grazing as observed in the field (see Klipple and Costello, 1960) are very confusing due to the multitude of external factors (climatic and otherwise) that obscure the successional patterns of the range under uncontrolled conditions. Nevertheless, the simulations demonstrate that the dynamic hypothesis is valid in the sense that it provides the feedback structure which generates secondary succession, and therefore the dominant modes of behavior which in the long run determine the condition of the range and its productive potential. It cannot be overemphasized that this appears to be the case under any set of circumstances short of irreversible site destruction by overgrazing. To illustrate the point further, consider the simulation of figure 6.1, which shows the successional transients that arise under joint natural and man-made perturbations. The simulation was conducted using a 20-year stocking cycle, with stocking density at the same level as in figure 5.17. Superimposed to this sustained perturbation, momentary perturbations further depleted plant biomass at 15-year intervals. These can represent the effect of natural phenomena such as fires or lack of rainfall; either one would result in destruction of part of the standing crop in addition to losses due to harvesting. Note that the "man-made" and "natural" perturbations do not coincide. Ten year periods of sustained grazing start at times zero, 20, and 40 years, while sudden natural destructions of biomass occur at times zero, 15, 30, and 45 years. As a result the neat successional patterns of figure 5.17 become somewhat obscured in figure 6.1, but they are not destroyed, and they continue to emerge in the long run because they are not produced by the exogenous inputs but by the internal feedback mechanisms of the ecosystem. Superimposing other external sources of variability (e.g., the effect of stochastic changes in climatic factors such as temperature or precipitation) would have the same effect as introducing noise; the dynamic trends of figure 5.17 would be further obscured, but the underlying trends would remain invariant as long as the feedback structure of the ecosystem is not altered. Therefore the dynamic hypothesis appears to be valid on the basis of the performance patterns that it generates endogenously, either in the presence of any set of reasonable exogenous perturbations or in their absence.

Needless to say, the model does not account for successional effects of grazing (or any other disturbance) whose analysis would require a different level of model aggregation. A good example is the trends known to arise in the species composition of grasses when they are grazed; generating these trends would require modeling the plant community at a lower level of aggregation, one which decomposes total plant biomass into palatable and unpalatable grasses, for example, and modeling the feedback interaction of these plant compartments with each other and with other sectors of the ecosystem. Therefore the simulations of chapter 5 simultaneously confirm the validity of the dynamic hypothesis and point out its limitations. While these limitations are suggestive of further modeling work needed in pursuing better ecosystem design, they in no way invalidate model performance

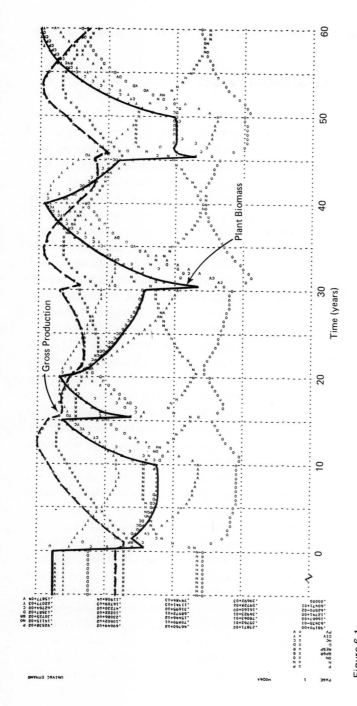

Figure 6.1
Successional dynamics under both transitory and sustained perturbations

with regard to the immediate research objective as set forth in the first chapter.

6.3 Conclusions about Model Validity and Use

It is appropriate to conclude with an assessment of what has been accomplished so far in this research. In so doing we shall be setting the stage for discussing what is yet to come, for it is hoped that this research does not lead to a dead end but, on the contrary, opens up an important area of research on the application of feedback dynamics to systems ecology.

This research has been concerned with successional dynamics as they arise from the endogenous feedback structure of ecosystems. More specifically, a feedback dynamics model of secondary succession in a grassland ecosystem has been structured, formulated in terms of first- and zero-order difference equations, and tested by means of simulation experiments. The research was motivated by strong evidence that ecological succession must be better understood if harmony between man and nature is to be established (Odum, 1969). At a time when intensive methods of ecosystem utilization for food production are becoming prohibitive due to short supply and soaring costs of fossil fuels (Pimentel et al., 1973), it is imperative to learn how to make efficient use of ecosystems by extensive methods, namely, by manipulation of secondary succession processes. The case of a grassland ecosystem used for grazing seemed an excellent place to start due to the availability of some structural and functional data, the fact that grasslands constitute a major source of meat production all over the world, and the fact that they are known to endure and even improve under grazing when the stockman works with the grassland rather than against it. Understanding why and how these desirable behavior patterns arise may lead to better utilization policies for grasslands and, by analogy, for other ecosystems as well.

The basic significance of the research is that it contributes (for the first time) an endogenic theory of secondary succession, a theory which accounts for secondary succession as generated by the endogenous structure of the ecosystem. It also provides a simulation model to test the theory, and the results of testing the model when quantified with grassland data. The simulations confirm that, within the limitations imposed by the physical environment and other open-loop factors, secondary succession is generated by the closed-loop structure of the ecosystem. They also show that successional *modes* of behavior are insensitive to parametric and exogenous perturbations as long as they are not unrealistically large, and that while climatic factors are certainly influential on range productivity in the short run, the endogenous feedback structure which is responsible for succession is also responsible for the performance of the range ecosystem in the long run. Indeed, these facts have been observed for a long time, and the resulting conclusions are not new; what is new is the knowledge gained as to what is the structure of the ecological mechanism which generates the observed dynamic patterns and the insights gained about secondary succession as the process to be manipulated in using ecosystems for productive purposes. Needless to say, the model produced by the research is by no means definitive. Let us attempt to qualify the model and the simulations with regard to their validity, generality, and utility.

It is felt that strong evidence has been provided on the validity of the dynamic hypothesis. It appears to be valid on the grounds that its structure is consistent with the full range of pertinent ecological knowledge and, furthermore, generates the successional modes of dynamic behavior it is intended to account for. By assuming a closed ecosystem boundary, the hypothesis restricts itself to explain secondary succession inasmuch as it is generated and controlled endogenously by the biotic community. Within this context, however, abundant documentary evidence is given on the adequacy of the feedback loop structure and the relationships coupling levels and rates within each loop. The actual quantification of the simulation model was arbitrary to the extent dictated by availability of data, but this is not a major source of concern in view of the model's insensitivity to parametric variations, at least as far as overall behavior patterns are concerned. The fact that the model is well behaved under both transitory and sustained exogenous disturbances further confirms the adequacy of the theoretical model. While these considerations increase our confidence in the soundness of the model, they do not, of course, constitute positive proof of its absolute validity. As Box and Jenkins (1970) have stated so well:

A model is only capable of being "proved" in the biblical sense of being put to the test. As was recommended by Saint Paul in his first epistle to the Thessalonians, what we can do is to "Prove all things: hold fast to that which is good."

Putting the model to the test beyond simulated experimentation is a matter of field research which is clearly beyond the scope of the present work. As it stands, however, the dynamic hypothesis holds fast to well-established ecological knowledge and principles. It results in a parsimonious yet comprehensive model, one which explains successional dynamics in terms of the fundamental ecological variables—energy, matter, diversity, space, and time—albeit that in a restricted sense for each. In other words, the model does not account for all possible implications of each one of these variables, but only those that were found to be indispensable to account for secondary succession. Thus the closed-loop recycling of matter between biotic and abiotic states was accounted for, but without differentiating between different kinds of minerals and assuming the existence of water, soil, and air. The open-loop flow of energy was accounted for inasmuch as its allocation to either plant production or other functions influences the unfolding of successional development. Only the variety component of species diversity was considered; while other aspects of diversity are also important, this component appears to be most directly associated with succession due to its influence on niche specialization. Space is considered in the functional sense only, in the sense of carrying capacity per unit area of soil surface. This simplification appears to be justified on the basis that, while succession takes place in time and space, it is a predominantly time-oriented process. Time is, of course, the independent variable of the model, and the simulations display performance patterns through time that are in complete consonance with actual successional dynamics.

With regard to generality, the dynamic hypothesis accounts only for secondary succession; primary succession, involving much longer time constants and the formation of soil out of bare rock, is clearly not covered since the existence of soil is taken for granted. In the context of secondary succession, the basic dynamic hypothesis of figure 3.1 possesses a high degree of generality. We feel that the feedback loops of figure 3.1 depict the fundamental structure responsible for secondary succession in both terrestrial and aquatic ecosystems. As more content is added to the hypothesis in sections 3.2 to 3.4 (in particular figures 3.2, 3.12, and 3.18) it ceases to be a general hypothesis of secondary ecosystem succession to become one of secondary autogenic terrestrial succession. Then, when the hypothesis is quantified in chapter 4, it becomes restricted to secondary autogenic succession in the shortgrass prairie. In other words, figure 3.1 provides a basic theory of secondary succession for ecosystems in general, but none in particular. As more content was added to it, the degree of generality was bound to decline, and we ended up with a simulation model of secondary succession in a shortgrass prairie ecosystem, one that can be exercised assuming either natural conditions or a single mode of utilization, such as grazing.

Subsequent research will have to proceed inductively in order to generalize the model with respect to successional time frame, class of ecosystems, and type of utilization. The theory needs to be extended to account for both primary and secondary succession, and to account for the longer term dynamics which sometimes would make the prairie develop eventually into a forest were it not for grazing and the periodic occurrence of fires. More generally, it needs to be extended to account for the dynamics of senescence, the dynamics whereby ecosystems sometimes grow, mature, age, and eventually decay, perhaps to start all over again (resulting in a cyclic climax) or to permit the emergence of a new ecosystem. The model needs to be extended and/or modified to account for successional dynamics in other grasslands (e.g., tall-grass and mixed prairies), in other terrestrial ecosystems, and eventually in aquatic ecosystems, by taking into account the similarities and dissimilarities that exist among them. Finally, the successional response of ecosystems to types of utilization other than grazing must be investigated, as well as the successional response in the most complex situation where the ecosystem is subject to multiple modes of utilization. These considerations point out both the limitations of the present model with regard to generality and the long road ahead, but they also stress the significance of this research in that it opens the way toward developing a more general feedback dynamic theory of ecological succession.

To conclude, let us discuss the matter of utility. Innis (1972) has pointed out that modeling complex biological systems may yield conceptual, developmental, and output utilities. Conceptual utility results from looking at the ecosystem through the framework provided by a given modeling philosophy. Developmental utilities arise during the learning process involved in accomplishing a precisely (if not accurately) formulated model. Finally, output utility is the useful information that exercising the model may produce for persons other than the modeler.

At this time, the only claim we can make with certainty is that both the dynamic hypothesis and the simulation model reported above possess conceptual and developmental utility in a significant degree; whether they really possess output utility or not is something that must wait the test of time. Conceptually, this research has integrated a vast amount of dispersed (and sometimes quite old) descriptive knowledge into a formal feedback structure that shows how all the pieces in the puzzle of tables 2.1 and/or 2.2 fit together and mutually interact to generate secondary succession. This conceptual utility is enhanced by the research emphasis on interpreting all these pieces in terms of energy, matter, diversity, space, and time as the fundamental ecological variables, which results in a highly parsimonious frame of reference. It goes without saying that the structuring of figure 3.1

into a dynamic hypothesis for secondary succession (as in chapter 3) and its
subsequent formulation as a precise simulation model (as in chapter 4) was
not a straightforward modeling process. A considerable amount of iteration
was necessary between hypothesis and model formulation, structural validation and performance validation (refer to figure 1.2) before the
hypothesis was cast into a model that generates the desired patterns. However, it is felt that the greatest developmental utility of the model is still to
come, and will materialize as seasoned ecologists study the model, find
faults with it, and, hopefully, improve upon it. Certainly, the model is not
ready for use as a self-sufficient planning tool by the range manager. It
accounts for closed-loop dynamics only, and this at a very high level of
aggregation. It ignores open-loop, short-term considerations which constitute the day-to-day, year-to-year concern of the stockman. Its numerical
quantification would have to be empirically worked out in the context of
ecosystem-specific applications. Still, it is felt that the output utility of the
model is significant in that it forcefully demonstrates that synthesis of
long-term grazing policies can and must be pursued on a successional-
dynamic basis; this is the way to go if extensive methods of land use are to be
developed whereby ecosystems can be productively used without prohibitive expenditures of scarce fossil fuel energy.

Generalizations and Extensions

If a man will begin with certainties he will end with doubts, but if he will
be content to begin with doubts he shall end in certainties.
—Francis Bacon (ca. 1626)

7.1 Allogenic Influences on Grassland Succession

Grasslands occur in both temperate and tropical latitudes where soil moisture and/or soil nutrients are unable to support trees but are adequate for
grasses. The grasses that predominate in the climax state are perennials,
while annual and biennial grasses dominate earlier successional stages.
Grass heights above ground increase with temperature and rainfall from
several inches to 20 feet (Robinson, 1972). Species diversity is extensive in
most grassland communities (Whitaker, 1975), and the range of biomass
(standing crop) and annual productivity may vary by a factor of 15 to 30
from a tundra meadow to a tropical savanna (Coupland, in Franklin, 1975).

Conclusive evidence is lacking for many of the above and following inferences. Authorities' opinions and data often differ and the International
Biological Programme (IBP) studies have not all been completed and
interpreted. Therefore, the suggestions offered in this chapter cannot be
considered to have been proved. However, an attempt has been made to
reflect the most widely held, the most reasonable, and the most empirically
documented positions relative to the present state of ecosystem knowledge
and the art of macroecosystem successional modeling.

Many factors influence the climax limits and the successional patterns of
grasslands without themselves being influenced by the grassland. Such
factors are called external, independent, or allogenic influences. Since
these factors are not direct elements in the endogenous feedback structure,
they are included in a model in the form either of constants and tabulated
values or of imposed, predetermined (input) time functions. In this model

there are no time function inputs. Four types of allogenic factors are described in this section. These include climatic, edaphic (soil), physiographic, and stochastic (fire) influences. Each has several aspects that are influential; and two, soil and fire, may be parts of the feedback structure, if the system boundaries and time scale are extended appropriately.

Climatic influences are the most obvious determinants of grassland structure and dynamics. Important climatic factors include moisture, temperature, sunlight, and wind (Cox, 1976; Robinson, 1972). The first three have a direct stimulating effect on plant growth while the latter is generally an inhibiting factor.

Rainfall appears to be the most important climatic factor. Grasslands generally occur in regions with an annual rainfall of 10 to 30 inches. The upper limit may be extended to 50 inches; if the rainfall is strongly seasonal, evaporation is abnormally high, and/or the soil is excessively porous. The rainfall isohyets are shown in figure 7.1 for the North American midland prairies, the western (shortgrass) section of which is the locale of the grassland site modeled here. It is fairly clear from this map, and many authors, that grass height, biomass, and annual primary production all increase with increasing moisture. However, when rainfall exceeds these rough limits, the grassland gives way to forest.

Since water is such an essential element in the plant, consumer, and decomposer life processes, additional moisture in the form of rainfall, snow, dew, humidity, or irrigation could be expected to stimulate all of the expressions of life. Increased rainfall does lead to a larger standing crop, greater production, and faster successional response. This is illustrated in table 7.1 where the probable effects of greater moisture (column 1) on the values of the model's constants and table values are estimated. The direction of influence is shown (larger, smaller, no change, or unknown effect) rather than a numerical value because so little is known about most of these details. In fact, many of the polarities are uncertain. Therefore the table is not meant to be a definitive assertion of fact. Rather, it is a suggestion for research and a reminder that many aspects of the system structure may be influenced by a change in almost any allogenic factor.

Temperature is also in influential climatic factor, though probably not as important as moisture. Higher temperature also encourages larger standing crop, greater productivity, faster nutrient cycling, and more responsive successional adjustment. Figure 7.2 shows the same North American midcontinent prairie as figure 7.1 with isotherms of seasonal temperature difference (average July minus average January temperature) replacing the rainfall isohyets. The isotherms do not determine the grassland boundaries.

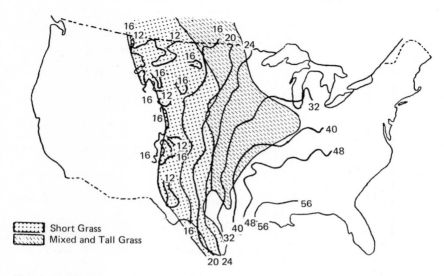

Figure 7.1
Isohyets showing lines of average annual precipitation (inches) for the North American midland prairies (From Paul C. Lemon, 1975, "Prairie Ecosystems Are Essential for Environmental Monitoring," in *Prairie: A Multiple View*, edited by Mohan K. Wali, Grand Forks: The University of North Dakota Press, p. 344. Reprinted with permission.)

Nevertheless, for a given rainfall, higher temperatures stimulate greater growth. Estimated temperature influences on model parameters are indicated in column 2 of table 7.1.

Growing season length is a climatic factor related to temperature. For annual plants the growing season usually is taken to be the period between the last spring frost and the first fall killing frost. Most perennial plants stop their growth but may not die when the mean monthly temperatures fall below, and remain below, 6°C (43°F), (Robinson, 1972, p. 175). Growing season extensions may produce greater climax standing crops if grasses requiring a long growing season have been excluded by a short season. However, yearly primary production and the speed of the successional response will increase with a longer growing season. Growing season influences on the model are estimated in column 3 of table 7.1.

Sunlight provides the input energy for the photosynthesis process that converts that energy to a usable, physical form—plant biomass. Incident energy may be increased through greater solar intensity or longer exposure. Species diversity is thought by some to increase with decreasing latitude. Since solar intensity increases with decreasing latitude, there may be a

Table 7.1
Estimated effects of changes in allogenic factors on the values of model constants and tables

Model Constants and Tables
L = larger or longer
S = smaller or shorter
O = no change
U = unknown change
mon = months, cal = calories

		Changes in External Factors															
		Climatic Factors					Soil Factors					Physiographic Factors					Fire
		(1) Greater Temperature	(2) Higher Temperature	(3) Longer Season	(4) Greater Sunlight	(5) Higher Winds	(6) Smaller Particles	(7) More Granular	(8) Thicker Soil	(9) Richer Minerals	(10) More Humus	(11) Less Alkaline	(12) Higher Altitude	(13) Less Level	(14) Greater Slope	(15) More South Exposure	(16) More Fires
PDD	Plant decay delay (months)	S	S	O	S	L	O	O	O	O	O	O	U	L	L	S	S
NAD	Nutrient absorption delay (months)	S	S	O	S	O	S	S	O	S	S	L	L	L	L	S	S
PDRSD	Plant decay sm delay (months)	S	S	O	S	U	S	U	U	U	S	U	L	L	L	U	U
INGAD	Indicated new growth adj delay (months)	S	S	U	S	L	S	S	O	S	S	L	L	L	L	S	S
DDMIN	Decomposition delay minimum (months)	S	S	O	S	L	S	S	U	S	S	L	L	L	L	S	S
DDS	Decomposition delay slope (months)	S	S	O	S	L	S	S	U	S	S	L	L	L	L	S	U
DRD	Decomposers response delay (months)	S	S	U	S	O	O	S	U	U	S	O	U	O	L	S	U
NCRD	Nat consumers response delay (months)	S	U	U	U	U	O	O	U	O	O	O	U	O	O	U	U
NPRC	Nutrient to plant req coeff (gn/gp)	O	U	U	U	U	O	U	O	L	U	O	U	U	U	U	O
ONDRC	Org nutrient to decomposer req (gn/gd)	U	U	U	U	U	O	O	O	U	U	O	U	O	U	U	U
PNCRC	Plants to nat consumers req (gp/gc)	U	U	U	U	U	O	O	O	O	O	O	O	O	O	S	U
NCPRC	Nat consumer-plant req coeff (gp/gc)	U	S	L	S	L	L	L	L	L	L	O	S	S	S	L	L
PPMT	Plant production multitable (1/month)	L	L	L	L	S	O	O	O	O	O	O	L	O	O	L	L
NCRT	Nat cons reproduction table (1/month)	L	L	O	O	O	O	O	O	O	L	O	S	O	O	O	L
NCMT	Nat consumer mortality table (1/month)	S	S	O	O	O	O	O	O	O	O	O	S	S	O	O	S
SED	Species emergence delay (months)	S	S	S	S	L	O	S	S	O	O	O	L	O	L	S	S
SMRN	Species extinction rate norm (1/month)	S	S	S	S	L	S	S	S	S	S	L	S	L	L	S	S
SSD	Species substitution delay (months)	S	S	S	S	L	S	S	S	S	S	L	L	L	L	S	S
ISEAD	Ind spec emergence adj delay (months)	U	U	U	U	U	U	U	U	U	U	U	U	U	U	U	L
SCCAD	Soil carrying cap adj delay (months)	S	S	S	O	U	S	S	S	S	S	L	L	U	L	S	S

ESRC	Energy to spec req coeff (cal/m²/spec)	U	S	U	O	U	U	U	U	U	U	L	S	U	S	U
EFR	Energy fixation rate (cal/gp/month)	L	L	S	U	S	S	L	L	L	L	S	L	L	L	L
EPRC	Energy to plant req coeff (cal/gp)	O	O	O	O	O	O	O	O	O	O	O	O	O	O	O
BSD	Total biomass smoothing delay (months)	O	O	O	O	O	O	O	O	O	O	O	O	O	O	O
PVDD	Plant vigor dissipation delay (months)	U	U	S	O	U	U	L	L	L	L	S	L	L	S	S
DIVMC	Diversity maint coeff (cal/m²/mon/spec)	O	S	L	U	U	U	O	O	O	O	L	S	O	S	S
PMC	Plant maint coeff (cal/gp/month)	O	L	L	O	O	O	O	O	O	O	U	U	U	U	U
SCCT	Soil carrying capacity table (gp/m²)	L	L	S	S	S	S	L	L	L	L	S	L	L	L	L
DIVT	Diversity table (species)	L	L	S	S	S	S	O	O	O	O	S	L	U	L	L
PPET	Plant production eff table (no dimen)	L	L	S	S	S	S	L	L	L	L	S	L	L	L	L

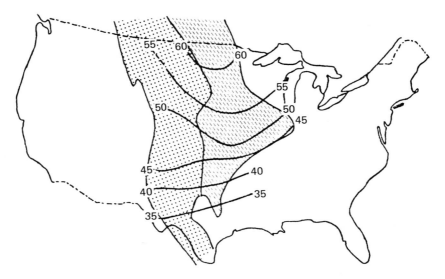

Figure 7.2
Average annual temperature change, July minus January (°F) for the North American
midland prairies (From Paul C. Lemon, 1975, "Prairie Ecosystems Are Essential for
Environmental Monitoring," in *Prairie: A Multiple View,* edited by Mohan K. Wali,
Grand Forks: The University of North Dakota Press, p. 344. Reprinted with permis-
sion.)

relationship between species emergence and sunlight. Biomass, primary
production, and successional rapidity are more obvious benefactors of
greater solar energy; however, if any other factor (e.g., nutrient exhaustion
or moisture inadequacy) is already limiting growth, additional sunlight may
be detrimental. Sunlight effects on model parameters are estimated in
column 4 of table 7.1.

Wind velocity is the final climatic factor to be considered here. The wind
imposes a physical pressure on the grasses which require internal energy to
withstand it. The wind also serves to accelerate the evapotranspiration of
moisture from the soil and plant surfaces; therefore increased winds retard
growth and slow successional adjustment. Actually, little has been done to
measure quantitatively the effect of the wind on primary production, consumption, and decomposition. Therefore the wind influences shown in
column 5 of table 7.1 are little more than guesses.

It should be noted that these macroclimatic factors are modified by the
grassland community to produce a microclimate. As one descends from the
upper tips of the grass culms to soil level, marked changes occur in tempera-

ture, humidity, sunlight, and wind velocity. Figure 7.3 shows this vertical variation for these four factors. This figure illustrates the moderating effect that the grassland has on the impact of external forces. This may partially explain the ecosystem's ability to sustain a climax state through fairly severe climatic irregularities.

Edaphic influences on grassland secondary succession are less visible, but significant nevertheless. The soil is a living community that engages in a mutually essential interaction with the rest of the ecosystem. The soil serves as a medium necessary to provide (1) root anchorage and physical support for the biomass, (2) seed germination and/or root division, (3) water for plant root sustenance, decomposition biochemistry, and conserving the above-soil humidity of the microclimate, (4) air, (5) important minerals such as phosphorus, nitrogen, potassium, iron, calcium, sodium, magnesium, sulfur, carbon, zinc, copper, manganese, and boron (Buol, 1973; Whittaker, 1975; Robinson, 1972), and (6) habitat for the organisms whose activities decompose and recycle nutrients from organic matter.

The soil characteristics that influence grassland secondary succession

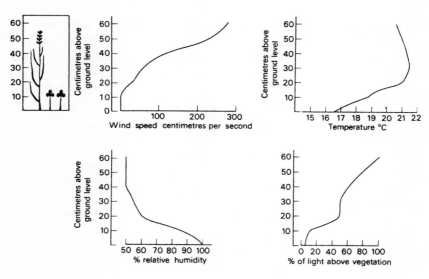

Figure 7.3
The structure of grassland vegetation and its effect on the ecosystem microclimate with respect to wind speed, temperature, percent relative humidity and percent light above vegetation (From Barry C. Cox, Ian N. Healy and Peter D. Moore, 1976, *Biogeography: An Ecological and Evolutionary Approach*, 2d. ed., New York: Wiley, p. 57. Reprinted with permission.)

include texture (particle size), structure (particle aggregates), thickness, mineral content, acidity, organic matter, and color (Buol, 1973; Robinson, 1972). All are discussed in the terminology used to designate different layers of soil composition. These layers (called horizons) are shown in figure 7.4. Not all soils contain all horizons, and different horizons are sometimes difficult to distinguish in a particular soil sample. A profile of chernozem, a soil typical of temperate tall grasslands, appears in figure 7.5. The A horizons generally contain the most active chemical and biological processes. Various salts and colloids are concentrated through leaching in the B horizons. The C and D horizons include bedrock material in weathered and undisturbed conditions, respectively, which only indirectly interact with the ecosystem. There are several soil horizon designation systems, but the soil survey staff method (Buol, 1973) is used here.

Shortgrass prairies often have brown to chestnut brown soils. Tallgrass prairies usually have chernozems (black, see figure 7.5) or brunizems (reddish) soils. Tallgrass soils are somewhat finer in texture, more uniform in structure (granular rather than ploty or blocky), thicker, richer in mineral and organic matter content, less alkaline, and darker in color than shortgrass soils. Estimates of some properties of traditional grassland soil groups are listed in table 7.2.

Texture indicates the size of soil particles that range from clay (less than 0.002 mm in diameter), to silt (0.002 to 0.05 and 0.02 mm), through sand

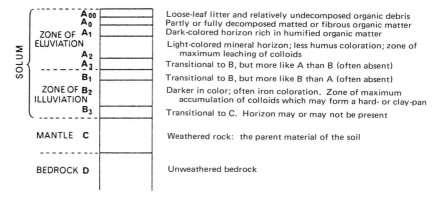

Figure 7.4
Idealized soil profile. The horizons are shown diagrammatically because not all soils are layered in this manner and the depths of both the soils and the horizons vary greatly. The A_2 horizon is absent in chernozems and chestnut soils. The B_2 horizon contains calcium carbonate or gypsum in chernozem soils. (From H. Robinson, 1972, *Biogeography,* London: Macdonald and Evans, p. 88. Reprinted with permission.)

Temperate Grassland

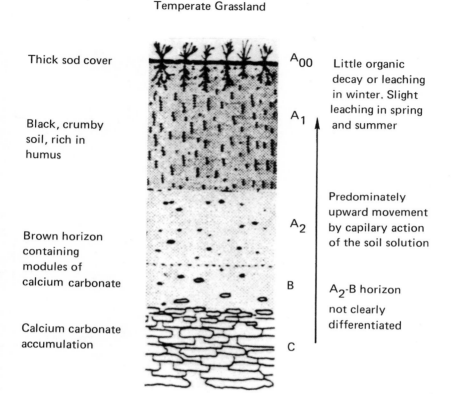

Thick sod cover

Black, crumby
soil, rich in
humus

Brown horizon
containing
modules of
calcium carbonate

Calcium carbonate
accumulation

A_{00} Little organic
decay or leaching
in winter. Slight
leaching in spring
and summer

A_1

Predominately
upward movement
by capilary action
of the soil solution

A_2

B A_2-B horizon
not clearly
differentiated

C

Figure 7.5
Profile of chernozem grassland soil (From H. Robinson, 1972, *Biogeography*, London: Macdonald and Evans, p. 100. Reprinted with permission.)

(0.05 or 0.02 to 2 mm), to gravel (2 to 76 mm). Larger sizes, cobbles and stones, are not ecologically important. Soils with mixtures of particle sizes are referred to with compound names (e.g., sandy clay). There are several classification systems that differ mainly in the size at the sand-silt boundary. The U.S. Department of Agriculture uses 0.05 mm (Buol, 1973), while European systems use 0.02 mm (Robinson, 1972). Larger particle sizes lead to faster water percolation (dryer, warmer soil) and easier root penetration. Both large or small particle size extremes are generally detrimental to vegetation. The given model parameters assume a shortgrass soil. The estimated influence of changes in soil characteristics on model constants as listed in table 7.1 assume changes from a brown or chestnut

Table 7.2

Estimates of some properties of mollisols of traditional grassland soil groups (From S. W. Buol, F. D. Hole, and R. J. McCracken, *Soil Genesis and Classification*, Ames, Iowa: Iowa State University Press, 1973. Reprinted with permission.)

	A1 Horizon					Development of Bt and Prisms	Development of Organs and Argillans	pH of B Horizon	O.M. Content of Horizons		Cca Horizon	Depth to Carbonates (cm)
	Thickness (cm)	pH	C/N	B.S. (%)	Structure				Ap (%)	B (%)		
Brunizems, Reddish Prairie soils (Argi-, Hapl-, and Verm-udolls)	30	5.1-6.5	10-11	70-90	granular	weak to none	moderate	5.3-6.7	4.5-2.0	1.5-1.0	absent	76-200
Chernozems (Agri-, Haplo-, Natri-, Vermiborolls)	20	6.0-7.5	11-12	85	granular	none to weak	moderate	6.5-7.5	4	2-3	usually present	38-60
Chestnuts, Reddish Chestnuts (Argi-, Hapl-, Verm-, Durustolls)	20	6.8-7.5	10-13	90	granular to blocky and prismatic	moderate to strong	weak to strons	7.5	3	2-3	present	30-90
Brown soils (Argi-, Haplustolls; Argi-, Dur-Xerolls)	10	6.9-7.5	11	95	platy to granular	weak to moderate	very weak	7.5	2	1.5	present	20-60
Sierozems (Haploxeroll)	7	7.5	8	100	fine platy, vesicular	none to very weak to moderate	very weak	9.1	1.3	1.3	present	17-30

Note: The purpose of this table is to identify in a general way the central concept of each of the traditional grassland soil groups of well-drained sites.

shortgrass soil. Therefore smaller particle size should improve moisture retention and influence succession. Smaller particle size should influence model constants (column 6 of table 7.1) in much the same way that greater moisture would (see column 1).

The cohesive property of particles to form aggregates is called soil structure. Productive natural grasslands have a uniform crumb-like structure (Robinson, 1972). Irregular clumping or plating interferes with moisture and air transmission; therefore greater granularity may be conducive to somewhat greater soil-carrying capacity and faster successional response, though no quantitative estimates exist for such effects. The influences suggested in column 7 of table 7.1 are probably small.

Thickness refers primarily to the depth of the mineral rich, organically active $A + B$ horizons. In a grassland, thicker soil is capable of supporting a greater standing crop and providing greater sustenance to a regenerating ecosystem through a larger nutrient base and a greater moisture reservoir. These effects, as shown in column 8 of table 7.1, probably will be similar to the influences of richer minerals (column 9), more humus (column 10), and greater moisture (column 1).

A soil's acidity also has an important effect on plant growth. The concentration of hydrogen ions is measured on the pH scale. Neutral is generally given a pH value of 7 with acidic soils having pH values of 6 or less while alkaline soils show pH values of 8 or above. Most grassland soils are in the roughly neutral range of 6.5 to 7.5. Small changes ought not to have a significant influence on constants (column 11) or successional patterns. Large changes, particularly in the acidic direction, may interfere with plant nutrient absorption and decomposition.

Physiographic influences on grassland succession include altitude, the flatness and slope of the topography, and the slope orientation direction. All of these are less important factors that modulate climatic or edaphic characteristics. Orientation direction (aspect), for example, influences sunlight intensity and duration, both climatic factors. Therefore the influence of physiographic factors on model constants and successional patterns will be similar to that of the corresponding climatic or edaphic factors.

Altitude and temperature are closely related. On average the air temperature falls by $0.6°C$ for every 100 meter rise in height (Cox, 1976, p. 34). Therefore the influence of higher altitude on model constants in column 12 of table 7.1 should be roughly the inverse of column 2. Atmospheric pressure also declines with increasing height, but very little is known about the effect of pressure on succession.

Levelness and slope are similar in that both relate to the topography, the former relative to small, short distance undulations; the latter relative to larger, longer distance variations. Small hills and valleys can create local differences in water drainage, wind shelter, sunlight, and temperature. These in turn produce variations in soil thickness, mineral and organic matter content, and pH. Decreasing levelness tends to decrease grassland productivity and responsiveness when measured as an average over the entire area. Column 13 of table 7.1 shows these expected effects. Increasing slope also usually has a detrimental effect on grassland productivity and responsiveness though the influence may be small for small slopes. However, there may be some advantage to small slopes, if they face south in the northern hemisphere. The influence of greater slope on model constants is estimated in column 14 of table 7.1 assuming an east–west orientation.

Aspect, a slope's directional orientation, has a fairly important influence on sunlight and temperature. In the northern hemisphere, south-facing slopes tend to be warmer, dryer, and more sunlit (Robinson, 1972) than other directions. Unless rainfall is very light, this should be an advantage to productivity and successional response. Column 15 of table 7.1 records the estimated effects of a more south-facing exposure in the northern hemisphere. Similar conclusions relate to northern aspects in the southern hemisphere.

Stochastic influences refer to accidental or unpredictable external events that seriously disturb the ecosystem state. Fire, flood, typhoon, hurricane, locust plague, prolonged drought, and tornado are some examples. Grasslands are most likely to experience fire or drought damage, with fire the most prevalent. Since controlled experiments are possible with fire, and fire damage is reasonably consistent in its effects, a great deal more is known about grassland response to fire than to other types of disaster. Therefore fire is the only stochastic factor treated here.

It has been fairly consistently demonstrated (there are a few contrary examples) that plant production is greater after a fire than would have occurred without it. In fact total biomass on recently burned prairie for a year or two may exceed biomass on unburned prairie. The results of a study by Hill and Platt (1972 in Wali, 1975) are presented in table 7.3 to show the rough magnitude of the biomass overshoot following fire damage. The reasons for this are not clear, but these authors suggest that burning removes ground litter that normally inhibits the growth of certain types of grass species. Litter removal permits a greater contribution from these types. Since these species types are always present, though less dominant, species diversity is not affected by fire. The response to fire is not a true secondary

Table 7.3
Plant production and moisture content on burned and unburned prairie for summer, 1972 (From Gerald R. Hill and William J. Platt, 1975, "Some Effects of Fire upon a Tall Grass Prairie Plant Community in Northwestern Iowa," in *Prairie: A Multiple View*, edited by Mohan K. Wali, Grand Forks: The University of North Dakota Press, p. 105. Reprinted with permission.)

Sampling Times	$\overline{WWB}$		$\overline{DWB}$		Ratio	
	Burned	Unburned	Burned	Unburned	Burned	Unburned
May	18.6 ± 2.5	112.0 ± 15.8	4.5 ± 0.7	37.3 ± 6.4	0.23 ± 0.01	0.35 ± 0.01
Early June	536.9 ± 49.4	409.2 ± 39.1	127.9 ± 14.8	111.9 ± 9.6	0.24 ± 0.10	0.28 ± 0.13
Late June	982.5 ± 70.9	757.7 ± 63.4	310.3 ± 21.9	269.5 ± 20.3	0.32 ± 0.09	0.36 ± 0.01
July	2244.02 ± 215.1	1482.65 ± 170.5	794.0 ± 70.1	520.2 ± 46.3	0.35 ± 0.08	0.35 ± 0.06
August	2198.6 ± 204.2	1311.1 ± 79.5	851.2 ± 79.4	520.5 ± 33.8	0.39 ± 0.08	0.40 ± 0.10
September	1332.2 ± 103.4	720.9 ± 48.6	562.4 ± 39.5	312.6 ± 29.8	0.43 ± 0.01	0.43 ± 0.02

NOTE:
$\overline{WWB}$ is mean wet weight biomass ± standard error.
$\overline{DWB}$ is mean dry weight biomass ± standard error.
Ratio is $\overline{DWB}/\overline{WWB}$ ± standard error.

succession because the regenerative parts of the grasses remain alive below ground so response is rapid. However, the accelerated productivity is similar to that in some stages of the secondary succession sequence. It is possible that frequent burning may permit a quasi-sustained hyper-climax standing crop. The influence of such persistent intervention on model parameters is estimated in column 16 of table 7.1. It has been suggested without quantitative demonstration that the probability of fire increases with the length of undisturbed climax. It is almost as if a senile grassland is more susceptible to fire to promote its rejuvenation. If this be true, then fire is an endogenous influence, not a true accident.

7.2 Grassland Primary Succession

Primary succession refers to the very long-term development of a terrestrial ecosystem starting with a bare bedrock surface. Secondary succession differs from this in that a soil cover already exists in which the developing vegetation can germinate seeds, anchor roots, and absorb nutrients. In order to understand and model primary succession, it is necessary to explore the nature of soil and the process of soil accumulation in some detail. Then some tentative relationships between primary and secondary successional models can be suggested. Since primary succession is not the primary focus of the study, a full primary model is not presented. However, primary succession is an important process that can be studied with feedback dynamics methods. It is hoped that this brief description may encourage others to model primary succession in detail or to introduce soil dynamics into secondary succession models.

Soil is a living community overlaying the rock base in which the primary producers (plants) grow. It is usually composed of an inorganic material base systematically interspersed with organic matter, living organisms (macro- and microflora and fauna), a complex water solution, and air. Each of these factors in important ways interacts with, and contributes to, the development and maintenance of the ecosystem. These factors exist in layers with different compositions and functions (see figure 7.4). Through time the soil factors and horizons change in their quantity, nature, and relative proportion just as grass biomass and species composition change above ground.

The inorganic material provides minerals that are dissolved by the soil water and transported to the plant roots. Such minerals are essential for plant growth. Some minerals are obtained through the decomposition of dead organic material, but until a stand of grass exists to provide decomposable litter, the minerals must all come from the base inorganic material. This is provided by weathered bedrock. Rock weathers through physical, chemical, and biological action. Wind, rain, ice, heat, hail, and lightning physically crack and break up the rock. Rain water is slightly acid. Its action weakens and dissolves the rock. Primitive organisms that establish themselves on the bare rock secrete acids that also contribute to rock disintegration. Later, plant roots crack the weakened rock. After an immature soil covers the rock, this weathering continues. Even deep, mature soils continue to interact with the buried bedrock to weather it and obtain its minerals.

Humus is the name given to the part of the soil's organic material that can decompose no further. As such it remains in the soil where it retains necessary elements for plant growth, modifies the soil's pH, and encourages soil bacteria to flourish (Robinson, 1972, p. 75). Other dead organic materials in the soil are being decomposed to yield their nutrients. All this important organic content can only develop through time as the plants and animals sustained by the soil die and return to enrich it. The development proceeds in stages as each simpler organic community prepares the soil for the more complex organisms that replace it. Grassland soil tends to be rich in humus and other organic material.

There are many species of soil flora and fauna and many individuals in even a small soil sample. A gram of soil may contain a million bacteria, a kilometer of fungal hyphae, and thousands of algae and protozoan cells (Buol, 1973, p. 144). These microorganisms serve many functions related to the decomposition and transformation of organic and inorganic materials. Larger animals, particularly worms and ants, aerate, mix, and fertilize the soil. In addition, the respiration of these organisms provides carbon dioxide for plant metabolism. Micro- and macroorganic communities arise only over substantial periods of time. This development is closely related to the availability of water, air, and dead organic material which in turn is dependent on the action of these organisms.

Water is the universal solvent. In the soil this is particularly true. Therefore soil water should really be called a soil solution. This carries minerals and organic substances to the plant roots and the soil's biotic community. The solution also breaks up the inorganic salts into electrically charged ions. Positively charged ions then are attracted to negatively charged particles of clay and humus. Thus potassium or other basic (positively charged) elements are separated from their negative bonds (usually carbonates) and are held in the upper A and B horizons by this so called clay-humus complex (Robinson, 1972). There they are available for plant nutrition. Without this electrical retention, important nutrients would be washed down to the inaccessible lower carbonate rich horizons. Even with this electrical force, excessive rain will leach (wash down) important positive ions because on its way down through the soil the slightly acid (H_2CO_2) rain trades its positive hydrogen ions to the negative clay-humus particles for the positive potassium ions previously held. High moisture climates thereby produce acid, mineral-poor soils.

In dry soils where evapotranspiration exceeds precipitation, ground water from the lower horizons is drawn up through capillary action. As a result calcium carbonate and other minerals are deposited near the surface and the soil becomes alkaline. Desert and grassland soils often have a high mineral content, but inadequate water and sometimes a nitrogen deficiency prevent full use of the minerals by natural ecosystems. However, when irrigated, many desert regions bloom, and cultivated former natural prairies have become the agricultural bread baskets of the world. There are other soil solution effects, but these are beyond the scope of this short overview.

Air is also essential in the soil because the action of bacteria in decomposition requires oxygen. Therefore a stagnant, wet soil with little air retains organic matter rather than recycling it (as in a bog). Worms and ants among other organisms aerate the soil through their burrowings.

The essence of primary succession is the continuing process of bedrock weathering to produce an inorganic particulate base and nutrients (minerals) coupled with the gradual development of more complex soil organisms, humus and plant biomass.

Weathering is dependent upon organic acid formation, clay-humus positive ion retention (after the bedrock is covered by soil), and natural forces. Soil organism development rests on the inorganic particulate base as a habitat and the availability of humus and dead organic nutrients. Humus is created out of dead organic material acted upon by soil organisms. Finally, plant biomass is supported by the inorganic particulate base with nutrients, humus, and soil organisms. Each step to greater quantity and complexity of any one variable must be preceded by appropriate development of the others.

These relationships form a feedback control system for primary succession. Some of these variables and relationships are already included in the secondary succession model (decomposers, plant biomass, etc.). The addition of five concepts to the grassland model (humus, bedrock weathering, clay-humus complex, inorganic particulate base, and soil suitability for plants) as shown in figure 7.6 would provide the basis for a simple, but general, primary succession representation. Fewer than twenty additional

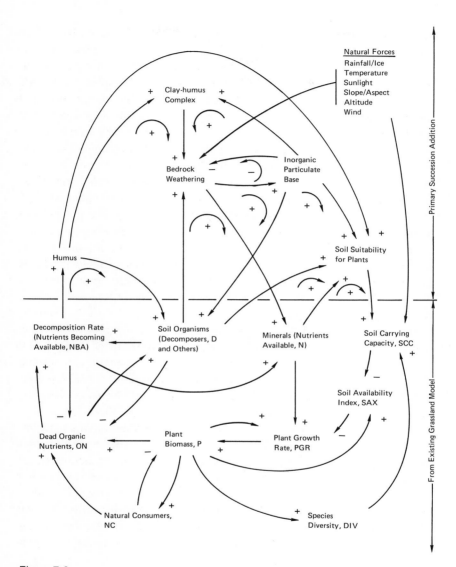

Figure 7.6
Influence diagram for the addition of primary succession to the grassland secondary
succession model

equations probably would be required, but many refinements have been omitted, and time constants and other parameters would need revision. Fortunately, there are only three existing equations (decomposers, nutrients available, and soil-carrying capacity) that would need revision to add a primary succession (soil) sector to the model. The general time pattern of primary succession probably would emerge even from this simple addition.

The influence diagram in figure 7.6 shows the feedback loops that are created by this extension of the model. All of the loops are positive except one in which a growing particulate base shields the bedrock from the direct attack of natural forces. Therefore this primary process acts to create a soil and ecosystem cover for any surface that is not too steep to retain a particulate cover, nor too cold nor too dry to sustain vegetation. The loops and table functions that limit a biomass to its climax maximum are already in the secondary model. However, even when the ecosystem is at a climax, soil may slowly increase in depth. This is particularly likely in low to moderate precipitation regions. Grasslands often develop thick soils. On the other hand, tropical rain forest soils tend to remain thin and acid.

Many of the new loops involve bedrock weathering, the primary activity early in development. For porous, weak parent rock (volcanic ash) weathering may proceed rapidly and lead to a vegetation climax in a few hundred to a few thousand years. Very hard granites with a high quartz content may resist for thousands or hundreds of thousands of years (Buol, 1973) depending on the climate. Dating of weathering and soil formation are very uncertain, so the numbers above are only very rough guides.

The principal weathering loops involve (1) the generation of particulate matter which serves as a habitat for organisms that secrete acids which weather the rock and (2) the generation of plant nutrients (minerals) which support plants whose dead litter both stimulates soil organisms that secrete acids and produces humus that removes positive ions from the soil solution leaving a weathering acid. While all of these loops are positive, their strength diminishes with time in the later developmental stages as the bedrock surface is covered more deeply and the acids reaching it become weaker.

Therefore, as the soil matures, dominance shifts from the weathering loops to loops related to soil suiability for plants. At this stage nutrient recycling becomes more important than mineral liberation from rock, and soil organism specialization responds more to the nature of the plant litter to be decomposed than to the rock to be disintegrated. Since plant community type (forest, grassland, etc.) is largely determined by climate, the nature of mature soil reflects more the ecosystem/climate type than the type of parent rock. The early Russian pedologists recognized this first (Buol, 1973), and modern soil classification systems are based on it. Zonal soils are those that are characteristic of an ecosystem type. The brown, chestnut, and chernozem (figure 7.5) grassland soils are examples. These soil-suitability loops are also positive, and their strength also diminishes as climax for the ecosystem is approached because plant biomass is a variable in all of these loops. Therefore, when plant biomass reaches a limit that prevents further expansion, the positive-soil loops cease to function though slow soil accumulation may continue.

7.3 Secondary Succession as a Control Process

Secondary succession is the action of an ecosystem that returns the system variables to a climax state. Any disturbance that removes the system from that climax state activates the restoration process. While humanlike volition cannot be attributed to a grassland, the restoration forces operate like a control system or servomechanism designed to approach and maintain the climax equilibrium. The form of the ecosystem control system is interesting because it differs from the form of control system usually designed by humans. Generally speaking, negative-feedback controls are used in human and engineering systems to maintain or achieve goals. Natural ecological control seems to take the form of positive loops that drive populations and related variables toward environmentally determined limits and hold them there. The difference is important because negative-loop control can result in a slow, oscillatory, and/or energy inefficient response unless the control system is very carefully and competently designed. Limited positive-loop control, on the other hand, tends to be rapid, efficient, and nonoscillatory within broad ranges of parameter values and relationship formats.

Negative-loop control usually consists of a variable of interest for which there is a goal or desired value. The difference between the two, called the error, is used to stimulate activities intended to correct or reduce the error. When the error is zero, the variable of interest coincides with its desired value and corrective action stops. In most human systems time delays occur between the time the variable of interest reaches a value and the time it is perceived and also between the time corrective action begins and the time the variable of interest begins to respond to the action. The existence of these delays makes it possible for more correction to be initiated than is required to return the variable to its desired value. The resulting over- and undershooting produce fluctuations of the variable above and below its desired value. To avoid oscillation, corrective actions often are taken in small, slow increments. However, this extends the time before the goal is reached. In the terminology of systems engineering a control process designed to return a variable to its desired value after a disturbance without oscillation in minimum time is said to be critically damped. Critically damped controls are difficult to design unless the response functions and system relationships are simple and linear. In most cases the controls are not well designed, so inefficient fluctuations or long expensive correction delays may occur. The only situations in which critically damped negative-feedback loop controls are consistently well designed arise in the design of better grade electrical, mechanical, aeronautical, and space hardware. Lunar landers and high speed elevators, for example, usually are meticulously designed, while inventory controls, urban-housing policies, and cattle-grazing decisions in many cases are not even recognized to be control points in feedback processes susceptible to quantitative feedback dynamics analysis.

Limited positive-loop control arises when a positive loop drives the variable of interest to larger and larger values until a limit is reached that prevents further increase. A hard limit, one that physically cannot be exceeded, may be approached in one of three ways. The first involves the dissipation of the energy generated by the positive loop to continue growth when the limit is reached. The second procedure reduces the gain (internal energy) of the positive loop as the limit or goal is approached. The third way simply introduces a reflecting boundary that changes the sign of the variable's momentum when it reaches the limit and causes the positive loop to begin an accelerating decrease in the variable's value (i.e., the variable bounces off the ceiling and then declines). The third limiting process prevents expansion above the limit but does not hold the variable at the limit as the first two limiting actions do.

Natural ecosystems use both the first and the second limits, particularly the second. Both methods use a negative loop coupled to the positive one. In a model the negative loop may be replaced by a saturating table function. The negative loops serve, respectively, to neutralize the positive loop's effect and to turn off the positive loop at the time that the limit is reached. The positive loop provides the primary upward correction while the negative loop fine tunes the approach to the limit. Rapid, nonoscillatory response can result.

In most ecosystems the primary variable of interest, the producers biomass, is driven to a climax maximum limit. This is the key variable because the transformation of solar energy to organic matter occurs in green plants which then sustain the other biological populations. Two major positive loops exist in the grassland model to represent the process of attaining and maintaining the maximum. In the first loop new growth occurs through the reproduction and extention of existing biomass—biomass regenerates itself (see figure 3.4). Indicated species diversity is positively dependent upon biomass in the second loop and in turn positively influences soil-carrying capacity to which biomass responds (see figure 3.12). These loops do not generate perpetual growth because both species diversity and soil-carrying capacity have upper limits appropriate to the climax state. In this case table functions (see figures 3.13 and 3.14) with horizontal asymptotes replace negative loops as limiters. The negative loop involving producers biomass and soil availability shown in figure 3.12 implements these limits (see figure 3.6).

Ecosystems can employ limited positive-loop control because the biomass goal is actually a physical maximum beyond which growth cannot be sustained (slight overshoots are possible, however). In human systems the desired values usually are not physical upper limits. Goals are often midrange values selected because both large and small extreme values create difficulties. A very large inventory, for example, is expensive to acquire and maintain, while a small inventory leads to inadequate customer service. While this difference is important, there may be human system situations where limited positive-loop control can be usefully employed. Cattle range management may be such a case, but designers of all types of systems should recognize the potential benefits of limited positive-loop control and use it when appropriate.

7.4. Secondary Succession in Other Ecosystems

The grassland is not the only ecosystem that experiences secondary succession. All major terrestrial ecosystems exhibit seral behavior. The IBP has identified four major terrestrial biome types and has supported research to study each (Holding, 1974). The four biomes are woodland, grassland, aridland, and tundra. Each has major and/or minor subdivisions. Authorities do not all agree on biome type classifications. However, a representative taxonomy is shown in tables 7.4 and 7.5 in which are estimated the global extent and productivity characteristics of both terrestrial and marine ecosystems. In this classification woodland includes tropical rain forest, tropical seasonal (deciduous) forest, temperate evergreen forest, temperate deciduous forest, boreal forest (taiga), and woodland and shrubland (Mediterranean woodland). The grassland designation covers tropical grasslands (savanna) and temperate grasslands with tall, mixed, and short

Table 7.4

Net primary production and plant biomass for the biomes of the earth measured in square kilometers, dry grams or kilograms per meter square, and dry metric tons (t) of organic matter (Reprinted with permission of Macmillan Publishing Co., Inc., from *Communities and Ecosystems*, 2d. ed., by Robert H. Whittaker. Copyright © 1975, Robert H. Whittaker.)

Ecosystem Type	Area* 10^6 km²	Net Primary Productivity, per Unit Area† g/m²/yr		World Net Primary Production** 10^9 t/yr	Biomass per Unit Area‡		World Biomass** 10^9 t
		Normal Range	Mean		Normal Range	Mean	
Tropical rain forest	17.0	1000–3500	2200	37.4	6–80	45	765
Tropical seasonal forest	7.5	1000–2500	1600	12.0	6–60	35	260
Temperate evergreen forest	5.0	600–2500	1300	6.5	6–200	35	175
Temperate deciduous forest	7.0	600–2500	1200	8.4	6–60	30	210
Boreal forest	12.0	400–2000	800	9.6	6–40	20	240
Woodland and shrubland	8.5	250–1200	700	6.0	2–20	6	50
Savanna	15.0	200–2000	900	13.5	0.2–15	4	60
Temperate grassland	9.0	200–1500	600	5.4	0.2–5	1.6	14
Tundra and alpine	8.0	10–400	140	1.1	0.1–3	0.6	5
Desert and semidesert scrub	18.0	10–250	90	1.6	0.1–4	0.7	13
Extreme desert, rock, sand, and ice	24.0	0–10	3	0.07	0–0.2	0.02	0.5
Cultivated land	14.0	100–3500	650	9.1	0.4–12	1	14
Swamp and marsh	2.0	800–3500	2000	4.0	3–50	15	30
Lake and stream	2.0	100–1500	250	0.5	0–0.1	0.02	0.05
Total continental	149.0		773	115.0		12.3	1837.0
Open ocean	332.0	2–400	125	41.5	0–0.005	0.003	1.0
Upwelling zones	0.4	400–1000	500	0.2	0.005–0.1	0.02	0.008

Continental shelf	26.6	200-600	360	9.6	0.001-0.04	0.01	0.27
Algal beds and reefs	0.6	500-4000	2500	1.6	0.04-4	2	1.2
Estuaries	1.4	200-3500	1500	2.1	0.01-6	1	1.4
Total marine	361.0		152	55.0		0.01	3.9
Full total	510.0		333	170.0		3.6	1841.0

Unit conversions

* Square kilometers x 0.3861 = square miles.

† Grams per square meter x 0.01 = t/ha, x 0.1 = dz/ha or m centn/ha (metric centners, 100 kg, per hectare, 10^4 square meters), x 10 = kg/ha, x 8.92 = lb/acre.

** Metric tons (10^6 g) x 1.1023 = English short tons.

‡ Kilograms per square meter x 100 = dz/ha, x 10 = t/ha, x 8922 = lb/acre, x 4.461 = English short tons per acre.

Productivities and biomasses expressed as carbon can be multiplied by 2.2 as an approximate conversion to dry matter.

Table 7.5
Other biosphere characteristics related to biome productivity. Units are in square kilometers and metric tons (t) of chlorophyll and organic matter (Reprinted with permission of Macmillan Publishing Co., Inc., from *Communities and Ecosystems*, 2d. ed., by Robert H. Whittaker. Copyright © 1975, Robert H. Whittaker.)

Ecosystem Type	Area* 10^6 km^2	Chlorophyll** 10^6 t	Leaf Surface Area* 10^6 km^2	Litter Mass** 10^9 t	Animal Consumption** 10^6 t/yr	Animal Production** 10^6 t/yr	Animal Biomass** 10^6 t
Tropical rain forest	17.0	51.0	136	3.4	2600	260	330
Tropical seasonal forest	7.5	18.8	38	3.8	720	72	90
Temperate evergreen forest	5.0	17.5	60	15.0	260	26	50
Temperate deciduous forest	7.0	14.0	35	14.0	420	42	110
Boreal forest	12.0	36.0	144	48.0	380	38	57
Woodland and shrubland	8.5	13.6	34	5.1	300	30	40
Savanna	15.0	22.5	60	3.0	2000	300	220
Temperate grassland	9.0	11.7	32	3.6	540	80	60
Tundra and alpine	8.0	4.0	16	8.0	33	3	3.5
Desert and semidesert scrub	18.0	9.0	18	0.36	48	7	8
Extreme desert, rock, sand, and ice	24.0	0.5	1.2	0.03	0.2	0.02	0.02
Cultivated land	14.0	21.0	56	1.4	90	9	6
Swamp and marsh	2.0	6.0	14	5.0	320	32	20
Lake and stream	2.0	0.5			100	10	10
Total continental	149	226	644	111	7810	909	1005
Open ocean	332.0	10.0			16,600	2500	800
Upwelling zones	0.4	0.1			70	11	4
Continental shelf	26.6	5.3			3000	430	160
Algal beds and reefs	0.6	1.2			240	36	12
Estuaries	1.4	1.4			320	48	21
Total marine	361	18.0			20,230	3025	997
Full total	510	244			28,040	3934	2002

grasses. Aridland refers to desert, semidesert scrub, and extreme desert. Tundra is not clearly defined, so the International Tundra Biome group includes true polar and alpine tundra sites, a number of forest tundra and temperate bog sites, because of the similarity of vegetation (Holding, 1974, p. 1). A map of the Earth's biomes is shown in figure 7.7. The map biomes do not exactly correspond to the table (7.4 and 7.5) biomes. For example, the map has no cultivated lands and the map's temperate deciduous forest includes temperate evergreen forest such as arises in the southeastern United States.

Each of these biomes has the same basic successional feedback loop structure as represented in the grassland model. Primary producers (plants) capture solar energy and convert it to biomass usable by consumers (vertebrate and invertebrate, herbivores and carnivores) who through their diversity provide structural stability. Decomposers close the loop by converting dead organic matter to inorganic nutrients that sustain the plants. In each biome the detailed nature of these components is somewhat different. The trees of the tropical rain forest obviously are different in shape and size from grasses and from the lichens of the tundra. Yet they all serve the same primary production function. Later the forest and tundra will be discussed in some detail and contrasted with marine ecosystems.

The differences between the functionally similar parts of different ecosystems are influenced primarily by differences in rainfall and temperature. The cold, dry tundra, for example, simply cannot support enormous quantities of plant biomass. A chart of the distribution of terrestrial biomes with respect to temperature (mean annual, °C) and precipitation (mean annual, cm) is provided in figure 7.8. As temperature and rainfall rise, the productivity per unit area of the resulting biome rises also. Thus tundra (cold desert) and desert are replaced by grassland, which in turn is replaced by forest of increasing density as moisture (most important) and temperature increase.

The mature soils of these climax biomes are primarily dependent upon climate and vegetation. The types of soils that arise under different climate/biome conditions are shown in figure 7.9. This suggests that the limited positive-feedback loops of the natural biosphere automatically generate (primary succession) and maintain (secondary succession) both soils and climax ecosystems even under the most inhospitable conditons to sustain life and stabilize the surface of the Earth.

Forests experience secondary succession similar to that of grasslands. The time histories for primary productivity, biomass, and species diversity in an oak-pine forest in New York for which successional changes were

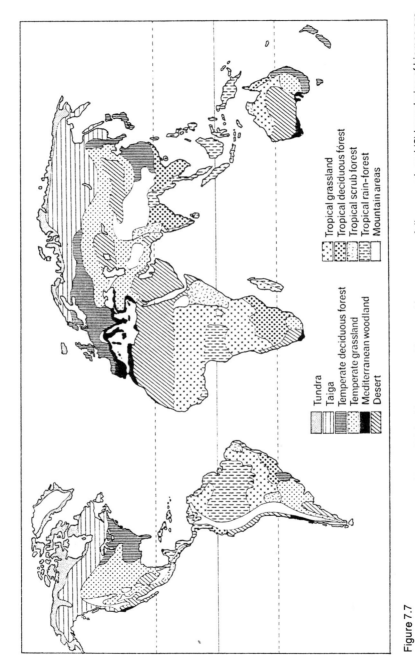

Figure 7.7
World map of the terrestrial biomes. Notes: (1) the biomes as yet have not been very carefully mapped, and (2) boundaries of biomes are always indefinite. (From H. Robinson, 1972, *Biogeography*, London: Macdonald and Evans, p. 438. Reprinted with permission.)

Tundra
Taiga
Temperate deciduous forest
Temperate grassland
Mediterranean woodland
Desert

Tropical grassland
Tropical deciduous forest
Tropical scrub forest
Tropical rain-forest
Mountain areas

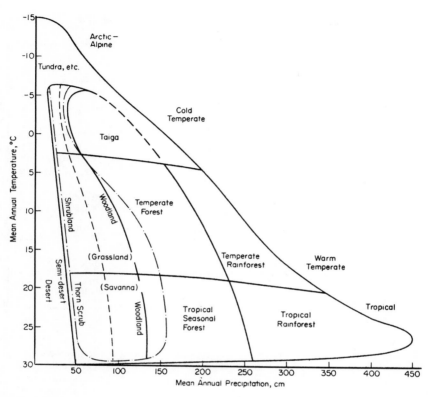

Figure 7.8
Distribution of the major terrestrial biomes with respect to mean annual precipitation
and mean annual temperature. Within regions delimited by the dashed line, a number
of factors, including oceanicity, seasonability of drought, and human land use, may
affect the biome type that develops. (Reprinted with permission of Macmillan
Publishing Co., Inc., from *Communities and Ecosystems* 2d. ed., by Robert H.
Whittaker. Copyright © 1975, Robert H. Whittaker.)

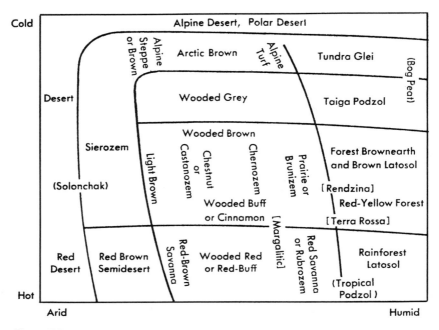

Figure 7.9
Great soil groups in relation to climate. Zonal great groups are shown by relative
positions along climatic gradients of humidity on the horizontal axis, and temperature
on the vertical. In intermediate climates both grass-dominated, and nongrass communities occur (figure 4.10) and form different soils. Soils formed in grassland communities are written on the vertical; soils formed by woodlands and shrublands (or, in
the Arctic, in tundra) are written on the horizontal for the same climates. Certain
nonzonal great soil groups are also shown; those formed on limestone or in high-
base situations are indicated in brackets, those formed with impeded drainage or
special conditions of water movement in parentheses. Terminologies and numbers of
great soil groups vary among authors. Forest brown earths as used here include
more than one group in most classifications; brown latosols occur in tropical mountain forests. (Reprinted with permission of Macmillan Publishing Co., Inc., from
Communities and Ecosystems, 2d. ed., by Robert H. Whittaker. Copyright © 1975,
Robert H. Whittaker.)

measured is presented in figure 7.10. The patterns of development are very similar to those produced by the grassland model, though the time to recover is longer and the climax magnitudes are different. The early dominance of annual plants (herbs) that are replaced by perennials as succession proceeds is the same in both ecosystems. Species diversity peaks correspondingly during the transition time when annuals and perennials coexist. Consumer and decomposer biomasses are not explicitly stated, but they are known to exist in sufficient quantity to sustain the nutrient recycling necessary for continued development toward the climax. An oak-pine forest is used to illustrate some of the similarities of structure and behavior between forests and grasslands, but any other type of forest would have served the same purpose. All experience secondary succession.

The ultimate climax condition associated with the secondary succession process may not always be the same as the primary climax condition. The model returns to the same climax each time a disturbance occurs just as real ecosystems do when the devastated areas are small, and the disturbances occur once or infrequently. But, if the affected area is large and/or disturbances recur frequently, deflected or arrested successions may result (Farnworth, 1973). This can mean a quantitatively smaller climax biomass and/or a qualitatively different type of ecosystem. There are reports of disturbed forests regenerating as grasslands that persist for long periods of time (Farnworth, 1973, p. 119). Generally, such biome switches occur in areas with annual precipitation close to the grassland maximum (30 inches). In some areas intentional burning is used to prevent forest encroachment on grazing or crop lands. Since very long-term observation has not been attempted, it is not clear whether the original type and magnitude of climax would ever return. Additional loops would be needed in the model to capture this phenomenon.

Tundra is the gently undulating plain of the arctic that appears barren, yet contains a functioning ecosystem that includes primary producers, such as dwarf trees, sedges, lichens, and mosses, consumers, and decomposers. Mountain areas above the tree line frequently have similar vegetation and sometimes are termed alpine tundra. With a few small exceptions Antarctica is ice covered and does not support tundralike life forms. On its southern boundary the tundra merges with the boreal forest in a broad, poorly defined transition zone.

Despite the sparse tundra vegetation consumers such as caribou and hares and carnivores, including wolves and owls among others, exist in some quantity. For some species there is a migratory pattern that removes them from the tundra during the winter months. With the absence of sunlight,

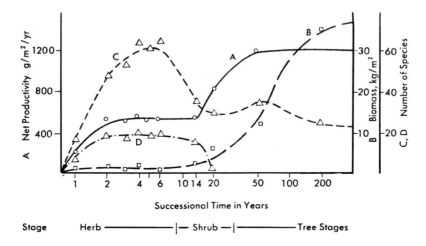

Figure 7.10
Productivity, biomass, and diversity during succession in the Brookhaven oak-pine forest, New York. These three community characteristics tend to increase during many successions, but such trends can be complex in detail. (A) Net primary productivity increases to a stable level in the herb stages, 2–6 years, then increases as woody plants enter the community, 14–50 years, to a stable level that may persist into the climax. (B) Biomass is low through the herb stages and then increases steeply with the accumulation of woody tissues of shrubs and trees; a stable climax biomass is probably not reached until after 200 years. (C) Species diversities—numbers of species in 0.3 hectare samples—increase into the late herb stages, decrease into shrub stages, 14–20 years, increase again into a young forest, 50 years, and from this decrease into the climax. (D) Numbers of exotic species; these are present only in the herb and early shrub stages.

Time is on a logarithmic scale to expand the earlier and contract the later part of the succession. (From B. Holt and G. M. Woodwell. Reprinted with permission of Macmillan Publishing Co., Inc., from *Communities and Ecosystems*, 2d. ed., by Robert H. Whittaker. Copyright © 1975, Robert H. Whittaker.)

intense cold ($-10°$ to $-60°$ F.), and strong wind for 3 to 6 months only the hardiest plants and animals can survive. Since growth and decomposition are slow, the tundra soils tend to be thin and deficient in humus and organic communities. As a result of the poor soil and environmental stress, secondary succession proceeds more slowly in the tundra than in more favored ecological areas. However, the same positive-feedback loops that regenerate biomass elsewhere exist and function in the tundra.

Desert, like the tundra, has little precipitation (less than 10 to 15 inches per year). However, the desert's high temperature makes this an extremely important problem, since the little available moisture evaporates quickly. Nevertheless, primary producers in the form of low growing ephemeral annuals, succulent perennials, and drought-tolerant nonsucculent perennials (Robinson, 1972) are scattered over the desert area. In most cases there is not a continuous ground cover, but sufficient vegetation exists to support both consumers and decomposers. Desert soil is usually immature in that organic content is low and the texture is loose and light (sandy). Minerals are often abundant but are not always present in the proper proportions. Since desert environmental stress is high, seral recovery is slow and subject to wide variability. Nevertheless, the secondary succession process functions to reestablish the desert climax when it is disturbed.

Woodland, tundra, aridland, and grassland all have the same type of organized interrelationships (feedback structure) that function to maintain or restore the climax state. The detailed nature of the primary producers, consumers, and decomposers is somewhat different in the different ecosystems. The time required for, and the precision of, the response also are somewhat different. However, since the processes and the patterns of response are similar, it is suggested that the grassland model can serve as a basis for the study of secondary succession in these other ecosystems after appropriate changes are made in the initial values of the accumulations and the values of the parameters and tables. In some particular cases more extensive modifications will be required. In any case that requires great accuracy; the model should be examined thoroughly to determine its suitability, and its parameter values should be estimated carefully with statistical procedures. It is hoped that substantial insight can be obtained in many ecological contexts through experimentation with this basic model. Table 7.6 provides estimates for the changes needed in model parameter and table values to create simulated successional patterns for other ecosystems. These estimates are not numerical values nor are they very reliable because little empirical work has been done to determine them. The table entries are intended only to suggest possibilities and encourage investigation.

Table 7.6
Estimated changes in model constants and tables for different terrestrial biomes

Model Constants and Tables

L = larger or longer
S = smaller or shorter
O = no change
U = unknown change
mon = months, cal = calories

Code	Description	Tropical Rain Forest	Tropical Seasonal Forest	Temperate Evergreen Forest	Temperate Deciduous Forest	Boreal Forest (Taiga)	Shrubland	Tropical Savanna	Temperate Tall Grassland	Temperate Short Grassland	Tundra	Desert
		Forest Biomes						Grassland Biomes				
PDD	Plant decay delay (months)	S	S	S	S	S	U	S	S		L	L
NAD	Nutrient absorption delay (months)	S	S	S	S	S	U	S	S		L	L
PDRSD	Plant decay sm. delay (months)	S	S	S	S	S	U	S	S		L	L
INGAD	Ind new growth adj delay (months)	S	S	S	S	S	U	S	S		L	L
DDMIN	Decomposition delay minimum (months)	S	S	S	S	S	U	S	S		L	L
DDS	Decomposition delay slope (months)	S	S	S	S	S	U	S	S		L	U
DRD	Decomposers response delay (months)	S	S	S	S	S	U	S	S		L	L
NCRD	Nat consumers response delay (months)	U	U	U	U	U	U	U	U	T	L	L
NPRC	Nutrient to plant req coeff (gn/gp)	U	U	U	U	U	U	U	U	H	U	U
ONDRC	Org nutrient to decomposer req (gn/gd)	U	U	U	U	U	U	U	U	E	U	U
PNCRC	Plants to nat consumers req (gp/gc)	U	U	U	U	U	U	U	U		S	S
NCPRC	Nat consumer-plant req coeff (gp/gc)	L	L	L	L	S	U	L	L		U	U
PPMT	Plant production multitable (1/month)	L	L	L	L	U	U	S	S	M	S	S
NCRT	Nat cons reproduction table (1/month)	L	L	S	S	S	U	S	S	O	L	L
NCMT	Nat consumer mortality table (1/month)	S	S	S	S	S	U	S	S	D	L	L
SED	Species emergence delay (months)	S	S	S	S	S	U	S	S	E	L	L
SMRN	Species extinction rate norm (1/month)	S	S	S	S	U	U	S	S	L	L	L
SSD	Species substitution delay (months)	S	S	U	U	U	U	S	S		L	L
ISEAD	Ind spec emergence adj delay (months)	S	S	U	U	U	U	S	S		L	L
SSCAD	Soil carrying cap adj delay (months)	S	S	S	S	U	U	S	S	B	L	L
ESRC	Energy to spec req coeff (cal/m²/spec)	U	U	U	U	U	U	U	U	I	U	U
EFR	Energy fixation rate (cal/gp/month)	L	L	U	U	U	U	L	L	O	S	S

Code	Description											
EPRC	Energy to plant req coeff (cal/gp)	U	U	M	U	U	U	U	U	U	U	U
BSD	Total biomass smoothing delay (months)	U	U	E	U	U	U	U	U	U	U	U
PVDD	Plant vigor dissipation delay (months)	L	L		S	S	U	S	S	S	S	S
DIVMC	Diversity maint coeff (cal/m²/mon/spec)				L	L	U	U	U	U	U	U
PMC	Plant maint coeff (cal/gp/month)	S	S		L	L	U	U	U	U	U	L
SCCT	Soil carrying capacity table (gp/m²)	S	S		L	L	S	L	L	L	L	L
DIVT	Diversity table (species)	S	S		U	U	S	S	S	S	U	L
PPET	Plant production eff table (no dimen)	S	S		L	L	U	L	L	L	L	L

Marine ecosystems are not as well understood nor as clearly structured as terrestrial ecosystems; therefore the relationship between the grassland model and marine succession is not obvious. The following brief review of marine ecology suggests that, while similarities to the grassland situation exist, the grassland model probably could not be used to simulate marine succession without several significant modifications.

Primary production in marine (and fresh water) ecosystems is accomplished by phytoplankton. These are minute (usually single-celled) plants of many species that are distributed in the surface waters where sunlight provides the energy for photosynthesis. Consumers include microcrustacea (copepods and cladocerans) and sedentary filter feeders (Crisp, 1975, in Franklin, 1975) that quickly consume the available phytoplankton (p. 76):

In contrast to the characteristic terrestrial situation in which herbivores are limited and vegetation permanent, in the marine environment herbivores control, and are controlled by, stocks of phytoplankton. Such a simple predator-prey relationship at the base of the food chain is likely to produce severe fluctuations in biomass and production, and may account for the preponderence of opportunistic life styles in the sea.

A series of predators of gradually increasing size prey upon the microcrustacea and each other. Detritus is consumed by bottom-feeding fish and crustacea to maintain the circulation of nutrients. Except in shallow water, there is no soil, and no plants to grow in it. It can be seen that the components and relationships of the marine system are different from those of the grassland. Continuing oscillation also contrasts with the grassland's persistent climax. This suggests that a predator-prey type of dynamic feedback model designed especially for marine conditions would be more appropriate than a modified grassland model for the study of marine succession.

7.5 Suggested Further Research

The research done to develop and analyze this model of grassland succession has disclosed much that remains to be done. General areas of additional needed investigation include data gathering and model validation; model extensions and refinements, including those involving strategies for human intervention in natural grasslands; use of the model for studies of other ecosystems; use of feedback dynamics to model other ecosystems; and the development of a natural environment sector for aggregate models of worldwide, socioeconomic dynamics.

Empirical studies of some aspects of natural grasslands do exist. However, they have not focused on many of the factors required to substantiate a complete feedback model. Table 7.1 lists the thirty parameters and tables that are used in this model. Few have been studied in sufficient detail to provide statistically reliable values. This table also shows estimated changes that might occur in parameter values for specified changes in various external factors related to climate, the soil, and frequent disturbances. If the parameter values are uncertain themselves, then the estimated changes must be even less clear. Empirical studies are required to clarify both the values and the influences of changes.

The successional performance patterns for grasslands have not been established clearly and quantitatively. Impressions and qualitative observation suggest the general shape of the time histories. However, regular, accurate, quantitative, long-run measurements are not available even for biomass. There are many other variables (consumer and decomposer biomass, species diversity, nutrient availability, etc.) for which time histories are needed to verify the phase relationships and pattern shapes. To statistically validate this or any model, sufficient data must be available for hypothesis testing. Since such data are not now available, this model cannot be said to be statistically valid. However, the model does pass many logical and qualitative tests. Under these circumstances it is probably the best model currently available. When data are obtained, additional validation is desirable.

Data relating to system structure and performance are needed for grasslands in several parts of the world and for other types of ecosystems. The recent uncertainty over the impact of the trans-Alaskan oil pipeline on tundra ecology demonstrates the practical importance of such information and the need to begin expeditiously. Some of this data may have been obtained through the IBP studies of the last decade. But much information almost certainly remains to be discovered.

The grassland model is a highly simplified, highly aggregated model of somewhat limited extent. Each of these constraints can be usefully relaxed. Factors associated with climate, soil, and natural disasters (see table 7.1 and figure 7.6) can be introduced into the model as variables. External variations could be systematic (trends and oscillations) and/or random. This would begin to recognize the variation in pattern and climax values that is known to exist in reality. Disaggregation is possible with respect to producer biomass type (annuals and perennials), consumer type (herbivores and carnivores), decomposer type (litter reducers and below-ground decomposers), and nutrient types available. Such expansion would improve the accuracy of the simulations, provide the ability to understand additional relationships, and introduce the possibility for validation with respect to variables not previously available.

One of the most unreliable assumptions underlying biological modeling is that functional relationships are always reversible. Frequently, they are not reversible. A phenomenon called hysteresis then arises. This is usually reflected in table function values. As an example, consider the relationship between indicated soil-carrying capacity (ISCC) and species diversity (DIV) as shown in figure 3.14. During times of rising diversity, carrying capacity will rise along the tabulated curve. If diversity should subsequently fall, the carrying capacity will reverse and fall along the same curve. However, it is quite possible that the curve for falling diversity is not the same as the one for rising diversity. Failure to recognize such differences can result in unrealistically consistent behavior or, in extreme cases, incorrect patterns. Hysteresis effects in the grassland have not been measured, though it is likely that they exist to some extent. Therefore, when observations are obtained, the relationships should be examined carefully.

There is a somewhat oversimplified representation of controlled cattle grazing in the natural grassland model and a limited analysis of grazing strategies. Since human utilization of natural ecosystems without destruction is so essential in this era of rising population and need for food, this analysis of intervention should be expanded substantially. Perhaps a combined model of the grassland and the entire cattle industry would be needed. Particular attention should be given to the determination of appropriate performance evaluation criteria and the future time horizon to be considered. Short-run profitability seems to be the present criterion in the operating system. Long-run environmental protection and consistent optimal food productivity are two other criteria of major importance. Whatever type and extent of study that is required to understand beneficial intervention should be undertaken, since the benefit to mankind from such an understanding would be enormous.

Other terrestrial ecosystems have successional feedback structures and performances similar to the grassland. Section 7.4 presents that concept in a general way without a complete detailed analysis. Ways that might be possible are suggested (table 7.6) for changing the grassland model parameters to facilitate the simulation of other ecosystems. Complete detailed analyses should be done for the other ecosystems, particulary those with high productivities which might be used for human benefit without destroying their operation. For example, some of the Amazonian tropical rain forest in Brazil is being cleared. With inadequate understanding of rain forest succession, the outcome of the clearing is not certain. Nor is a recommended optimal procedure for clearing and future management available. A combined natural ecosystem succession analysis and a human intervention and management analysis seems essential.

Similarly, a soil dynamics analysis as discussed in section 7.2 would be most desirable. Vast areas of the Earth are affected by soil erosion especially in places where climatic changes are altering the precipitation patterns such as in the southern part of the Sahara Desert. While some soil conservation procedures have been known for thousands of years, terracing and water runoff channeling for example, it is possible that an integrated analysis of soil and ecosystem dynamics would reveal other helpful procedures and management policies. The importance of such studies is underscored by Robinson's comment (1972, p. 501):

Only 29 per cent of the Earth's surface is dry land. Of this only a very small proportion is fertile and capable of being used agriculturally . . . The conditions which limit the use of the Earth's land surface for cultivation may be summarised as follows: approximately one-fifth of the total land area is too mountainous, one-fifth is too cold, one-fifth is too dry, and one-fifth is forested or marshy. Thus a mere 20 per cent of the land area is available for agricultural use. Most of the best land is already being used. A proportion, possibly as much as a quarter, of the 80 per cent of the Earth's surface that is too high or dry or cold or forested could be made suitable for farming purposes, but only through a large capital investment. The picture that emerges from this very brief summary is of a shortage of land fit for cultivation. With the rapid growth in world population and the need to produce more food, together with the ever-increasing acreages being gobbled up by urban expansion, industrial development and modern communications, land is becoming increasingly precious.

It is suggested in section 7.4 that marine and fresh water ecosystems are different from terrestrial ecosystems in several important respects. Therefore the grassland model is not an appropriate basis for simulating marine succession. However, marine succession does appear to result from the functioning of ecological feedback processes which could be modeled through the application of the feedback dynamics methodology. Considering the severe limits on terrestrial food production and the vast extent and productivity of marine habitats, it would seem desirable, if not essential, to develop a dynamic feedback model or models of marine succession. Of course, the oceans have been fished for many years, but inadequate understanding and control have resulted in declining yields and fears of extinction for a number of marine species. Clearer insight into marine ecosystem dynamics would probably result in increased yields without threats to species survival or productivity. In addition, recent large-scale oil spills have created major ecological disruptions, the long-run outcomes of which are uncertain. Some of the uncertainty might be dispelled and beneficial restoration procedures discovered through the analysis of a marine succession model. In all likelihood a marine model could be used for studies of lake succession as well, if appropriate changes were made in the initial, parameter, and table values. Unfortunately, marine systems are not well documented quantitatively and data gathering is difficult. However, the intensity of the population pressures anticipated for the coming decades make imperative timely empirical studies and model analyses of such a large area with such a high productivity.

In recent years much concern and modeling have focused on the Earth's limited nonrenewable resources and arable land. Several quantitative models have attempted to represent the relationships at the world-level of aggregation that have in the past and will in the future determine the time histories of significant variables such as world population, food production, industrial production, services output, pollution, standard of living (average), and resource utilization. These and other variables are important at a time when the world socioeconomic system is experiencing the transition from a growing to a steady-state performance pattern. Natural ecosystems either are omitted from such models or are included in an over simplified way. Perhaps because natural systems historically have regenerated themselves automatically and dependably, it is easy to assume that they will continue to generate oxygen, support the indigenous life forms, regulate the water cycle, create soil, absorb human waste, and sustain various forms of ever-growing human intervention, including logging, hunting, grazing, farming, and fishing. If that assumption is true, the superficial ecosystem sectors for world models are justified. However, it is suggested here and elsewhere that the natural biomes have limits that are being approached now, just as nonrenewable resources and arable lands are becoming limited.

Natural ecosystem influences and limitations are essential to the understanding and prediction of future world system operation. Therefore meaningful natural system representations should be included in world models. Such representations need to be ecologically accurate, appropriately aggregated, dynamic representatives of different ecosystems, large enough to include the variables needed for interaction with the world system, and simple enough to understand easily. While the grassland succession model does not possess all of the characteristics, in all likelihood it could be modified easily to serve as a natural ecosystem sector for a world model. The details of the extension must be left to the particular situation. However, since the model was developed to capture the essence of ecosystem function, its generality and flexibility should make it an ideal base for the world application.

Bibliography

Albertson, F. W., and Tomanek, G. W. 1965. "Vegetation Changes During a 30-Year Period in Grassland Communities Near Hays, Kansas." *Ecology* 46:714–720.

Albertson, F. W., Tomanek, G. W., and Riegel, A. 1957. "Ecology of Drought Cycles and Grazing Intensity on Grasslands of Central Great Plains." *Ecological Monographs 27:27–44.*

Allen, D. L. 1967. *The Life of Prairies and Plains.* New York: McGraw-Hill.

Bagley, S., and Odum, H. T. 1976. "Simulation of Interrelations of the Everglades' Marsh, Peat, Fire, Water and Phosphorus." *Ecological Modelling* 2:169–188.

Barnard, C., ed. 1964. *Grasses and Grasslands.* London: Macmillan.

Bartos, D. L. 1973. "A Dynamic Model of Aspen Succession." IUFRO Biomass Studies, pp. 11–25. Orono: University of Maine Press.

Bledsoe, L. J., and Van Dyne, G. M. 1971. "A Compartment Model Simulation of Secondary Succession." *Systems Analysis and Simulation in Ecology.* Vol. 1. Edited by B. C. Patten. New York: Academic Press, pp. 480–511.

Bledsoe, L. J., Francis, R. C., Swartzman, G. L., and Gustafson, J. D. 1971. "PWNEE: A Grassland Ecosystem Model." *US IBP Grassland Biome Study Tech. Rep. No. 64.* Colorado State University, Ft. Collins.

Borman, F. H., and Likens, G. E. 1967. "Nutrient Cycling." *Science 1955:*424–429.

Borman, F. H., and Likens, G. E. 1970. "The Nutrient Cycles of an Ecosystem." *Scientific American 22:*92–101.

Bougis, Paul. 1976. *Marine Plankton Ecology.* Amsterdam: North-Holland Publishing Co.

Box, G. E. P., and Jenkins, G. M. 1970. *Time Series Analysis, Forecasting and Control.* San Francisco: Holden-Day.

Brinkhurst, Ralph O. 1974. *The Benthos of Lakes.* New York: St. Martin's Press.

Brown, G. W., Jr., ed. 1968. *Desert Biology: Special Topics on the Physical and Biological Aspects of Arid Regions.* Vol. 1. New York: Academic Press.

Buol, S. W., Hole, F. D., and McCracken, R. J. 1973. *Soil Genesis and Classification.* Ames: Iowa State University Press.

Carpenter, J. R., 1940. "The Grassland Biome." *Ecological Monographs 10:*617–684.

Clawson, M., Held, R. B., and Stoddard, C. H. 1960. *Land for the Future.* Baltimore, Md.: The Johns Hopkins University Press.

Clements, F. E. 1916. *Plant Succession: An Analysis of the Development of Vegetation.* Carnegie Inst., Publ. 242. Washington, D. C., pp. 1–512.

Coleman, D. C., Dyer, M. I., Ellis, J. E., French, N. R., Gibson, J. H., Innis, G. S., Marshall, J. K., Smith, F. M., and Van Dyne, G. M. 1973. "Grassland Ecosystem Evaluation." *Bulletin of the Ecological Society of America 54:*8–10.

Cooke, G. D. 1967. "The Pattern of Autotrophic Succession in Laboratory Microcosms." *Bioscience 17:*717–721.

Cooper, W. S. 1926. "The Fundamentals of Vegetational Change." *Ecology 7:*391–413.

Costello, D. F. 1944. "Natural Revegetation of Abandoned Plowed Land in the Mixed Prairie Association of Northeastern Colorado." *Ecology 25:*312–326.

Costello, D. F. 1957. "Application of Ecology to Range Management." *Ecology 38:*49–53.

Costello, D. F. 1969. *The Prairie World.* New York: Crowell.

Coupland, R. T., Zacharuk, R. Y., and Paul, E. A. 1969. "Procedures for Study of Grassland Ecosystems." *The Ecosystem Concept in Natural Resource Management.* Edited by G. M. Van Dyne. New York: Academic Press, pp. 25–47.

Cowles, H. C. 1899. "The Ecological Relations of the Vegetation on the Sand Dunes of Lake Michigan." *Botanical Gazette 27:*95–117, 167–202, 281–308, 361–391.

Cowles, H. C. 1901. "The Physiographic Ecology of Chicago and Vicinity." *Botanical Gazette 31:*73–108, 145–182.

Cowles, H. C. 1911. "The Causes of Vegetative Cycles." *Botanical Gazette 51:*161–183.

Cox, C. Barry, Healey, Ian N., and Moore, Peter D. 1976. *Biogeography: An Ecological and Evolutionary Approach.* 2d ed. New York: Wiley.

Cushing, D. H., and Walsh, J. J., eds. 1976. *The Ecology of the Seas.* Philadelphia: Saunders.

Dale, M. B. 1970. "Systems Analysis and Ecology." *Ecology 51:*2–16.

Daubenmire, R. 1968a. "Ecology of Fire in Grasslands." *Advances in Ecological Research.* Vol. 5. Edited by J. G. Cragg. New York: Academic Press, pp. 209–266.

Daubenmire, R. 1968b. *Plant Communities: A Textbook of Plant Synecology.* New York: Harper and Row.

De Vos, A. 1969. "Ecological Conditions Affecting the Production of Wild Herbivorous Mammals on Grasslands." *Advances in Ecological Research.* Vol. 6. Edited by J. B. Cragg. New York: Academic Press, pp. 137–183.

De Wit, C. T., and Goudriaan, J. 1974. *Simulation of Ecological Processes.* Centre for Agricultural Publishing and Documentation, Wageningen, The Netherlands.

Drury, W. H., and Nisbet, I. C. T. 1973. "Succession." *Journal of the Arnold Arboretum 54:*331–368.

Dyksterhuis, E. J. 1949. "Condition and Management of Range Land Based on Quantitative Ecology." *Journal of Range Management 2:*104–155.

Dyksterhuis, E. J. 1958. "Ecological Principles in Range Evaluation." *Botanical Review 24:*253–272.

Ellison, L. 1960. "Influence of Grazing on Plant Succession of Rangelands." *Botanical Review 26:*1–78.

Evans, F. C. 1956. "Ecosystem as the Basic Unit in Ecology." *Science 123;*1127–1128.

Farnworth, Edward G., and Golley, Frank B., eds. 1973. *Fragile Ecosystems: Evaluation of Research and Applications in the Neotropics.* New York: Springer-Verlag.

Forrester, J. W. 1961. *Industrial Dynamics.* Cambridge, Mass.: MIT Press.

Forrester, J. W. 1968a. *Principles of Systems.* Cambridge, Mass.: Wright-Allen Press.

Forrester, J. W. 1968b. "Industrial Dynamics After the First Decade." *Management Science 14:*398–415.

Forrester, J. W. 1968c. "Industrial Dynamics—A Response to Ansoff and Slevin." *Management Science 14:*601–618.

Forrester, J. W. 1971. *World Dynamics.* Cambridge, Mass.: Wright-Allen Press.

Franklin, Jerry F., Goodale, David W., and Reichle, David E., eds. 1975. *Productivity of World Ecosystems.* National Academy of Sciences, Washington, D C.

Fricke, Haus W. 1973. *The Coral Seas.* New York: Putnam's Sons.

Fridriksson, S. 1972. "Grass and Grass Utilization in Iceland." *Ecology 53:*785–796.

Frischknecht, N. C., and Harris, L. E. 1968. "Grazing Intensities and Systems on Crested Wheatgrass in Central Utah: Response of Vegetation and Cattle." *USDA Technical Bulletin No. 1388.*

Gates, D. M. 1968. "Toward Understanding Ecosystems." *Advances in Ecological Research.* Vol. 5. Edited by J. B. Cragg. New York: Academic Press, pp. 1–35.

Gelfant, S., and Smith, J. G., Jr. 1972. "Aging: Noncycling Cells an Explanation." *Science 178:*357–361.

Gilmanov, T. G. 1977. "Plant Submodel in the Holistic Model of a Grassland Ecosystem (with Special Attention to the Belowground Part)." *Ecological Modelling 3:*149–163.

Golterman, H. L. 1975. *Physiological Limnology: An Approach to the Physiology of Lake Ecosystems.* Amsterdam: Elsevier.

Good, R. E., Whigham, D. F., and Simpson, R. L., eds. 1978. *Freshwater Wetlands: Ecological Processes and Management Potential.* New York: Academic Press.

Goodale, David W., ed. 1976. *Evolution of Desert Biota.* Austin: University of Texas Press.

Gutierrez, L. T., and Fey, W. R. 1975a. "Simulation of Secondary Autogenic Succession in the Shortgrass Prairie Ecosystem." *Simulation 24:*113–125.

Gutierrez, L. T., and Fey, W. R. 1975b. "Simulation of Successional Dynamics in Ecosystems." *New Directions in the Analysis of Ecological Systems.* Edited by G. S. Innis. Simulation Councils Proceedings Series 5:73–82.

Gutierrez, L. T., and Fey, W. R. 1975c. "Feedback Dynamics Analysis of Secondary Successional Transients in Ecosystems." *Proceedings of the National Academy of Sciences 72:*2733–2737.

Haeckel, E. 1866. *Generelle Morphologie der Organismen.* Berlin: Reimer.

Hall, Charles A. S., and Day, John W., eds. 1977. *Ecosystem Modelling in Theory and Practice: An Introduction with Case Histories.* New York: Wiley.

Hanson, H. C. 1938. "Ecology of the Grassland, I." *Botanical Review 4:*51–82.

Hanson, H. C. 1950. "Ecology of the Grassland, II." *Botanical Review 16:*283–361.

Holding, A. J., Heal, O. W., Maclean, S. F., Jr., and Flanagan, P. W., eds. 1974. *Soil Organisms and Decomposition in Tundra.* Stockholm: Tundra Biome Steering Committee.

Horn, H. S. 1975. "Forest Succession." *Scientific American 232:*90–98.

Humphrey, R. T. 1962. *Range Ecology.* New York: Ronald Press.

Hutchinson, G. Evelyn. 1957, 1967, and 1975. *A Treatise on Limnology.* Vols. 1, 2, and 3. London: Wiley.

Innis, G. S. 1972a. "ELM: A Grassland Ecosystem Model." *Proc. Summer Computer Simulation Conference,* San Diego, Calif.

Innis, G. S. 1972b. "Simulation of Ill-Defined Systems: Some Problems and Progress." *Simulation Today 9:*33–36.

Jaeger, Edmund C. 1957. *The North American Deserts.* Stanford: Stanford University Press.

Jameson, D. A. 1963. "Response of Individual Plants to Harvesting." *Botanical Review 29:*532–594.

Jameson, D. A. 1970. "Land Management Policy and Development of Ecological Concepts." *Journal of Range Management 23:*316–321.

Jameson, D. A., and Bement, R. E. 1969. "General Description of the Pawnee Site." *U.S. IBP Grassland Biome Study Technical Report No. 1.* Colorado State University, Ft. Collins.

Kinne, Otto, ed. 1970, 1971, 1975, 1975, 1976, 1977, and 1978. *Marine Ecology: A Comprehensive, Integrated Treatise on Life in Oceans and Coastal Waters.* Vol. 1, pts. 1, 2, vol. 2, pt. 1, vol. 3, pts. 1, 2, 3. Chichester: Wiley.

Kira, T. and Shidei, T. 1967. "Primary Production and Turnover of Organic Matter in Different Forest Ecosystems of the Western Pacific." *Japan Journal of Ecology 17:*70–85.

Klapp, E. 1964. "Features of a Grassland Theory." *Journal of Range Management 17:*309–322.

Klipple, G. E., and Costello, D. F. 1960. "Vegetation and Cattle Responses to Different Intensities of Grazing on Short-Grass Ranges on the Central Great Plains." *USDA Technical Bulletin No. 1216.*

Kormondy, E. J. 1969. *Concepts of Ecology.* Englewood Cliffs: Prentice-Hall.

Larson, F. 1940. "The Role of the Bison in Maintaining the Short Grass Plains." *Ecology 21:*113–121.

Lewis, J. K. 1969. "Range Management Viewed in the Ecosystem Framework." *The Ecosystem Concept in Natural Resource Management.* Edited by G. M. Van Dyne. New York: Academic Press, pp. 97–185.

Lindeman, R. L. 1942. "The Trophic-Dynamic Aspect of Ecology." *Ecology 23:*399–418.

Longman, K. A., and Jenik, J. 1974. *Tropical Forest and its Environment.* London: Longman Group.

Macan, T. T. 1970. *Biological Studies of the English Lakes.* New York: American Elsevier.

MacFadyen, A. 1957. *Animal Ecology: Aims and Methods.* London: Pitman and Sons.

MacFadyen, A. 1969. "The Systematic Study of Soil Ecosystems." *The Soil Ecosystem: Systematic Aspects of the Environment, Organisms and Communities.* London: The Systematics Association.

MacIntosh, R. P. 1967. "The Continuum Concept of Vegetation." *Botanical Review 33:*130–187.

Maguire, L. A., and Porter, J. W. 1977. "A Spatial Model of Growth and Competition Strategies in Coral Communities." *Ecological Modelling 3:*249–271.

Major, J. 1969. "Historical Development of the Ecosystem Concept." *The*

Ecosystem Concept in Natural Resource Management. Edited by G. M. Van Dyne. New York: Academic Press, pp. 9–24.

Margalef, R. 1963. "On Certain Unifying Principles in Ecology." *American Naturalist 97:*357–374.

Margalef, R. 1969. "Diversity and Stability: A Practical Proposal and a Model of Interdependence." *Brookhaven Symposium of Biology 22:*25–37.

McNaughton, S. J., and Wolf, L. L. 1973. *General Ecology.* New York: Holt, Rinehart and Winston.

Meadows, D. L. 1970. *The Dynamics of Commodity Production Cycles.* Cambridge, Mass.: Wright-Allen Press.

Monsi, M., and Oshima, Y. 1955. "A Theoretical Analysis of the Succession Process of Plant Community, Based Upon the Production of Matter." *Japanese Journal of Botany 15:*60–82.

Moore, I. 1966. *Grass and Grasslands.* London: Collins.

Odum, E. P. 1959. *Fundamentals of Ecology.* 2d ed. Philadelphia: Saunders.

Odum, E. P. 1963. *Ecology.* New York: Holt, Rinehart and Winston.

Odum, E. P. 1969. "The Strategy of Ecosystem Development." *Science 164:*262–270.

Odum, E. P. 1971. *Fundamentals of Ecology.* 3d ed. Philadelphia: Saunders.

Odum, E. P. 1972. "Harmony Between Man and Nature: An Ecological View." *Symp. on Limits of Growth.* New Haven, Conn.: Yale University Press.

Odum, H. T. 1960. "Ecological Potential and Analogue Circuits for the Ecosystem." *American Scientist 48:*1–8.

Odum, H. T. 1971. *Environment, Power and Society.* New York: Wiley-Inter-science.

Olson, J. S. 1958. "Rates of Succession and Soil Changes on Southern Lake Michigan Sand Dunes." *Botanical Gazette 119:*125–170.

Osborn, B. 1956. "Cover Requirements for the Protection of Range Site and Biota." *Journal of Range Management 9:*75–80.

Parker, K. W. 1954. "Application of Ecology in the Determination of Range Condition and Trend." *Journal of Range Management 7:*14–23.

Patten, B. C. 1971. "A Linear State Space Model in Grassland." Research Report, University of Georgia, Athens.

Patten, B. C. 1972. "A Simulation of the Shortgrass Prairie Ecosystem." *Simulation 19:*177–186.

Patten, Bernard C., ed. 1976. *Systems Analysis and Simulation in Ecology."* Vol. 4. New York: Academic Press.

Paulsen, H. A., Jr., and Ares, F. N. 1962. "Grazing Values and Management of Block Grama and Tobosa Grasslands and Associated Shrub Ranges of the Southwest." *USDA Technical Bulletin No. 1270.*

Phillipson, J. 1966. *Ecological Energetics*. London: Arnold.

Pickford, G. D. 1932. "The Influence of Continued Heavy Grazing and of Promiscuous Burning on Spring-Fall Ranges in Utah." *Ecology 13:*159–171.

Pimentel, D., Hurd, L. E., Bellatti, A. C., Forster, M. J., Oka, I. N., Sholes, O. D., and Whitman, R. J. 1973. "Food Production and the Energy Crisis." *Science 182:*443–449.

Preston, F. W. 1969. "Diversity and Stability in the Biological World." *Symp. on Diversity and Stability in Ecological Systems*. Upton, N.Y.: Brookhaven National Laboratory.

Pugh, A. L., III. 1963. *DYNAMO User's Manual*. Cambridge, Mass.: MIT Press.

Ranwell, D. S. 1972. *Ecology of Salt Marshes and Sand Dunes*. London: Chapman and Hall.

Raunkiaer, C. 1934. *The Life Forms of Plants and Statistical Plant Geography*. Oxford: Clarendon Press.

Reed, M. J., and Peterson, R. A. 1961. "Vegetation, Soil and Cattle Responses to Grazing on Northern Great Plains Range." *USDA Technical Bulletin No. 1252*.

Reichle, David E., ed. 1970. *Analysis of Temperate Forest Ecosystems*. Berlin: Springer-Verlag.

Robinson, H. 1972. *Biogeography*. London: Macdonald & Evans.

Sampson, A. W. 1919. "Plant Succession in Relation to Range Management." *USDA Technical Bulletin No. 791*.

Semple, A. T. 1970. *Grassland Improvement*. Cleveland: CRC Press.

Shantz, H. L. 1906. "A Study of the Vegetation of the Mesa Region East of Pikes Peak; the Bouteloua Formation." *Botanical Gazette 42:*16.

Shantz, H. L. 1917. "Plant Succession on Abandoned Roads in Eastern Colorado." *Journal of Ecology 5:*19–42.

Shelford, V. E. 1911a. "Ecological Succession: Stream Fishes and the Method of Physiographic Analysis." *Biological Bulletin 21:*9–34.

Shelford, V. E. 1911b. "Ecological Succession: Pond Fishes." *Biological Bulletin 21:*127–151.

Smith, D. R. 1967. "Effects of Cattle Grazing on a Ponderosa Pine-Bunchgrass Range in Colorado." *USDA Technical Bulletin No. 1371*.

Sneals, J. G., ed. 1969. *The Soil Ecosystem: Systematic Aspects of the Environment, Organisms, and Communities*. London: The Systematics Association.

Sneath, P. H. A. and McKenzie, K. G. 1973. "Statistical Methods for the Study of Biogeography." *Organisms and Continents Through Time*. London: The Palaeontological Association.

Spedding, C. R. W. 1971. *Grassland Ecology*. Oxford: Oxford University Press.

Steger, R. E. 1970. "Grazing Systems for Range Care." *Cooperative Extension Service Circular No. 427*. New Mexico State University, Las Cruces.

Stern, Klaus, and Roche, Laurence. 1974. *Genetics of Forest Ecosystems*. New York: Springer-Verlag.

Tansley, A. G. 1929. "Succession: The Concept and Its Values." *Proc. First International Congress of Plant Sciences*. Geo. Banta, Menasha, Wisc., pp. 667–686.

Tansley, A. G. 1935. "The Use and Abuse of Vegetational Concepts and Terms." *Ecology 16:*284–307.

Tedrow, John C. F. 1977. *Soils of the Polar Landscapes*. New Brunswick, N.J.: Rutgers University Press.

Vallentine, J. F. 1971. *Range Development and Improvements*. Provo, Utah: Brigham Young University Press.

Van Dyne, G. M., ed. 1969. *The Ecosystem Concept in Natural Resource Management*. New York: Academic Press.

Wali, Mohan, ed. 1975. *Prairie: A Multiple View*. Grand Forks: University of North Dakota Press.

Walter, Heinrich. 1971. *Ecology of Tropical and Subtropical Vegetation*. New York: Van Nostrand Reinhold.

Watt, K. E. F., ed. 1966. *Systems Analysis in Ecology*. New York: Academic Press.

Watt, K. E. F. 1968. *Ecology and Resource Management—A Quantitative Approach*. New York: McGraw-Hill.

Watt, K. E. F. 1973. *Principles of Environmental Science*. New York: McGraw-Hill.

Whittaker, R. H. 1953. "A Consideration of Climax Theory: The Climax as a Population and Pattern." *Ecological Monographs 23:*41–78.

Whittaker, R. H. 1969. "Evaluation of Diversity in Plant Communities." *Symp. on Diversity and Stability in Ecological Systems*. Upton, N.Y.: Brookhaven National Laboratory.

Whittaker, R. H. 1970. *Communities and Ecosystems*. 1st ed. London: Macmillan.

Whittaker, Robert H. 1975. *Communities and Ecosystems*. 2d ed. New York: Macmillan,

Whittaker, R. H., and Woodwell, G. M. 1968. "Dimension and Production Relations of Trees and Shrubs in the Brookhaven Forest, New York." *Journal of Ecology 56:*1–25.

Whittaker, R. H., and Woodwell, G. M. 1969. "Structure, Production and Diversity of the Oakpine Forest at Brookhaven, New York." *Journal of Ecology 57:*155–174.

Wilde, S. A. 1958. *Forest Soils*. New York: Ronald Press.

Williams, R. B. 1971. "Computer Simulation of Energy Flow in Cedar Bog Lake, Minnesota, Based on the Classical Studies of Lindeman." *Systems Analysis and Simulation in Ecology.* Vol 1. Edited by B. C. Patten. New York: Academic Press, pp. 543–582.

Woodwell, G. M. 1970. "Effects of Pollution on the Structure and Physiology of Ecosystems." *Science 168:*429–433.

Index